COLD WAR SECRETS

TRUE CRIME HISTORY

COLD WAR SECRETS

A VANISHED PROFESSOR, A SUSPECTED KILLER, AND HOOVER'S FBI

EILEEN WELSOME

 The Kent State University Press   KENT, OHIO

© 2021 by The Kent State University Press, Kent, Ohio 44242
All rights reserved
Library of Congress Catalog Number 2021005745
ISBN 978-1-60635-425-4
Manufactured in the United States of America

Library of Congress Cataloging-in-Publication Data
Names: Welsome, Eileen, author.
Title: Cold War secrets : a vanished professor, a suspected killer, and Hoover's FBI / Eileen Welsome.
Description: Kent, Ohio : The Kent State University Press, 2021. | Series: True crime history | Includes bibliographical references and index.
Identifiers: LCCN 2021005745 | ISBN 9781606354254 (paperback) | ISBN 9781631014550 (epub) | ISBN 9781631014567 (pdf)
Subjects: LCSH: Riha, Thomas. | Missing persons--Investigation. | Tannenbaum, Galya, 1931-1971. | United States. Federal Bureau of Investigation--History. | Cold War.
Classification: LCC HV6762.U5 W45 2021 | DDC 363.2/336--dc23
LC record available at https://lccn.loc.gov/2021005745

25 24 23 22 21   5 4 3 2 1

To Jim

Thomas Riha and Hana Hruskova before the wedding. (Courtesy Hana Riha)

CONTENTS

PART IV: "WHAT WOULD THE RUSSIANS THINK?"

19 Torpedoes and Submarines 199
20 The Fink 204
21 Misspellings and Murder 212
22 The Informant and the "Useful Idiot" 220

Epilogue 226
Notes 230
Index 258

ACKNOWLEDGMENTS

I first heard about Thomas Riha almost a decade ago from a friend and fellow journalist named Julie Hutchinson, who had written about the case for the *Boulder Camera*.

Julie pulled up a photograph of Riha on her cell phone. He was a handsome man with a head of thick, dark hair and a carnation in his lapel. "I was surprised nobody bothered to look for him after the Berlin Wall fell," she said.

"I'm going to find him," I responded spontaneously.

At a local history conference a couple of months later, I happened to meet Vonnie Perkins, the mother-in-law of Becky Perkins, Galya Tannenbaum's youngest child.

Vonnie arranged an interview for me with Becky, who came to the meeting with documents and Galya's jewelry box. When I opened the jewelry box, the theme song from *Doctor Zhivago* started to play. In one of the trays were several small-caliber bullets.

I picked them up and rolled them in my hand. They were real. I looked questioningly at Becky.

She shrugged noncommittally.

Initially, I thought Galya was an innocent woman who had been made a scapegoat by federal and local law enforcement officials. It didn't seem plausible that a woman who was nearly forty years old, had four children, and no history of violent crimes would begin murdering people—with cyanide no less. But as I began reading the case files, many of which have been unavailable for decades, I realized that Galya was a darker and more complex person than I had imagined. I also realized that finding Thomas Riha—or his body—was going to be nearly impossible, but I was too deep into the story to quit.

Many other people shared their memories and insights with me, including Zdenek Cerveny and Jarmila Zakova, Thomas Riha's nephew and niece, who both now live in Prague. Zdenek had just emigrated from Czechoslovakia to the United States when Riha disappeared and was plunged into the middle of the unfolding mystery. Jarmila remained in Prague and showed me the flimsy, blue airmail letters that Thomas had written to her in earlier years.

Although the Church Committee and former Colorado senator Gary Hart released a statement in the 1970s saying Riha was probably living in eastern Europe, Zdenek and Jarmila long ago gave up hope that Riha was alive and would one day coming knocking at their door.

I am also indebted to Hana Riha, Thomas's ex-wife, who had looked forward to a happy marriage in Boulder only to flee her home forever on a cold spring night in March 1969. Hana spoke candidly of her brief marriage and loaned me many of the photographs used in this book.

I also owe a big thanks to Pete Ingwersen, one of Gustav Ingwersen's grandchildren, who shared his memories of Gus and allowed me to use Gus's photo in this book.

I also was fortunate enough to meet Fred Gillies a few weeks before he died. Fred covered the Riha story for the *Denver Post* for a decade. After his death, his nephew, Randy Gillies, loaned me a box of documents that Fred had kept on the case. Going through those records was an unforgettable experience: an investigative reporter picking up the trail of another investigative reporter. Fred had served in the military during World War II and he typed and dated most of his interviews. Reading his notes was almost like being present for those long-ago interviews.

I would not have been able to obtain information on Thomas Riha's childhood or the background of his relatives without the assistance of David Kohout, a researcher and translator who lives in the Czech Republic. David and I went together to the Czech National Archives and to the Institute for Totalitarian Regimes in Prague. Afterward we photographed every home in Prague where members of the Kress and Riha families had lived.

Beth Rashbaum made invaluable suggestions early in the project, as did several readers later on. I am also indebted to the many academics who recalled what they know about Thomas Riha, particularly Joyce Lebra, who cotaught a history class with Thomas and fearlessly demanded that law enforcement officials investigate Riha's sudden disappearance. Donald Fanger, Riha's longtime friend, was also helpful, as were Richard Wortman, Jim Jankowski, Boyd Hill, Elisabeth Israels Perry, and Francis Randall and Oren Jarinkes.

Gerald Caplan, Hana's divorce lawyer, and John Kokish, Galya's defense lawyer, provided valuable insight. John Kokish is now deceased but his voluminous files on the case have been deposited with History Colorado and are available to the public. Robert Schwind and Dennis Blewitt, also lawyers, shared their impressions of Thomas Riha with me.

Law enforcement officials were also accommodating. From the Boulder Police Department, I received a stack of documents nearly a foot deep. The Denver Police Department's Mary Dulacki promptly supplied me with the investigative files of Gustav Ingwersen and Barbara Egbert. Retired DPD detectives Tom Lohr, Phillip Villalovos, and Charlie McCormick, all of whom had been present for one or more interviews with Galya, were also generous with their time.

Silvia Pettem, a Boulder historian and author, also lent her support to this project. As a volunteer at the Boulder Police Department, Silvia had organized the voluminous Thomas Riha files and had tracked down and interviewed many of the people involved in the case.

On a beautiful fall day, Silvia, Charlie McCormick, and I hiked up into the foothills above Dumont, Colorado, looking for the Lucky Find Mine, once owned by Gustav Ingwersen. It had been mentioned in police reports and I thought it possible that Riha's body had been dumped in the mine.

Gerald Schinke, the present-day owner, gave us permission to go onto the property. We didn't find the Lucky Find, but we did discover the nearby Ohio mine, which resembles a bottomless pit that is slowly collapsing upon itself. The Ohio—or a mine like it—could well be the final resting place of Thomas Riha, which is a wretched ending to contemplate.

I am also deeply indebted to the staff of the Kent State University Press. William Underwood, the acquiring editor, first recognized the potential of this book. His successor, Susan Wadsworth-Booth, has been equally enthusiastic and has brought abundant energy to the project.

I am deeply indebted to the other members of the publishing team, including Mary Young, managing editor; Christine Brooks, design and production manager; and Valerie Ahwee, copy editor. Valerie, who has the eyes of an eagle, patiently went through the manuscript, plucking out errors. Those that remain are mine.

Finally, I want to thank my husband, Jim Martin. Without his love and support, this book could not have been written. And to my two patient dogs and my new puppy, I owe you lots of walks.

If anyone really knew me they'd know

I was the biggest softie in the West.

—Galya Tannenbaum

July 30, 1970

PROLOGUE ★
THE SMELL OF ETHER

On the evening of March 8, 1969, Thomas Riha sat in his Boulder study waiting for his estranged wife to return home.[1] A light snow had begun to fall and the majestic Flatirons that rose behind his house had become indistinct as the wind drove the snow flurries eastward. Light from a streetlamp entered through the study, illuminating his face, which was frowning slightly and absent the geniality with which he normally greeted his students and colleagues. Glimmering faintly on the walls behind him were the spines of hundreds of books that he had purchased from book stalls in Moscow, Prague, and Montreal.

Thomas wore his usual weekend garb—a brown turtleneck and tweed jacket—which was informal by European standards but not in Boulder, where bell-bottom jeans and olive army jackets were the norm. Periodically, he stood to stretch and peer out the window. By watching the flakes tumbling down, he could calculate how fast the snow was falling and if there would be any accumulation by morning. He hoped there would be; he loved the snow that swept down from the Rockies. So light and dry, it seemed more like air than water and was one of the reasons why he never wanted to leave Boulder.[2]

A faculty party was under way next door and the sound of laughter easily penetrated the walls of his home. There was a time when Thomas would have been in the thick of things at his neighbor's house, singing "Mack the Knife"[3] in German or reciting Carl Sandburg's "Twelve Days of Marxmas" ("seven Lenins leaping, eight Stalins staring, nine bloody purges"). But he had become paranoid of late, convinced that he was being followed by several men and worried about important papers that seemed to be missing from his home.[4]

Thomas also had a visitor that evening—a tall, confident woman named Galya Tannenbaum, who had arrived earlier that afternoon, her cheeks flushed with cold and a wintry freshness issuing from her ankle-length mink coat. She tossed a manila envelope containing some immigration documents onto the table in the dining room and went into the kitchen to make coffee.

Even before Thomas had closed the front door, Galya had begun talking. She talked constantly, her conversation often fueled by the methamphetamines she took when she was tired.[5] Her chatter annoyed Thomas, but he let her prattle on. Other than the fact they were both about forty years old, they seemed to have little in common. She was a head taller than him, arranged her blondish hair in a careless bun, and wore cat's-eye glasses that swept up into points. Galya liked cars and guns and walked with a manly stride. Sometimes she even referred to herself as a "he."[6] But her body remained stubbornly female and she still carried some of the weight she had acquired during her four pregnancies. Her two younger children—a three-year-old girl and a ten-year-old boy—still lived at home with her.

Thomas was an associate professor of Russian history in the University of Colorado's newly created Slavic Studies Department. He was raised in a cosmopolitan Prague family that had been torn asunder in 1939 when the Nazis occupied Czechoslovakia. Hitler himself, riding in a heavy, open-topped Mercedes, had passed within feet of Riha's family flat as the car climbed the hill to the Prague Castle.

Galya grew up in St. Louis in a large, extended Catholic family.[7] Her father had abandoned the family when she was a little girl and she had a difficult and complex relationship with her mother. Although she didn't have Thomas's marvelous education, she was exceptionally good at math, like her eldest brother, who worked at Sandia National Laboratory.[8] She had taught herself bookkeeping and the principles of real estate investing, and her Rolodex contained the names of scientists, doctors, politicians, and celebrities, including Art Linkletter.[9] Galya's real talent, though, lay in painting and she filled her canvasses with thick slashes of green and white paint that evoked the ice and gloom of the Rockies.

Galya told people she was an intelligence officer and spoke darkly of assassinations, secret missions, and far-off assignments in places such as Vietnam. Many of Riha's friends were skeptical of her claims, but Thomas believed her. "You don't know these people," he would say.[10]

Thomas spoke five languages, including flawless Russian and equally excellent English, which had made him an attractive candidate for intelligence work.[11] Almost immediately after the Cold War began, at a time when the Soviets already had an expansive network of agents and collaborators in place in the United States, the CIA and FBI found themselves in the position of having to play catch-up. Both intelligence agencies scouted the country for citizens who could speak Russian, and both had approached Riha. They were not the only ones. When he stopped in Czechoslovakia to visit his father in 1958 on his way to the Soviet Union as an exchange student, the StB, or Státní bezpečnost—the Czech secret police—had courted him. "He was surrounded by agents," his niece, Jarmila Zakova, would say many years later.[12]

Galya had smooth, fine-grained skin and radiated a warmth that some men found sexually attractive. But Thomas preferred women who were young and beautiful. Nevertheless, they appeared to have some sort of intimate relationship and he had given her a key to his house. Galya felt so comfortable there that she often put her three-year-old down for a nap in one of his bedrooms.

Galya told people that she and Thomas planned to marry. The plan—if indeed there was one—had fallen apart five months earlier when Thomas had suddenly married Hana Hruskova, a young Czech woman he had met in New York City on his way home from one of his trips to the Soviet Union. Hana was twenty-five years old and beautiful, with large brown eyes and thick, chestnut hair that curled around her shoulders.

Hana moved from Prague to Brooklyn in 1966 to live with her father's brother and his wife.[13] The couple had no children and treated Hana as if she were their own daughter. She enrolled in a business school and began taking English classes. In August 1968, she was introduced to Thomas and two and a half months later, they were married in a wedding ceremony in Boulder.

On his wedding day, Thomas stuck a pale flower in his lapel and pronounced marriage forever. But theirs began to disintegrate immediately. The difference in their ages, their personalities, and their educational and cultural backgrounds created a chasm too wide to bridge. "They were misaligned from the beginning," Thomas's nephew, Zdenek Cerveny, would say.[14]

Thomas had filed for divorce in February 1969,[15] hoping Hana would return to Brooklyn so that he could resume his quiet life as a professor. Instead, with the help of her aunt and uncle in New York, Hana had hired Boulder lawyer Gerald Caplan, who had filed a counterclaim probing every aspect of Thomas's financial affairs.

The divorce proceedings had grown so rancorous that Hana had begun sleeping in a small guest bedroom. Occasionally she had coffee with Veva Nye, a young married woman who had become her confidante since Hana moved to Boulder to start her life with Thomas. Mostly, she wrote letters home in local coffee shops and walked the streets of her new hometown.

Boulder had the charm of an alpine village, but exploded in rowdiness when hundreds of students gathered to protest the Vietnam War, the nearby Rocky Flats nuclear weapons plant, or a CIA recruiter who happened to set up shop on campus.

★   ★   ★

The splendid snowfall that Thomas had hoped for did not materialize. The flurries slowed and then stopped, leaving a cloud-streaked sky and a handful of hard, white stars. When Hana reached the corner of Sixth and College Avenue, where Riha's house was located, she saw Galya's car and hesitated, debating whether to go in or wait until Galya left.

The night before, when she was in the kitchen drinking coffee with Veva Nye, Galya had barged in, carrying a brown grocery sack containing a hunk of sausage covered with white speckles. She offered some to the two young women, but they declined, saying they weren't hungry.

Galya reached into a manila envelope that she was carrying and pulled out Hana's passport. "Remember this, doll?" she asked. "You haven't seen this for a while, have you?"[16] Galya pointed at one of the forms in the envelope and told Hana to sign it or she would contact the Pentagon on Monday morning and have Hana deported.

"No, Mrs. Tannenbaum, I will not sign this paper—until Monday—and we will go together to my lawyer and we will sign it in his presence. And this is my last word," Hana said.[17]

Hana had obtained a student visa soon after she arrived in the United States. She had applied for a permanent resident immigration visa while living in New York, but before the application was processed, she had met Thomas and moved to Colorado. Immigration authorities in New York had told her to reapply for permanent status once she was settled in Colorado.[18]

Galya had offered to help Hana with her paperwork, so Hana had given Galya most of her documents. But Hana's aunt and uncle back in New York kept getting mail from the Immigration and Naturalization Service under Hana's maiden name. The INS, in its most recent letter, had instructed Hana to report to their offices immediately.

It was the first time Veva had met Galya and she observed her closely. "She has to be at least five ten, and she is massive," she would say. "She has gray hair, and it was fixed in a rather unattractive flat bun on the top of her head. She wears glasses. I would say she was a little slovenly in appearance—not a very neat woman, a heavy woman, but dresses as though she weren't really too interested in how she looks; and as far as her talk is concerned, she is foul-mouthed, because she uses rather curt language and vulgar terms."[19]

When Veva announced she had to go home, Galya insisted upon giving her a ride. Hana decided to go along. Galya backed the car out and turned in the direction of Buckeye Court, where Veva lived.

"You weren't kidding," Veva said. "You do know where I live."[20]

"I know everything," Galya responded.

Galya drove fast, explaining that speeding was one of the "fringe benefits" of her job.[21] When they reached Veva's house, Veva asked Hana to accompany her up to the door. Once they were out of earshot of Galya, Veva reminded Hana not to sign anything. Hana reassured her friend that she wouldn't and then returned to the car and slid into the front seat next to Galya. It was about ten o'clock in the evening. For the next six hours, Galya would keep Hana virtually captive in the car.

Their first stop was the Boulder Charcoal Chef. Hana went into a phone booth and called her New York attorney, David Regosin, thinking that Galya would be placated if she talked directly to him. When the lawyer answered the phone, Galya snatched the receiver away and went into a vitriolic tirade, shouting so loudly that other people in the restaurant looked up.

It was "like a raging torrent," Regosin would say in a sworn affidavit. "There was no stopping or interrupting her. With the greatest difficulty I asked her who she was and in the torrent of words, I made out the name, 'Galwa [sic] Tannenbaum.' She practically screamed out that she had gone out of her way for this girl; that she was not going to take a 'kick in the ass' from her; this girl is here illegally and 'I will have her deported.'"[22]

Regosin told Galya that the government offices were closed until Monday morning and that he saw no reason why papers needed to be signed that night.

Galya slammed down the phone.

"He's stupid, just unbelievably," she fumed to Hana. "How can you have around such a stupid lawyer, such stupid people? He told me I was hysterical—hysterical!"[23]

Galya stormed out of the restaurant, with Hana following her. She backed her Chevrolet *Bel Air* out of the parking lot, but instead of turning toward Riha's house, she drove in a southerly direction toward Denver. "Please, Mrs. Tannenbaum, stop. If you don't feel like to bring me home, please would you be so kind and stop the car and I can take a taxi and I can walk. It's not so far, but I really feel I would like to go home. I am tired," Hana said.[24]

Galya ignored her. She drove past restaurants and gas stations and large swaths of farmland that would one day become suburbs. As her rage subsided, she began talking in a sad voice about the results of some medical tests that Hana had recently taken.

"Baby, you are going to die," Galya said mournfully.[25]

Alarmed, Hana demanded to know more, but Galya simply shook her head and repeated the words.

When they reached Denver, Galya pulled into the parking lot of another restaurant and went inside to get coffee. A few minutes later, Hana followed, hoping to find a telephone where she could call for help. Galya waylaid her and asked her what she was doing.

Looking for the bathroom, Hana responded.

Galya followed her to the bathroom and waited outside the door, then the two women returned to the car together. Galya drove on through the darkness, talking in a low voice about how she didn't sleep at night and why it didn't matter anyway because her job required her to work at night.

"Oh, baby dear, I know you are tired," Galya said, glancing over at Hana. "I'm glad you are because you are playing with me a game many months, so now I can play with you a few hours. You are complaining about being tired. It's just a few hours, but I am sick and tired of your playing so many months, so stop. Now be quiet. I am having fun. Listen to me and do what I tell you."[26]

"So now tell me what actually you really want me to do right now, because I don't know," Hana said. "You are talking to me all the time and I really don't know what you want. What do you want?"[27]

"You don't know, baby? It's all right. I think you know," Galya responded.

Eventually Galya turned the car around and headed back to Boulder. As she approached the city limits, she swung off the highway onto an access road. She turned off the engine, pulled a large white pill from her pocket and held it out to Hana, saying the pill would help her sleep. Hana, who rarely even took an aspirin, declined.

"Take it!" Galya ordered.

Hana refused.

"No, no, baby, you will eat it right now! Right now!" Galya said, lunging across the seat and trying to force the pill down Hana's throat.[28]

The two women grappled with each other in the front seat for a few minutes. When Galya realized that she couldn't overpower Hana, she tossed the pill out the window and suddenly became friendly.

"Oh, baby. All right. Now I will let you sleep and promise me you will sleep tonight."[29] Galya held out her hand, but Hana refused to take it.

When they reached Riha's house, Galya said she would be back at eleven o'clock that morning and they would go hiking in the mountains. "Promise me you will be here exactly at eleven o'clock—you will take your slacks and we will go for hiking somewhere and I will buy champagne. Don't you like champagne? We will have a good time."[30]

★ ★ ★

As Hana stood in front of Riha's house, the cold mountain air penetrating her coat and stockings, she may have thought about the strange car ride. She shifted back and forth on her feet, trying to stay warm. Finally, she decided to go inside.

Quietly, she pushed open the front door and hurried down the hall. She thought she heard voices and the door of her husband's study closing. When she reached the spare bedroom, she locked the door and flipped on the overhead light.

Blankets lay heaped on the bed, a plate of partially eaten cabbage sat on top of the bureau, and a bag of doughnuts lay on a bedside table. She climbed into bed with most of her clothes on. At 10 P.M., Veva called to make sure she had gotten home safely. Hana assured her she was okay and hung up quickly because she thought Thomas and Galya were listening on an extension in the study. A few minutes later, Hana heard someone jiggling her doorknob.

"Who is there?"

"This is me," Thomas responded.

"What do you want?"

"I want to talk to you."

"I will not open the door," Hana said.

"Open the door," he ordered. "Mrs. Tannenbaum wants something from you."

"What you want to tell me, we can speak through the door," she answered.[31]

Riha kept banging on the door, ordering her to open it. Finally, he wandered back to his study where Hana heard him having a furious argument with Galya. Then Hana heard Galya's car start up and drive away. Relieved, she nibbled on a doughnut and began reading a book. After a while, she turned out the light and tried to go to sleep.

Suddenly, she detected a strong, solvent-like odor wafting through an overhead heating vent and seeping into the room from under the door.[32] She began to panic and went to the door and began jabbering to her husband in Czech. "Please stop these dangerous things, because it is going to be a crime."[33]

On the other side of the door, Hana could hear Thomas translating what she was saying. Belatedly, she realized Galya hadn't left the house after all. They had tricked her. Thomas and Galya began pounding on the door, demanding that she come out.[34]

"Open the door! We want to talk to you!" they screamed.

"I won't open the door!" Hana shouted back. The door began to splinter.

"Don't worry, honey baby, we will get you," said Galya.[35] Then she told Hana that she had a pistol and would shoot her through the door.[36]

Hana looked around wildly, dashed to the window, opened it and began screaming. "Please help! Help, help, help!"[37]

Alarmed, Galya and Thomas sprinted out the front door and around to the side of the house where they intended to grab Hana through the open window. Hana saw them coming and started to slam shut the window, but at that moment she spotted Robert Hanson, a sociology professor who had been at the neighbor's party, veering toward her from the other side of the yard.

The faculty party was breaking up and the departing guests had heard her cries. Hana had enough presence of mind to grab her coat and her purse, which contained all of her important documents and telephone numbers, and clambered out the window. As she started across the snow-covered lawn, Hanson grabbed her by the arm. He was nearly overcome by the fumes emanating from her clothing and kept reaching up and putting his hand over his nose.

Hana pulled him along, sobbing and pleading with him to hurry. Riha caught up with them and tried to wrest Hana from his grasp, but Hanson stopped him. "Go away! Don't touch her!" he shouted.[38]

Thomas, normally so decorous, followed them into the neighbor's foyer, where the owner of the house, Richard Wilson, a professor of political science, was watching the altercation along with two wives from the party. Everyone immediately noticed the heavy odor clinging to both Riha and his wife. Thomas explained to the alarmed neighbors that Galya was a colonel in military intelligence and was armed with a pistol.[39]

"It would be dangerous for you to become involved in this situation," he warned.[40]

"We don't live in a police state yet," retorted Richard Wilson, who had gotten into a dispute with Riha a few weeks earlier. He ordered Thomas to leave his house.

Incensed, Riha returned home. Galya, meanwhile, called the Boulder Police Department and the call went out over the police radio as a 1096, the code for a disturbance involving a mental patient.[41] A few minutes later, two patrolmen—Douglas J. Dorsey and Dale Stange—pulled up to the curb in separate police cars. They went to Riha's house first. Intimating that she had connections with immigration authorities, Galya told the officers that Hana was in the country illegally and subject to deportation. She added that Hana had been taking some kind of narcotic and had locked herself in her room.

The two officers then walked over to the neighbor's to get Hana's side of the story. Despite the cold, the windows had been thrown open to get rid of the heavy odor emanating from Hana's clothing. Hana was sobbing, telling the neighbors in almost incomprehensible language that her husband and Galya were trying to kill her.

The doorbell rang. It was Thomas again. He asked Officer Stange to accompany him back to his house. The two men walked across the lawn, their exhalations white and frosty in the night air. When the patrolman went inside, he saw that Hana's bedroom door was now open and noticed an old blue t-shirt with paint stains lying on the floor.[42] He picked it up and held it to his nose. It had the same heavy odor that clung to Hana and her husband. "I then searched further in the room, in the closets, in the chest of drawers looking for a bottle, a container of some sort," he would say.[43] "I noticed the blankets on the bed were all rummaged together, piled on one another. I picked up the blankets and underneath the blankets was a jar. Just a plain fruit jar, with a substance in it. This jar also contained a bundle, or bandage, of gauze stuffed in the jar. I noticed the jar contained approximately three to four inches of liquid."

Clearly, he was meant to believe that Hana put the jar there, but it seemed just as possible that Galya or Thomas had placed the jar under the blankets after Hana fled the room and before the police arrived.

The police officer returned to the neighbor's house. He told his partner, Officer Dorsey, about the fruit jar and said he suspected the liquid was ether. Dorsey shrugged. "There wasn't any law against having it, possessing it, or using it, so it was of no concern, really, as a police matter," he would later say.[44]

The two patrolmen walked back to the Riha residence. Galya was in the study talking on the telephone. When she hung up, she told the officers that she had been talking to immigration officials in Denver.

"I understand that you have some official capacity in this case?" Officer Dorsey asked her.

"Oh, yes," responded Galya.

"Could I see some identification?"

Galya said her ID was in her car.

"Fine. Let's go—let's go see it," the policeman responded.[45]

Officer Dorsey followed Galya out to her car, where she kept her purse. She rummaged through it and pulled out her vehicle registration and an old Illinois driver's license, telling the policeman she must have left her official identification at home. She added that she owned a Boulder company called Universal Graphics and did government work on the side. "You know how these things are. I do some extra-curricular-type work for certain people at times."[46]

Dorsey advised Galya to go home. The two patrolmen departed the scene, taking the fruit jar with them. "A bunch of kooks," they thought.[47]

Hana, meanwhile, had decided to spend the night at the Boulderado Hotel and returned to Riha's house with Robert Hanson and his wife, Margaret, to pick up some overnight toiletries. Contrary to the policeman's advice, Galya had also returned. Although the temperature was approaching zero, she was coatless and red-faced. She asked everyone to sit down at the table so she could explain what was going on. "And boy, was she agitated," Margaret Hanson would say. "I would say she was not drunk, but she was very upset. I thought this large, powerful woman was scared."[48]

The house still reeked of ether. Thomas Riha sat silently at the table listening to the conversation. "He was white, like a white wall. He was shaking, he was staring," Hana recalled.[49] Then Thomas leaned over to her and whispered, 'I'm sorry. I love you."

Finally, the Hansons departed, taking Hana with them.

★   ★   ★

On Monday morning, March 10, 1969, Hana went to see her Boulder attorney, Gerald Caplan, a tall, athletic man and avid mountain climber. Accompanying Hana were Veva Nye and Rose Grossman, her aunt, who had flown in from Brooklyn the day before. Although Caplan wasn't a divorce lawyer, he had agreed to take Hana's case after New York attorney David Regosin assured him it was a simple case.

He ushered the three women into a quiet conference room and listened as Hana and the other two women described the weekend's events. Although Hana was visibly upset, Caplan saw no evidence of the dissolute wife that Thomas Riha had described. "She was under a lot of pressure and showed considerable courage under the circumstances," he recalled.[50]

Caplan already knew who Galya Tannenbaum was. She had breezed into his office soon after Riha had filed for divorce, claiming she was Hana's sponsor and that she was helping her with her immigration problems.[51] Her hair was pulled back in a severe ponytail and she projected an air of authority.

Galya told Caplan she was associated with MI4, the military intelligence division of the army,[52] and that she had "friends" in the Justice Department, the Immigration and Naturalization Service, and the US Postal Service, which enabled her to postdate documents for which the filing period had passed.[53] Caplan listened politely to what she had to say and then asked to see her identification. Galya said she would bring it to their next meeting.

After listening to Hana's story, Caplan took an unusual step of asking a court reporter to come to his office at nine thirty that evening so he could begin taking depositions. He wanted to preserve a record while memories were still fresh. He took Hana's and Veva's depositions that night. In the days to come, he would also take Rose Grossman's deposition, the depositions of Boulder Police Department officers Douglas Dorsey and Dale Stange, and the depositions of three neighbors who had been at the party—Robert Hanson, who had helped Hana out the window; his wife, Margaret Hanson; and Richard Wilson, who had curtly ordered Riha to leave his house.

Caplan also looked over two letters purportedly written by Hana to immigration authorities that were dated March 8 and March 9, 1969. He noticed that the word "consider" was spelled "concider" in both letters.[54] There were other peculiar misspellings, including "freedome," "arround," "scheem," and "misserable."

One of the police officers who had been at Riha's house had given Caplan the fruit jar and its contents. Caplan asked a university chemist to analyze the contents. The scientist concluded the liquid was indeed ether, a powerful chemical once used to anesthetize patients undergoing surgery.[55] Thomas and Galya apparently wanted to render Hana unconscious. But what were they planning to do with her afterward?

Hana was convinced they were planning to murder her. "If I hadn't locked the door, if the neighbors hadn't heard me call for help, I would be dead and they would say I committed suicide," she said in an interview.[56]

The idea seemed preposterous. Riha was a respected professor, with a promising career and a book that had just been published. He had no criminal record, no history of violence, and went out of his way to avoid confrontations. Galya's past was not so unblemished—she had been arrested and convicted on various forgery and embezzlement charges—but her criminal record contained no history of assault or violence.

★　★　★

While Gerald Caplan was taking depositions, Thomas Riha went about his business as if nothing were amiss. He taught his classes and exchanged pleasantries with his colleagues in the history department. He did tell a close friend, Joyce Lebra, a professor of Japanese history who cotaught a class with him, that Hana had gone on a "trip" on ether.[57]

"I didn't know people took trips on ether," she said.

"Well, that's the kind of person she is," Thomas replied.

On Thursday, March 13, Thomas had lunch with Carol Word, an accomplished pianist who had played at his wedding.[58] Word, who was studying Russian literature and the Russian language, was one of Riha's favorite students and lunched with him nearly every day.

Later that evening, he drove to Galya's house in Denver for dinner and invited his nephew, Zdenek Cerveny, to join them. "They were cozy. I don't know whether he was having an affair with her or what. He was running around the house in a kimono. She was wearing some kind of Japanese outfit, too," Cerveny recalled.[59]

On Friday evening, Thomas went to the home of Jan Sorensen, one of his teaching assistants, who was throwing a birthday party for one of her children. Riha liked children, but he was impatient for the party to end so he could speak to her privately. When they were finally alone together, Riha told her that he thought someone had followed him to her house that night.[60] When Jan saw how frightened he was, she suggested that he spend the night and offered to make up a bed in a spare bedroom.

Thomas shook his head, saying he had to go home. He donned his coat and gloves and walked out to his car. The temperature was in the teens, the night bright with light from the stars. He loved the purity of Boulder's nights almost as much as he loved its snow. He started his car, letting the engine warm for a minute or two, and drove off down Mapleton Avenue. A dense silence engulfed the street. Frost fell upon the lawns and the fir trees shone a ghostly gray.

Thomas Riha was gone, vanished into the night. It was twelve thirty on the morning of March 15, 1969.

PART I ★
BEGINNINGS

1 ★ CRAZY BILLY

There were days when William Sullivan, the head of the FBI's domestic intelligence division, couldn't get the lines from Sir Walter Scott's poem out of his head. "Oh what a tangled web we weave when first we practice to deceive," he would chant as he reviewed a particularly devious counterintelligence operation.[1] Now, as he scanned the FBI reports describing the ether incident and the sudden disappearance of Thomas Riha, the lines may have floated into his head again. Oh, what a tangled web we weave, / When first we practice to deceive![2]

Bill Sullivan had always suffered from anxiety and with the rise in protests and demonstrations against the Vietnam War, the pressures of the job had grown almost unbearable. He had the hollow-eyed appearance of the chronically sleep-deprived, his skin seemed to have absorbed some of the fluorescent light from his office, and his compact body had grown soft from putting in twelve- to fifteen-hour days. By 1969, he was classified as a GS-18 and making $30,239 a year.[3]

He had been an FBI man for thirty years and nothing surprised him anymore. But there were aspects of the Riha case that he no doubt found intriguing. It seems that the two Boulder patrolmen who answered the domestic disturbance call at Riha's house on the evening of March 8–9, 1969, were not as blasé about the evening's activities as they pretended. On Monday, March 10, they informed the campus police of the incident.[4] The campus police, in turn, alerted the FBI's Denver office, which was headed by Special Agent in Charge Scott Werner, one of J. Edgar Hoover's favorites, a handsome man with bushy white hair and a bristly white mustache.

In keeping with FBI procedures, Werner would have then forwarded the report to FBI headquarters in Washington, DC, which FBI agents called the Seat of Government, or SOG. The information would then have been distributed to a handful of high-level FBI executives, including William Sullivan.

As the FBI's intelligence chieftain, Sullivan oversaw all matters relating to espionage, counterespionage, and internal security. At the time, he had 61 double agents working against Soviet-bloc countries;[5] 64 informants monitoring Chinese Communist intelligence activities;[6] more than 300 paid informants covering Communist Party USA activities,[7] and 1,180 informants who kept the Bureau informed of activities relating to the so-called "New Left" and "Black Hate" groups.[8]

Sullivan mentally reviewed the various scenarios that could have accounted for the professor's disappearance. Had the FBI overlooked something in Riha's file when he was admitted to the United States in 1947? Or could the Bureau have missed something thirteen years later, when two agents in Cambridge, Massachusetts, vetted him as a possible double agent?

Perhaps Thomas Riha was an "illegal," that is, a covert agent supplied with a false identity and sent abroad to live in a host country for years before being activated. The FBI had been able to uncover a number of "illegals" through a secret mail-opening program, which was operated by the CIA and code-named HTLINGUAL. Agents also spot-checked savings accounts, looking for unusual sums of money coming from Soviet-bloc countries, and periodically checked death records against the names of new immigrants in selected cities. But the programs were time-consuming and many of these illegals had managed to slip into the country anyway, waiting like viruses until they were activated.[9]

Then, too, there was the remote possibility that the Czech StB or the Soviet KGB had sent an assassin to kill Thomas. Sullivan knew that the Soviets indeed had an assassination squad and that they had killed at least two people in the United States, running over one man with a car in New York City after he was already dead and murdering another Soviet defector in his hotel room in Washington, DC.[10] Thomas spoke multiple languages and had traveled widely in the Soviet Union and Czechoslovakia at a time when such travel was infrequent, but he hardly seemed important enough to merit such an extreme measure.

There were many military and civilian installations within driving distance of Boulder—including the Rocky Flats nuclear weapons plant—but Riha was a history professor with no apparent access to military or scientific intelligence. Still, he could have served as a courier, a recruiter, or even what Sullivan called an "agent of influence."

Finally, there was the strong possibility that Riha's disappearance had nothing to do with espionage at all; he was going through a tumultuous divorce and perhaps he just needed to get away from Boulder for a few days. But that didn't make much sense either. Riha was a responsible man and it seemed unlikely that he would have left Boulder just as spring break was ending and the final weeks of the semester were about to begin.

⋆ ⋆ ⋆

Aside from Clyde Tolson, J. Edgar Hoover's Number Two man and longtime confidant, there was no one in the FBI that Hoover trusted more than Bill Sullivan. Together they had fought the Communist Party USA, the Ku Klux Klan, and La Cosa Nostra.

The Reverend Dr. Martin Luther King was one of their longtime targets. At Hoover's urging, Sullivan and his aides tapped King's telephone, put listening bugs in his hotel rooms, and attempted to discredit the civil rights leader by exposing his sexual relations with other women.[11]

Hoover addressed most employees by their last name, but he had grown fond of Sullivan and in many memos simply called him "Bill." (Other men in the FBI who knew Sullivan's mercurial ways and hair-trigger temper called him Crazy Billy.)[12]

In 1941, when he applied for an agent's job, Sullivan was twenty-three years old and stuck in a dead-end job with the Internal Revenue Service. The FBI did an extensive background check, interviewing employers, friends, neighbors, and even grade school teachers. All of them described Sullivan as intelligent, industrious, and honest. But he had one defect: he was only five feet six inches tall, which was a strike against him in the all-white, all-male FBI.[13] However, being short was not as bad as being bald or possessing, say, an excessively large nose. (The former would all but guarantee rejection and the latter once resulted in a letter of censure to an FBI man who had failed to notice the offending feature in a prospective employee.)[14]

The son of a dairy farmer from Bolton, Massachusetts, Sullivan had a thick mop of dark brown hair and a faint sprinkling of freckles. His parents, who were both from Ireland, were also above reproach, though his father was known to drink a little.[15] Sullivan was offered a starting position at $3,200 a year and accepted immediately. Six months later, Pearl Harbor was bombed and the United States entered World War II. Sullivan and other agents in the FBI were not drafted because Hoover insisted his men were integral to maintaining order at home and hunting down Nazi spies who had infiltrated the United States.

Sullivan was a quick study, rapidly absorbing the FBI culture and enduring without complaint the transfers from field office to field office. They were hellish for young families, but necessary for agents who wanted to work at headquarters.

One of Sullivan's first supervisors was a crusty agent named Charlie Winstead, who had gunned down John Dillinger. In Sullivan's autobiography, he quotes Winstead as saying, "If Hoover ever calls you, dress like a dandy, carry a notebook, and write in it furiously whenever Hoover opens his mouth. You can throw away the notes later. And flatter him. Everyone at headquarters knows Hoover is an egomaniac, and they all flatter him constantly. If you don't you'll be noticed."[16]

The FBI's rules were mind-boggling: Agents were expected to put in long hours of overtime. (Overtime was never rounded up or down but recorded to the exact minute.) Hoover wanted everyone out in the field and agents were often censured for TIO, or too much time in the office. Resourceful agents like Sullivan learned to carry their paperwork with them, completing it in the local library or a coffee shop. FBI agents were also censured for grammatical and spelling errors in memos and reports; for failure to answer the telephones promptly; for failure to keep their cars clean; and for failures related to their appearance, which included such things as being overweight or suffering from a bad case of acne.

Crafty agents like William Sullivan and W. Mark Felt, a contemporary who joined the Bureau at about the same time and one day would admit he was Deep Throat, the *Washington Post*'s anonymous source in the Watergate scandal, learned to censure themselves even before Hoover or Clyde Tolson had a chance to write their stinging rebukes.

Sullivan had a knack for writing and public speaking and Hoover was pleased by the heroic way he characterized the Bureau's fight against communism. He carried out Hoover's orders with zeal and never forgot to flatter him. In return, Hoover rewarded him by giving him promotions and bonuses and occasionally, a few words of warm praise. After ten years of service, Hoover sent him a pro forma congratulatory letter and Sullivan responded with a heartfelt, three-page letter of his own, saying, "You spoke generously of my contribution to the FBI during the past decade. May I take this occasion to remind you of the FBI's contribution to me."[17]

As a boy, Sullivan had often been sick and poor health continued to plague him into adulthood. He suffered from sore throats, fevers, sinus infections, pneumonia, bronchitis, asthma, peptic ulcers, and anxiety. During the mid-1950s, he suffered from such serious respiratory ailments that he was reassigned to the Tucson office.[18] Hoover was as solicitous as Sullivan's own mother, reassuring him in notes and letters that his work could wait and that his main task was to regain his health.[19]

In Sullivan's annual employee evaluations, Hoover urged him to recruit more informants and double agents. Just two months after Thomas disappeared, in a May 26, 1969, letter, Hoover wrote, "Your accomplishments in the continuing penetration of Soviet-bloc operations, effective counterintelligence action against the Communist Party, and detection of illegal agents are gratifying. I am greatly concerned, however, with the lack of Soviet defectors being operated in the United States. This is a serious gap in our intelligence coverage and great efforts are essential if we are to achieve full effectiveness in the counterespionage field."[20]

Now, as the 1960s were drawing to a close, the FBI was facing its most serious challenges ever. The protests against the Vietnam War had grown increasingly violent and almost every day, there were reports of bombings, sniper shootings, and arsons, which were attributed to groups such as the Weather Underground and the Black Panthers. From January 1969 to April 1970—when opposition to the Vietnam War was at its highest—4,330 bombings occurred in the United States.[21] The Weather Underground, which had purportedly renounced violence after a series of spectacular explosions killed three people and destroyed a townhouse in Greenwich Village in New York City, was responsible for only a fraction of the bombings. Splinter groups and lone individuals were responsible for the rest.

The FBI had not been prepared for the rise of the Black Panthers and the Weather Underground and it was also behind when it came to the counterculture lifestyle and lingo. Nevertheless, Hoover warned Sullivan to keep abreast of protest marches and demonstrations as well. "I am deeply concerned by the mood of violence involving both black and white extremist groups," he advised Sullivan. "We must be aware in advance of impending violence, bombings and other terroristic acts. The President and the general public expect this type of effective action on the part of the Bureau and I will accept nothing less."[22]

Sullivan found his investigative resources stretched thin. To compound matters, Hoover had cut back on many of the tools that the FBI had relied upon in the past to combat the Communist Party USA, the Klan, and the Mob. Those tools, often referred to as "technicals," "sensitive techniques," or "technical surveillance," included black bag jobs, buggings, wiretapping, and mail-opening programs. Hoover had grown wary of the practices around 1965 because he was worried that the public might find out and come to view the FBI negatively.[23]

Without these tools, which Sullivan believed were essential, he was having difficulties keeping abreast of threats. Nor were his more than one thousand informants particularly helpful. He had begun venting his frustrations to a twenty-nine-year-old lawyer named Tom Charles Huston, who worked in President Richard M. Nixon's White House.

Huston was a tall, slender man who spoke with a slight twang and had the thoughtful air of a scholar. He had been chairman of Young Americans for Freedom, a national conservative youth organization, and had come to Nixon's attention in 1967 when Nixon was preparing to run for president.[24] Armed with a bachelor's and law degree from Indiana University, Huston had joined Nixon's speechwriting staff in 1968 after completing a stint at the Pentagon with the Defense Intelligence Agency.

Huston had gotten to know William Sullivan after Nixon had asked Huston to undertake several sensitive investigations for him, including one directed at finding out whether foreign agents were behind the civil unrest occurring on college campuses and in America's cities. The FBI and the CIA had already investigated that issue for President Lyndon B. Johnson and had found little evidence of foreign involvement. But Nixon, whose own inauguration ceremonies had been marred by stone-throwing youths and hecklers, couldn't accept those conclusions.[25] "I don't think that's what the president wanted to hear," Huston recalled in a 2008 oral history interview. "He was a lot like Johnson in that, I mean, they looked out their window and they saw all of this stuff going on out there, and, you know, they couldn't imagine why a policy that was so much in the national interest, as they perceived it, could be opposed by all this rabblerousing group without some foreign or subversive outfit having their finger in the pot."[26]

President Nixon considered Huston to be one of the toughest operatives in the White House, but he didn't much like him. In one conversation with his chief of staff, H. R. Haldeman, he called Huston "a son-of-a-bitch."[27] In another, he referred to him as an "arrogant little bastard."[28]

Bill Sullivan was accustomed to dealing with sons-of-bitches and bastards. Moreover, he saw none of those qualities in Tom Charles Huston. As the months passed, their relationship deepened. Though decades separated the two men, Sullivan was attracted to Huston's quiet demeanor. "As we talked, I found myself admiring him more and more," he would say.[29] Huston was similarly impressed with Sullivan. "I don't think there was anyone in the Government who I respected more than Mr. Sullivan," he would tell a Senate panel that undertook an historic review of the nation's intelligence activities in the 1970s and became known as the Church Committee.[30]

★ ★ ★

After reading about the events surrounding Riha's vanishing, Sullivan probably went to the FBI's vast filing system and pulled up Riha's dossier. Thomas had been assigned the number 105-78256. (The 105 prefix stood for foreign counterintelligence.)[31]

The file was unremarkable save for a couple of pages describing a decades-old interview that FBI agents conducted with Riha when he was living in Cambridge, Massachusetts, and studying Russian history at Harvard. The FBI men were interested in finding out whether Riha had been recruited by the Soviets or Czechs during his 1958 trip abroad and whether he had the makings of a good double agent. Riha was described as a cooperative subject and proud of his US citizenship, but the FBI report doesn't disclose whether he went on to become a double agent.

William Sullivan needed more information about Riha's disappearance, but he no doubt wanted to obtain the information quietly, through unofficial channels, so no one would know of the FBI's involvement. That might mean using informants or some of the surreptitious surveillance techniques that Hoover had grown leery of.

In a memo from FBI headquarters to Denver, Special Agent in Charge Scott Werner was instructed *not* to do any investigation. "Any pertinent information received concerning this matter should be forwarded to the Bureau by LHM [letterhead memorandum] and no investigation need be conducted by your office."[32]

Galya also had an FBI dossier, but Bill Sullivan may not have been aware of that. She had changed her last name when she moved from Chicago to Colorado.

2 ★ GALYA

As the summer mist from the Mississippi River rolled across south St. Louis, Gloria Forest watched her cousin playing on a swing set with other neighborhood children.[1] She desperately wanted to join them, but was afraid one of the kids would suddenly notice her and call his playmates over to make fun of her haircut, her wool stockings, or the tight-fitting bodice of her dress. So she grabbed her "doll"—a broken porcelain statue that she kept wrapped in blankets—and ducked under the porch.

Gloria Forest was a bright child who could draw lifelike images almost before she could walk. In spite of her abundant talent, she believed she was inferior to other children. From almost the moment she could talk, she thought of herself as a misfit and outsider. She felt alienated from friends and family, especially her mother. Sometimes she even felt alienated from her own self and that was the most painful feeling of all. She began to erect a protective wall around herself, which kept out the hurtful things, but also kept out the love she craved and the skills that she needed to learn how to overcome obstacles.

Gloria Ann Forest, who one day would go by the name Galya Tannenbaum, was born on March 30, 1931, in Chicago's Presbyterian Hospital. When she was about two years old, her parents, Margaret and Joseph Forest, returned to St. Louis, where they moved into a four-story house at 3406 Meramec Street with a family consisting of aunts, uncles, and cousins. Built in 1894 by her grandfather, the brick house had been originally designed for one family, but had been converted into a multifamily dwelling. One of Galya's widowed aunts, Theresa, a dressmaker and seamstress, lived on the first floor with her daughter, Antoinette. Galya's grandfather and two unmarried aunts occupied the second floor. Galya's family lived in the third-floor attic.

The house on Meramec Street was Galya's home throughout much of her childhood, but she thought of it as a kind of a House of Usher. She was filled with unnameable fears and projected those fears onto her surroundings. She was terrified of the shadowy attic and even more frightened of the basement, where a huge coal-burning furnace emitted a flickering light and the nearby rooms were heaped with cast-off bassinets, baby carriages, and stiffened mops. Even the steep wooden stairs connecting the levels of the house held a kind of terror for her. In one of several biographical sketches that she wrote in 1970, she remembered, "The steps were steep and frightening—I'd come tumbling down and collide with the door at the bottom. *Once* my Aunt Mary made an attempt to catch me—but generally I was left there alone untill [*sic*] I managed to get up by myself."[2]

The Meramec Street residence was located in a south St. Louis neighborhood known as Dutchtown, which had been settled by the Germans in the previous century and took its name from the word *deutsch,* which means *German.* Dutchtown was a relatively prosperous neighborhood, with churches, schools, parks, and small businesses, including grocery stores and drugstores. Streetcars provided access to the rest of the city and the Mississippi River was a few blocks away. Though the neighborhood's economic fortunes would decline precipitously over the next fifty years, at that time it was a pleasant part of St. Louis where many first- and second-generation immigrant families made their homes.

Galya's father worked as a window decorator and paint salesman. Galya was the oldest child and had two brothers, Peter and Charles. (A third brother, Paul, died in infancy.) When her brother, Pete, was born, he was given her bed in the attic and she was forced to sleep on a pallet on the floor. Consequently, she developed pneumonia, an illness that recurred frequently throughout her life, along with strep throat, earaches, sinus infections, and mysterious headaches. As Galya grew older, she wound up being the de facto babysitter, maid, and yard person. She resented the role and grew more alienated from her family. Sometimes she walked down to the Mississippi River, where she fantasized about throwing herself off the bluffs.

Her parents argued with each other and with other relatives in the house. When her father landed a job at Thomas Bros. Paint Company, which paid fifteen dollars a week, the Forests decided to move out of the house on Meramec Street and into their own flat.[3] The new apartment had radiator heat and consisted of four rooms and a bath. A junk man clip-clopped up and down the alley in a horse-drawn wagon and often let Galya climb on board.

Galya's brother Pete vandalized property and got into fistfights with other neighborhood kids. Yet he remained his mother's favorite and when he returned home with scratches and bruises, Galya was reprimanded for not protecting him.

School brought more misery. She could barely squeeze into her small desk and felt so self-conscious and clumsy when she was called upon to answer a question that she often became mute. "I was like a little old lady, I did not make friends and it was extreemly [sic] difficult for me to have to come in and be there each day."[4]

Over time, her family's financial condition improved. Her father bought a car and the Forests moved to a new flat on Louisiana Street, which had large airy rooms and an enclosed front porch. In the summertime, the family went to Galva, Illinois, a small farming community where Galya's maternal grandparents lived. (One journalist speculated that Galya could have taken her first name from that of the small town because when the downward dash on the y was removed, it became Galva.)

Located 160 miles southwest of Chicago, Galva had been settled by Swedish immigrants in the previous century and took its name from a sister city in Sweden called Gävle. Victorian homes lined the streets and swaths of open land had been set aside for parks.

One summer, while the family was vacationing in Galva, her father announced that he was leaving. His departure devastated Galya, who saw her father as an ally in the growing psychological struggle with her mother. Mrs. Forest and her three children returned to St. Louis and moved into the first floor flat on Meramec Street. One of Mrs. Forest's sisters, Mary, moved in with them. Galya's Aunt Mary felt free to scold Galya as much as her mother.

In one of Galya's autobiographical sketches, she claims she was beaten by her mother with belts, broomsticks, or razor strops. Her mother, Margaret Forest, a benign-looking woman who wore floral-patterned dresses and thick eyeglasses that reflected the milky Midwestern sky, found the allegations painful. Mrs. Forest had a business degree, but worked in school cafeterias when Galya was growing up and later in the kitchen of a large hotel. She began her day at four thirty in the morning, firing up huge wall ovens for meat dishes and then rolling out the dough for bread, rolls, pies, cobblers, and pastries. She finally called it quits when an oven exploded and blew her into a meat locker. "She worked very hard. She was an educated woman. She had graduated but in the town where she was living there were no job opportunities," said one granddaughter.

When Galya reached adolescence, arguments with her mother and her Aunt Mary escalated. When she misbehaved, she writes, the two women would drag her down to the basement and tie her to a post. There, in the humid darkness, her imagination bloomed with fearful images and her thoughts circled obsessively, digging new pathways in her brain:

I spent a lot of time in that ominous basement terrified and feeling as though everything crawling down there had found me & was crawling on me & I couldn't get loose to swat them off. It's strange what a child can imagine, but the basement experience, which always started with me screaming & begging not to have to go down there, and kicking & fighting my amazon-strength aunt all the way with my mother swinging a stick or a strap, would dissolve into a different world:[5]

I could smell the fragrance of flowers and touch the soft textures of everything around me. All sorts of things happened then, from being a scholar, admired by all in a beautiful school with teachers who liked me, to feeling the sensations of having my hair curled and made pretty. There were no dark, fearful things in my illusionary world, and I'd stay there untill [sic] someone in my family came to drag me back up the stairs.[6]

Galya attended Catholic schools throughout her childhood. Under the nuns' guidance, she developed an unusually beautiful penmanship. But her writing was marred by misspellings, as if on some unconscious level she were trying to undermine herself.

She possessed genuine artistic talent and on Saturday mornings, she would take the streetcar across town for art lessons. Once she spent her fare on a candy bar and trudged home through an ice storm. She wasn't wearing mittens and when she stopped at a relative's house to warm up, she writes that her fingers split open like "ripe tomatoes." In the kitchen, she knocked a pan of pea soup from the stove, which ran into her shoes and scalded her feet. A neighbor took her to the hospital, where she remained for the next six weeks.

When she returned to school, she was hopelessly behind. Her feet remained tender and sensitive to the cold, so she began ducking into churches on the way to school to get warm. In the dim interior of the churches, a strange thing happened: Saints walked down from their pedestals to converse with her. "They were gentle people and would go with me anywhere I desired to go—but vanish with the appearance of anyone else."[7]

Once she left church, fear gripped her. She was afraid of everything—the attic, the basement, her classmates, the Mississippi River, the neighborhood swimming pool, two-wheel bicycles, weeds, roaches, barnyard hens, and dogs of any kind. Galya desperately wanted a pair of roller skates and when her mother refused to buy them, she simply took a pair from the local hardware store, telling the clerk that her mother would pay for them. She paid for the brazen act. While skating on Louisiana Street, she was struck by a car and wound up in the hospital. The doctors quizzed her about the head-aches she was having, which surprised her, for she had had headaches all her life. Simply walking from a warm to cold room could trigger the pain, but only the doctors seemed interested in finding out what caused them.[8]

As the years passed, a corrosive self-pity continued to grow within her. "I saw most everyone as being more valuable than I was—accepted—popular—and most of the time I tried to stay away—out of sight where I would not become—or at least, wouldn't hear myself being ridiculed—laughed at for looking funny."[9]

At home, the physical and verbal abuse continued. "There was seldom a day that passed that I was not struck with the broomstick by my mother & having her tell me she couldn't wait until I was old enough to get married & get out of her house, and my aunt going into tyrades [sic] telling me how sinfull [sic] I was for everything I was supposed to have been doing or *thinking*."[10]

★ ★ ★

Galya's life was about to change. She met a young dance bandleader named Robert "Mack" McPherson, who became infatuated with her. Galya was only sixteen, but Mack thought she was much older and invited her to dinner at the fanciest place in St. Louis—the Jefferson Hotel dining room—where a camera girl took their picture. Her mother and aunt approved of him because he taught music at a nearby music school. Eventually they fell into a routine; Mack would spend the evening playing cards with Mrs. Forest and Galya's Aunt Mary while Galya sat behind them, watching. On August 15, 1947, they got married in Illinois before a justice of the peace.[11] Galya was now Mrs. Robert Stuart McPherson. She was ecstatic, but her family was furious because she had married outside of the Catholic Church.

Mack reenlisted in the military and the couple moved to Bolling Air Force Base outside Washington, DC. It was the first time Galya and Mack had been alone together for any length of time and the adjustment was difficult. While they were in the Washington, DC, area, Galya said she met Thomas Riha for the first time. Although Galya was younger than Thomas, she spoke of him as if he were one of her children. "I'll tell you something," she would tell Boulder journalist John R. Olson in 1970, "Thomas at the age of seventeen was like a little old man, after the experiences he'd had. His education had been aborted because of all this mishmash of war and he was in the process of trying to put the pieces together."[12] She continued,

"It was sorta help him get settled here, dragging up blankets so he'd have something to have in the school dormitory, dragging things together sorta like that and we sort of kept in contact. . . . Thomas Riha was a messed up kid that we liked and we kept contact with. Like I said, it was off and on."[13]

Other than Thomas Riha, Galya and Mack didn't socialize much. Mack was often gone on music gigs on weekends and Galya stayed up all night waiting for him. "It seemed as though he had lost some of his love for me, and I didn't know what to do to attract him to me," she writes.[14] Galya became pregnant and took to her bed, waiting for her husband to come home. Once, she looked up and saw a spider descending from the ceiling toward her face.[15] She was petrified and pulled the blankets over her head. The following morning, she couldn't move her left arm or left leg.

When the paralysis persisted, an ambulance was called and she was taken to the base hospital. The physicians didn't know what to make of her condition. "Patient talks very fast but her words were distinct," one wrote. "Voice breaks from time to time and patient intersperses many profane expressions. There are many small fibrillary twitching of facial and extremity musculature."[16] Galya was injected with sodium amytal, a truth serum, and afterward she was able to get up and walk around her hospital room. The doctors concluded she was suffering from a "hysterical conversion reaction," a condition in which paralysis is thought to be due to an underlying psychological disturbance.

Afterward, she went to Galva, Illinois. Although she was visibly pregnant, her mother made it clear that she was not welcome, so she went to live with Mack's parents in Danville, Illinois. On March 20, 1949, she gave birth to a daughter, Margaret Ann McPherson.[17] Her husband, meanwhile, had moved to Lackland Air Force Base in San Antonio, Texas, and seemed to be in no hurry to be reunited with his wife and newborn daughter. When Galya's relatives threatened to contact his commanding officer, he drove to Illinois and picked up Galya and Margie and drove them back to Texas. It was a miserable trip; Margie had colic and cried the entire way. They set up housekeeping in a kitchenette motel near the base. While Mack was working, Galya bundled up Margie in a secondhand stroller and they visited the Alamo and other sights in downtown San Antonio. Eventually they moved into a duplex.

One evening, after she had fed and bathed Margie and put her to bed, she went out to visit a neighbor. When she returned, "Mack was all huffed up & in the living room—and said he knew how to put that kid to sleep—I asked him what he did and he said he spanked her."[18]

Margie was quiet that night and Galya didn't check on her. The following morning, the infant still had not stirred. "I went to see how she was and found her sopping wet and black and blue from the back of her head to her heels. I almost threw up on the spot, I was furious and crying and terribly upset. I couldn't get her to wake up at all."[19]

A neighbor took Galya and the baby to the base hospital. By then, Margie was beginning to awaken and the doctor told her to take the infant back home. "I put my precious baby on a satin blanket on the floor on her tummy—Mack came in and without any apparent provocation flung a potty chair right at Margie, and missed hitting her head by inches. I picked up my baby & had her in the crib with the side up and dumped the food cooking on the stove down his back—he lit out toward the back door & I grabbed for the car keys & he tripped & went out head first down the stairs. I jumped on top of him pounding on him—the sheriff came & Margie went to the Brooke Army hospital, Mack to Lackland Base Hospital and I went to jail."

When Mack admitted to authorities that he was the one who had spanked Margie, Galya said she was released from jail. But their relationship was over. She found herself alone and penniless in a strange city. In desperation, she forged her husband's name to a $336 payroll check that had been mailed to their address. She was subsequently charged with mail theft and forgery of a government check. On March 19, 1950, she was sentenced to three years' probation in lieu of a one-year prison sentence.[20]

★ ★ ★

Depressed and confused, she returned once more to Galva, Illinois. She worked the night shift at the Lilly Tulip Cup Corporation and made friends with a man named Clayton Lind, who showed her how to use a gun and took her hunting. She began carrying a gun and a badge in her wallet, boasting to townspeople that she was an FBI agent. That didn't sit well with a resident named Norma Blewitt, who decided to contact the FBI. "She is probably a 'big bag of wind,' but I don't like the idea of her going around posing as any kind of special agent any more than you probably do, so if nothing more I hope you can scare the heck out of her," she wrote.[21]

The FBI opened an impersonation case and an agent in J. Edgar Hoover's squeaky-clean Bureau was assigned to look into the matter. He interviewed the postmaster and justice of the peace and a probation officer assigned to Galya's case. The justice of the peace said Galya had appeared before him on a concealed gun charge. The gun was inoperable and he gave it back to Galya and fined her $14.10.[22] The postmaster described Galya (who was still going by the name Gloria) as a frustrated woman, a gun enthusiast, and harmless "crank."[23]

When the FBI caught up with Galya, she conceded that she could have made some misleading statements, but signed a sworn affidavit saying she never told anyone she was an FBI agent or any other government employee. "The most I ever did was to tell someone that I intended to apply for a position with the government," she admitted. "I have never acted as a government employee or led anyone to believe I was a government employee. I have never received any money or anything else of value from anyone by pretense of being a government employee."[24] Since Galya had not illegally enriched herself while posing as an agent, the FBI closed the case.

In April 1954, she was rushed to St. Louis County Hospital, where she was treated for an overdose of bichloride of mercury and barbiturates. She told the medical staff she was a captain in the Air Force and a certified public accountant and had undergone surgery for cancer of the pancreas. The doctors diagnosed her with an "inadequate personality" and "sociopathic personality disturbance" and urged her to get counseling.[25]

Galya had no money for counseling and instead went to work as a bookkeeper for the city of Wellston, Missouri, a suburb of St. Louis. While there, she was indicted by a grand jury for embezzling six thousand dollars by forging the name of the town's mayor and treasurer on eleven checks made out to herself or to a fictitious entity.[26] Her picture appeared in the *St. Louis Globe Democrat* where she looked cool and defiant in her cat's-eye glasses. Before the indictment was handed down, she breezed into a St. Louis hotel with Margie, demanded a suite and an extra phone line, and gave the hotel employees the distinct impression she was an FBI agent.

The FBI subsequently opened a second impersonation inquiry. Galya said she was innocent of the embezzlement charges and denied trying to pass herself off as an FBI agent. The Bureau closed the case again.

On March 2, 1955, Galya gave birth to a second daughter named Deborah. When she realized she did not have the emotional or financial resources to care for the infant, she gave the baby up for adoption to a relative. She wanted her baby back, but knew the legal costs would be prohibitively expensive and let the matter drop. "I didn't want to give my baby up but it seemed hopeless."[27]

Galya made preparations to end her life again. She drew up a will and last testament and gave away her possessions. On June 2, 1955, she took an overdose of morphine, Nembutal, and insulin. Luckily a friend saw her injecting the drugs and called an ambulance, which took her to St. Louis's Jewish Hospital. By then, she was in a deep coma and a spinal tap was done to rule out brain hemorrhage. When she came out of the coma, she was released from the hospital. Three days later, she attempted suicide again and once again was revived. "Patient was not likely a psychopath, but all that can be definitely said is that she has an inadequate personality. Psychiatric help not wanted," a doctor wrote in her medical chart.[28]

3 ★ THOMAS

The Czechs have a proverb that says there is no rumor without a grain of truth in it. Thomas Riha could have had a proverb of his own saying there is no truth without a grain of falsehood in it. He had a rich and dramatic story to tell—a half-Jewish boy forced to hide from the Nazis during World War II, seemingly abandoned by his mother, who managed to bootstrap his way up into the finest universities in the United States. Still, he felt it necessary to tweak the details, especially when it came to his relatives, making them seem grander or more tragic than they really were.

He was, by all accounts, a dedicated teacher, charming, handsome, a meticulous dresser, orderly in his personal habits. Yet there was a moodiness about him that led one of his fellow history professors to wonder if he possessed a "split personality."[1] He was surrounded by women—they were his students, teaching assistants, and confidantes—but he seemed incapable of developing a long-lasting and healthy relationship. Academic colleagues saw him as a harmless flirt who had schoolboy crushes on women who were beyond his reach. Yet an army buddy described him as a man with an insatiable sexual appetite.

Galya would chalk up the dysfunction to the fact that his mother had abandoned him during the war. "She claimed that he hated his mother and that a lot of his behavior with women showed this hatred for his mother—some kind of mother complex," Carol Word, Riha's favorite student, would say. "She claimed that his mother had never been close to him and that he wasn't concerned with his mother and therefore his treatment of her and other women manifested itself in strange and unusual ways."[2]

Thomas was born in Prague on April 17, 1929, the year the US stock market collapsed and Europe's economic and political woes deepened. His mother, Ruth, was a beautiful woman with thick blonde hair, which she sometimes wore flapper style or done up in an elegant French twist. Her waist was small, her teeth were white, her eyes gray. Educated in a convent, she practiced yoga and read philosophy books.

Thomas Riha's father, Viktor, who had a grown daughter from his first marriage, was equally handsome. He had a slight cleft in his chin, a firm mouth, and arching eyebrows, which gave him a thoughtful and appraising demeanor. Ruth and Viktor both had doctorates in the law, but only Viktor worked as a lawyer. Ruth spent most of her career teaching languages in private schools.

Thomas lived with his parents in a lovely, three-story flat on the stone steps below the Prague Castle. The castle, which actually consists of a complex of gardens, courtyards, palaces, and the magnificent St. Vitus Cathedral, sits on a high hill overlooking the city of Prague and the Vltava River. Viktor purchased the flat in 1924 and gave half of it to Ruth when they married.[3] The ceilings were covered with Renaissance paintings. Across the cobblestone steps was a ledge where the family could look out over Prague's red-tiled roofs and white chimneys. A balcony at the rear of the flat jutted out over the castle's manicured grounds. Ruth and Viktor drew admiring glances as they walked down the stone steps and over the Charles Bridge to Old Town, where they could listen to street musicians or watch the medieval astronomical clock chime the hour.

Ruth's parents, Karel and Josepha Kress, were Jewish, but had converted to Catholicism in the early part of the twentieth century. They lived in a more residential and less conspicuously wealthy Prague neighborhood together with their other child—Pavel Peter—who was about seven years younger than Ruth and possessed the family's handsome looks. Karel Kress was the president of the Austrian Bank of Industry and Commerce. Sometime before 1914, he had changed his surname from Kohn to Kress.[4] He was a sober, serious man who wore wire-rimmed spectacles and fine woolen suits and traveled throughout Europe. He doted on his wife, Josepha, who had the harried appearance of a woman who was perpetually late for appointments and was once cited by the Prague police for honking her automobile horn excessively.

Occasionally, Mrs. Kress took her children and grandson Thomas to Seeboden, Austria, a resort town in the Alps next to a fjord-shaped lake. Doted on by parents and grandparents, Thomas attended a French school and carried himself like a young prince while he was still in schoolboy shorts.[5] "He belonged to the last generation that enjoyed a particular kind of privileged, cosmopolitan, middle-European childhood," Donald Fanger, a professor of Russian literature at Harvard and close friend of Thomas, would write.[6]

That world began to crumble on the morning of March 15, 1939, when Hitler invaded Czechoslovakia. As the Führer rolled through Prague, flipping up his hand in greeting, thousands of Czechs returned his salute and unfurled from their windows huge flags sewn with swastikas. Other bystanders stood silent, aware of the surging anti-Semitism in neighboring Germany. Accompanying Hitler was his bloodthirsty companion, Reinhard Heydrich, who in 1941 would be appointed Reich protector of the protectorate of Bohemia and Moravia.

A workaholic and physical fitness buff, Heydrich was tall and muscular, except for a feminine flare to his hips. The son of a professional musician and a musician himself, Heydrich built the Gestapo into a ruthless and efficient weapon of terror across Europe. He is viewed as one of the key architects of the Final Solution, the Nazis' plan for the mass murder of Europe's Jews. In Prague, the Gestapo's administrative headquarters was located in a large stone palace on Wenceslas Square. Behind the thick stone walls were interrogation rooms and instruments of torture, including a guillotine.

When the German Army bogged down on the Eastern Front and the Allied bombers turned the Third Reich's magnificent cities into rubble, Heydrich would dispatch thousands of people to their death throughout Prague and the rest of Europe.

The Nazis took control of all aspects of the Czech government, including police departments, which had files containing much of the history of Prague's Jews—where they lived, how much property they owned, if, and when, they converted to Christianity. (The conversion date would become an important factor in evaluating how "Jewish" the children of mixed-marriages—such as Thomas Riha—were and whether they should be sent to death camps.)

The Nazi war machine immediately set about stripping the country of its natural resources. "It is terrible, terrible in Czechoslovakia," said John Beneš, the brother of Czech president Eduard Beneš, who had fled to London, where he established a government in exile. "The Czechs have nothing. Everything is German. They are cutting the forests of Bohemia to the ground to get wood fiber for their 'Erzatz' shirts, gasoline, everything they make from wood. Everything from the mines and factories is shipped back to Germany. You see the loaded trucks on the roads to Germany and the empties coming back." Prague, he added, was crawling with Gestapo agents and spies. "They would try to pick fights with Czechs so the German press could write stories about the oppressed Germans."[7]

Czechoslovakia was also important to the Nazi war effort because of its central location in Europe and its large armaments industry, which included the Skoda Works. Initially the laborers in these heavy industries were left alone while the Gestapo rounded up enemies of the Nazi regime—Jews, Communists, Gypsies, homosexuals, the mentally and physically handicapped—and packed them off to concentration camps. As for the Czech people themselves, Heydrich divided them up into categories. Writes author Robert Gerwath: "'Racially good' and 'well-intentioned Czechs,' he announced, would certainly become Germans. 'Racially bad' and 'ill-intentioned' Czechs would be 'removed' to the 'wide spaces' of the East. Racially inferior Czechs with good intentions would be sterilized and then resettled in the Old Reich where they would be exploited as slave laborers. 'Ill-intentioned' but 'racially good' Czechs, the 'most dangerous of them all,' would be 'put up against the wall.'"[8]

Czech Jews were allowed to emigrate until September 1939. After that, their lives became miserable. Their property was confiscated, they were expelled from their jobs, and their children were not allowed to attend school. They were banned from theaters, restaurants, trams and taxis, and could shop for groceries only during restricted hours. In 1941, when Heydrich officially took control of the Protectorate, about one thousand Jews were rounded up daily and transported to Terezín, a ghetto and SS prison forty miles north of Prague. From Terezín, thousands were herded onto transports going to Auschwitz and other death camps. In all, more than 155,000 men, women, and children passed through the gates of Terezín, Roughly 35,000 people died there and another 83,000 perished when they were deported to extermination camps.[9]

Thomas Riha's father, Viktor, often took his daily walk in Vodickova Street with the chancellor of former president Thomas Masaryk, a beloved politician who built Czechoslovakia into a vibrant democracy following World War I.[10] From his discussions with the chancellor and others, Viktor was acutely aware of the dangers facing his beautiful wife, his son, and his in-laws.

Less than two weeks after Hitler rolled into Prague, the Kress family packed up their belongings in their elegant flat on Na Magistrale Street—beds, mattresses, tables, chairs, writing tables, cabinets, carpets, mirrors, paintings, china, linen, and kitchenware—and fled. For Josepha, born in Prague in 1880, the departure was agonizing.

An angry Nazi would write that Mr. and Mrs. Kress were last seen heading toward Seeboden, Austria, the resort town where Mrs. Kress had vacationed in happier times.[11] But that may have been a ruse designed to throw off the Nazis. With the help of Viktor, they actually departed from a port in Hamburg, Germany. "They were rich people so they could pay their way out,"

Thomas's nephew, Zdenek Cerveny, recalled.[12] The trip was long; their first
stop may have been Scotland and later an island in the Caribbean. (Ruth's
passport application indicates she was planning on going to Cuba after the
war.) Eventually they entered the United States by way of Mexico and settled
in California.

For the first two and a half years of the Nazi Occupation, Thomas continued to live with his father in Prague. On a police form, Viktor wrote that his
son was not Jewish.[13] But under Germany's complicated Nuremberg laws,
Thomas could be classified as a mischlinge because he had two Jewish grandparents. Many of these so-called hybrid children, or "mongrels," wound up in
Terezín.

The city became increasingly dangerous for anyone of Jewish blood. In
1942, Thomas was sent to a boarding school in Zlin, a town located two
hundred miles to the southeast of Prague and home of the Bata shoe factory, a global footwear company that is still thriving today.[14]

President Beneš, who presided over the Czech government in exile in
London, actively encouraged a resistance movement. Rail lines and utilities
were sabotaged and factory workers slowed their output. Outraged by the
opposition, Hitler sent resistance fighters to death camps or had them sum-
marily executed.

On May 27, 1942, two Czech paratroopers attempted to assassinate Reinhard Heydrich as he headed to the Prague airport for a meeting with Hitler.
When his black Mercedes slowed down for a curve in the northeast section
of the city, paratrooper Josef Gabčik stepped in front of the car with his
Sten submachine gun and tried to spray the vehicle with bullets. The gun
jammed. A second paratrooper, Jan Kubiš, stepped forward and lobbed a
grenade that exploded on the running board in front of the right rear wheel
of the Mercedes. Shrapnel and horsehair from the vehicle's seat were blown
into Heydrich's body. In spite of his wounds, he managed to stagger from the
Mercedes and fire back at the attackers. Then a passing vehicle was hailed
down and he was transported to the hospital, where he was operated on by
two German surgeons. Several days later, he died from infection caused by
his wounds.

Hitler and other high-ranking Nazis were enraged by his death. His body
lay in state in the Prague Castle for two days while dutiful Germans and Czech
collaborators lined up to bid him farewell. Then his coffin was transferred to
Berlin for one of the most elaborate funerals ever held by the Third Reich. "It
is absurd and once more our disgust is aroused by this mixture of brutality
and shrieking whininess that has always been a hallmark of Nazism," wrote

Thomas Mann. "Wherever this killer went, blood flowed in rivers. Everywhere, even in Germany, he was simply called: The Hangman."[15]

Afterward, the Nazis launched an intensive manhunt for the assassins, rounding up and murdering thousands of suspects. Claiming the paratroopers had received aid from residents in the village of Lidice, a settlement of five hundred people located northwest of Prague, they razed the entire village. All the men were killed and women and children sent to concentration camps, with the exception of Aryan-looking children, who were placed in German foster homes. But that was not sufficient revenge for the Nazis. They filled fishponds with stones and dug up the bones of the village ancestors, removed their gold crowns, and scattered the remains in the fields. "Killing one hundred percent of the people was not enough for the Nazis," Milan Pelant, a Czech guide and historian, said. "It must be one thousand percent. Even the fish had to be punished."[16]

Thomas returned to Prague a year later, but the city was still unsafe. His father sent him first to the village of Pocaply and later to the small town of Jihlava to live with Ludmila Cervena, who was Thomas's half sister and Viktor's daughter from his first marriage.[17] Ludmila was married to a man named Jiri Cerveny and they had two children—Zdenek and Jarmila—who were much younger than Thomas. "It was for his protection," Zdenek Cerveny said. "The danger was that they would start picking up the half-Jews in Prague and send them off to Auschwitz."[18]

The town of Jihlava was not immune to Nazi fervor either. Located eighty miles southeast of Prague, Jihlava was an ancient mining town with a large German-speaking population. Many of those Germans welcomed Hitler's annexation of Czechoslovakia and were imbued with the same anti-Semitic fervor. The local synagogue was torched, Jewish shops were ransacked, and many Jews were transported to extermination camps. "It was complicated in Jihlava because some people collaborated with the Nazis," remembered Jarmila Zakova.[19]

Fortunately, her father was a well-liked and influential man who protected Thomas and managed to get him a job in a sawmill. The elder Cerveny, who was also a lawyer, was questioned by Nazis in his summer home and arrested in a railroad station for antifascist activities. After four months of imprisonment, he was released. "Fortunately, he was not sent to a concentration camp," Jarmila said.[20]

Thomas's beautiful mother, Ruth, remained in Prague for the first year of the Occupation and had the unsavory job of assembling the lists of Jews who had to report to Terazín. "She was making lists until the time she felt she would be on the list. Then she procured false documents and went to Vienna," said Zdenek.[21]

When the war was over, she divorced her husband, Viktor, and moved to California to join her parents. Before she departed, the Czech government issued Ruth a "good citizenship" document, which stated she had done nothing improper during the war.[22]

Thomas finished high school in Prague and in 1946 was sent to the Czechoslovakia College in London to learn English. When the school recruiter absconded with the funds, his mother sent him money for his passage to the United States. In 1947, he boarded the Queen Elizabeth in Southampton, England.[23] When the ship docked in New York, he made his way west to the Bay Area, where his mother, grandparents, and thousands of Slav refugees had settled.

With its abundant sunshine, year-round flowers, and slate-blue Pacific, California must have seemed a paradise to him. For nearly half his life, Thomas had known the uncertainty and terror of war. Now he could fill up on familiar foods at local Czech restaurants, order a bowl of savory soup in Chinatown, or ponder the years of his lost childhood in the afternoon quiet of Russian teahouses.

Riha enrolled as a freshman at the University of California in Berkeley. His yearbook picture shows a strikingly handsome young man with his mother's white teeth and her thick hair and clad in an old-fashioned suit. The yearbook picture taken a year later shows a more wolfish and guarded young man who has jettisoned the suit, but is still wearing a tie.

Riha worked his way through college by babysitting, gardening, stocking shelves at the local supermarket, and busing tables in Lake Tahoe and Yosemite during summer vacations.[24] He was careful with money and put his meager earnings in five different banks.[25]

He dated the Berkeley co-eds, but when he was unable to satisfy his sexual needs, he occasionally slipped across the Bay to visit prostitutes. "I was unaware of him having a relationship with a woman who would be appropriate for him, that is, a relationship of equals," said his close friend, Donald Fanger. "If that signifies the difficulty in establishing intimate connection, that would drive him all the more into the arms of someone who could give him physical relief without challenging him to enter a relationship."[26]

In 1951, Riha graduated with a degree in political science. His whereabouts during the next two years are not known. He may have been traveling, working some nonacademic job that he didn't consider important enough put down on his résumé, or possibly being trained as an intelligence agent.

Between 1947 and 1956, the CIA was hiring many agents from Czechoslovakia, Bulgaria, Romania, and other Communist countries. The Soviets were simultaneously trying to convince these new CIA recruits to become double agents, remembered Sam Papich, an FBI agent who worked closely with Bill Sullivan and served as longtime liaison to the CIA.[27] "Many of these individuals kept their attachments to their previous culture and were socialistically inclined," Papich said. "The FBI was always very leery when dealing with these aliens, always questioning whether they were being loyal to the United States. This caused some difficulties between the CIA and the FBI."[28]

On December 19, 1952, while living at 2630 Etna Street in Berkeley, Thomas became a naturalized citizen and changed his name from Tomáš Ondřej Karel Řiha to Thomas Riha.[29] He then enrolled in Columbia University's Russian Institute, where he studied from September 1953 to February 1954 and again from September 1955 to February 1956.[30]

The Russian Institute, which was founded in 1946 with support from the Rockefeller Foundation, trained students in the Russian language and history. Many of the students went on to become diplomats, academics, and spies. Spotters for the CIA and other intelligence agencies roamed the hallways looking for potential recruits. "The urgent demand for intelligence—not to say information—on the USSR and its satellites was intense and relentless," former CIA director Richard Helms would write of that period.[31] One CIA veteran, Duane Clarridge, remembered having tea and red caviar at the Russian Institute with Alexander Kerensky, who served as prime minister during Russia's brief fling with democracy following the abdication of Czar Nicholas II.[32]

After studying at the Institute for a little over a semester, Riha enlisted in the army. The three-year Korean War was drawing to a close and the Cold War was deepening. Following basic training, Riha was assigned to the 6th Radio and Leaflet Group at the Psychological Warfare Center at Fort Bragg, North Carolina. A Defense Department official writes that Riha "occupied a non-sensitive position and did not have access to classified documents."[33]

Oren Jarinkes, a skilled linguist who served with Riha in the army and later worked at the United Nations, described their military tasks in blunter terms: "We scrubbed garbage cans." When asked why their language skills weren't used, Jarinkes said, "You don't know the American Army. I knew Russian, German, French, and Italian and they had me scrubbing garbage cans." Thomas was "pretty much" doing the same thing, he added.[34]

Robert Schwind, a Georgia lawyer who also served with Riha in the army, has a different recollection of Thomas's duties. In 1954, after the French were decisively defeated in Vietnam at Dien Bien Phu, the US military believed it wouldn't be long before they would be sending ground troops into Vietnam. But nearly everything they knew about Indochina had been written in French, so Riha and his colleagues were tasked with translating French documents into English. "They took a large number of us, particularly those proficient in French language and put us in a library under command of a college professor who had the rank of corporal and we set about translating French materials," Schwind said in an interview in 2014.[35]

Riha's group had been operational for only several months when President Eisenhower held a press conference and emphatically stated that no US troops would be sent to Vietnam. "The question came up: Will the United States intervene in Indochina for the French who were withdrawing? And I remember his words as if they were uttered yesterday: He said, 'No US forces in Indochina as long as I'm president. All Indochina is not worth the life of a single GI,'" Schwind said. "Our group was scattered. I went to Germany for the rest of my tour. I don't know what happened to Riha after that."[36]

Riha remained in the army and then returned to Columbia University. One of his friends was a cheerful young man named Ted Curran, who often dined with him at Sokol Hall, a crowded Czech restaurant on Manhattan's East Side. Curran, who went to the Soviet Union in the mid-1950s and later joined the Foreign Service, remembered Riha as an innocent youth who liked to give the impression he was a ladies' man, but may have actually been clueless when it came to women. "He was kind of a butterfly," Curran said in a 2013 interview. "He was very cute and sweet and played the mandolin. He was a life-of-the-party type guy."[37]

Riha told his fellow students conflicting stories about his father. Peter Bridges, who met Riha at Columbia, said Riha told him that his father worked for Bata Shoes and that the family had emigrated from Canada. Both statements were untrue.[38]

By 1956, Riha was back in Berkeley and working on his master's degree at the Slavic Center. He lived in an apartment owned by his grandmother and shared it with Donald Fanger. "We paid almost nothing in rent," said Fanger. Thomas was a happy, outgoing student, he said.[39] "I can remember going to a large auditorium in Berkeley in the evening and some famous speaker was supposed to be making a speech. The person didn't show up and Tom, to my great shock, walked up on the stage and said, 'Since our speaker isn't here, let's sing some songs' and he had the whole auditorium singing American folk songs and Berkeley college songs." (The Berkeley performance may have been spontaneous, but Riha took his singing seriously and wrote down in a notebook the Czech, Russian, German, and French lyrics to folk and popular songs.)

Fanger met many of Riha's relatives, including Ruth and her second husband, Howard Cook Jr., whom she married in 1948. Cook was fourteen years younger than Ruth and only seven years older than Thomas. He was lean and energetic, with short-cropped, blond hair, and always smiling. As soon as he graduated from high school, he went to work for San Bernardino's *Sun-Telegram*. From there, he enrolled in the University of California at Berkeley, where he became editor of the *Daily Californian*, the university's prestigious student newspaper.[40]

In February 1943, the year he was scheduled to graduate, he enlisted in the Army Air Forces. He was assigned to the Pacific theater, where he flew ten combat missions over Japan as a radar-navigator with the Twentieth Air Force's B-29 bombing squadrons. The B-29s rained down destruction over Japan, culminating with the dropping of atomic bombs on Nagasaki and Hiroshima. Cook was awarded three battle stars and a Presidential Unit citation ribbon.[41]

When he mustered out of the air force, he completed his undergraduate degree and returned to journalism. In the summer of 1958, he was hired to become the top public affairs adviser to Clark Kerr, the president of the sprawling University of California system, who in a few years' time would be dealing with some of the most radical student activists in the United States.

Shortly after his appointment, Cook stopped his vehicle in the middle of the Golden Gate Bridge, walked swiftly to the ocean side, and disappeared over the rail. US Coast Guardsmen saw his body strike the water and sink immediately, leading them to theorize that he had weighed himself down. President Kerr was shocked by the news and refused to believe it until positive confirmation had been made. "As a student and as an important member of the staff, he made a significant contribution to the life of the university and particularly to the development of the Riverside campus," he said in a statement.[42]

Berkeley police found evidence in Cook's apartment that he had attempted to kill himself by breathing gas, slashing his wrists, and swallowing sleeping pills. He left an envelope containing sixty-six dollars for Ruth and a note, which said, "Ruth, I am no good really. You are. Howard."[43] Ruth told reporters that she had no idea why her husband decided to take his life. "We had just bought a new home," she said. "We were full of plans."[44]

Thomas told his nephew, Zdenek Cerveny, that Cook was consumed with guilt because he took part in the atomic bombing of Nagasaki.[45] "That's what Thomas told me. He said Cook's conscience bothered him," Zdenek Cerveny recalled.[46]

In graduate school, Riha had three prominent advisers, including Gleb Struve, a renowned poet and literary historian and friend of novelist Vladimir Nabokov. In his master's thesis, Riha writes sympathetically of the Russian émigrés who settled in Prague between the two world wars.[47]

Master's degree in hand, Riha went east again, this time to obtain his PhD in Russian history from Harvard. "There was something captivating about him. He knew that and played it up," remembered Loren Graham, a respected scholar and author.[48] Riha's adviser was Richard Pipes, a conservative historian and Polish émigré who served as a member of the National Security Council during the Reagan administration. He described Riha as an average student. "Of all my students, he was one of the quietest and least obtrusive," Pipes said. "I certainly have had other students who were much more brilliant."[49]

4 ★ BEHIND THE IRON CURTAIN

In the early summer of 1958, Thomas Riha flew to Paris on the first leg of a trip that would ultimately take him to Moscow University. He was one of a handful of exchange students who had been selected to study in the USSR under a new program designed to promote cooperation between the United States and the Soviet Union. During the exchange program's first three years, roughly one-third of the US students, including Thomas Riha, had some sort of intelligence background.[1]

The exchange students were of great interest to spy agencies both in the United States and the USSR. The American students were briefed by the FBI before they left, followed by the KGB overseas, and occasionally thrust into the unwitting position of informant for the FBI when they returned home. "I found the whole procedure odious," said Richard Wortman, one of Riha's colleagues and an exchange student in the early 1960s.[2] "They started to ask questions about people I was with—not Russians—but Americans. I didn't see myself as a spy on my friends so I avoided the questions."

In the Soviet Union, foreigners were placed under intense surveillance. "It is difficult to comprehend the extent to which the Soviet security organs monitored the movement and activity of foreigners," former CIA director Richard Helms writes.[3] "This level of surveillance made it possible for the KGB to launch provocations and blackmail operations on a uniquely sophisticated level. I recall at least two foreign ambassadors, various high-ranking embassy and military personnel, and numerous clerks who fell victim to these operations. Tourists and others without diplomatic immunity were also at risk of arrest and blackmail."

Robert Byrnes, a leading expert on Soviet affairs who helped shape the careers of many students, including former CIA director Robert M. Gates, chaired the organization that administered the student exchange program, originally called the Inter-University Committee on Travel Grants and located at Columbia University.[4] Byrnes, a former CIA consultant, was the author of more than twenty books and served on the board of Radio Free Europe, which was funded by the CIA.

"He hated all Communists. He hated the Soviet people and their representatives. He really was quite fierce," recalled Donald Fanger. "I remember running into him on a Moscow street. I was there for a conference and he dragged me along to some negotiations he was having with the Russians. It was clear to me as I listened to the Russians and listened to him that he was getting everything he wanted and yet he rubbed their noses in it and made it as unpleasant as he could for them."[5]

Anne Fisher, whose husband, Stephen Fischer-Galati, worked with Riha in CU's history department, said Byrnes once visited them in their Boulder home. She took an immediate dislike to him as he prowled through their bookshelves. "He was so damned snoopy," she remembered.[6]

Administrators of the exchange program were hesitant about letting Riha go to the Soviet Union because they were afraid he might be snatched up and jailed.[7] Grudgingly, they approved his application, but warned him not to visit Czechoslovakia during his fellowship year. Riha assured them he had no intention of doing so, but as soon as his plane landed in Paris, he made arrangements to continue on to Prague.[8]

According to Riha's StB file, which is available at Prague's Institute for Totalitarian Regimes, Riha had been charged in 1947 with the crime of leaving the country without permission.[9] He should have been arrested as soon as he crossed the border into Czechoslovakia, but instead, he was assigned by the Czech Housing Bureau for Foreigners to stay at the Flora Hotel, an arrangement that suggests the Communist government knew he was coming and had authorized his visit.

Riha's StB file, which consists of only four or five pages, doesn't explain how or why these arrangements were made. (Officials at the Institute for Totalitarian Regimes said most of Riha's file, along with the files of thousands of other people, were destroyed after the 1989 collapse of the Communist government.)

At the time of Riha's 1958 visit, Czechoslovakia was just beginning to recover from a ten-year wave of violence. The Communists had seized control of the government in 1948 and had spent a decade expelling nonbelievers from government posts and universities. They conducted show trials and executions and banished thousands of people to work camps and uranium mines. Between 1948 and 1954, approximately a hundred thousand people had been captured by Czech security forces and executed or given lengthy prison sentences.[10]

The StB was the foundation and scaffolding of the repressive Czech government and over time would develop an elaborate network consisting of two hundred thousand collaborators, informers, and agents. Equipped with state-of-the-art cameras, StB agents and collaborators observed and photographed thousands of unwitting Czech citizens in pubs, train stations, parks, and streets. If a resident spoke out against the regime or was related to someone who had defected, their homes were searched for incriminating literature and listening devices installed. "They were people who were morally twisted and wicked at heart," a Czech author would write.[11] "They were employees of a psychotic state apparatus."

To stave off bankruptcy, the Communist government in the 1950s had seized personal assets and bank accounts of innumerable Czech citizens. The Kress family home on Na Magistrale Street was seized and even the boyhood bank account of Zdenek Cerveny was confiscated. Farms and factories, businesses and banks, were appropriated and became state-operated. "With collectivization of agriculture nearing completion, in 1959 probably nine-tenths of the national wealth and almost one hundred percent of the means of production were in Socialist ownership; if socialism can be defined simply as collective ownership of the means of production, Czechoslovakia has become a full Socialist country," writes author Jan Michal.

The cobblestone streets of Prague and the centuries-old buildings were falling into disrepair. Statues and facades crumbled, balconies toppled over, roofs leaked, pipes and electrical fittings became worn and unusable. The alleys were filled with trash. "It is a grey dark city with empty streets, at first glance dead," writes a Czech historian. "This is a world that has come to a complete 'stop.'"[12]

Each citizen was allotted between ten and twelve meters of living space. Thus, a family of four like the Cervenys would have been entitled to an apartment of fifty square meters.[13] Housewives waited in long lines for food. Oranges, bananas, and potatoes were scarce. Canned goods were almost nonexistent. Demand was so much greater than what shopkeepers could supply that merchants trying to supplement their own meager incomes set aside delicacies for customers who were willing to pay a little extra. Consequently, a thriving black market developed.

★   ★   ★

Thomas Riha spent seven days at the Flora Hotel before he ventured out to see his father and the Cerveny family. It's not clear what he did during those seven days or why he waited so long to visit his relatives. He may have walked the streets, visited old friends, done research in the libraries, or undergone intensive debriefing. Although he didn't appear to have access to top-secret information, the StB had a voracious appetite for any scrap of information about the United States.

Thomas's once prosperous and politically connected father lived in a small pension on Rimska Street. By then, Viktor was in his early seventies and had seen his fortunes decline greatly in the aftermath of World War II and the 1948 Communist putsch. Gone was the elegant flat on the stone steps beneath Prague Castle. Gone was his beautiful wife with the slender waist. Gone, too, was his handsome son. He had to descend several flights of stairs to reach the bathroom and most likely shared his small room with another pensioner. In just four months' time, Viktor would be dead of a heart attack.

While Riha was visiting his father, a mysterious Czech by the name of Karel Chrpa loitered in the street in his automobile, offering to give Thomas a ride to wherever he was going.[14] Mr. Chrpa also followed Riha to the Cerveny residence, pacing back and forth in front of the house while Riha was inside visiting with the family.

Thomas found the surveillance amusing and often accepted Chrpa's rides. "He stayed with us and often his keeper from the StB would pick him up. Thomas liked it. He thought it was friendly attention. He asked to look inside a Czech library that wasn't open to Czech historians and they let Thomas look," Zdenek Cerveny said.[15]

Chrpa tried hard to convince Thomas to return to Czechoslovakia, offering to return to him the family's magnificent flat and to secure a professorship at a university in Bratislava. "They made all kinds of promises. They offered him the house on the castle steps—they would have kicked out whoever was living there—and given it to Thomas if he defected," Cerveny said.[16]

But Thomas told them he wasn't interested. After three weeks in Prague, he traveled to Vienna, Copenhagen, and Helsinki. On September 27, 1958, he entered the Soviet Union by way of Vyborg and made his way to Moscow. "When he got to Moscow by train, Comrade Chrpa was there, waiting to hand him over to the Russians," Cerveny said.[17]

Stalin had been dead for five years and the young Russian students were in a celebratory mood. "There was a kind of effervescence in post–Stalinist Russia," remembered Richard Wortman.[18] "They were singing songs, playing guitars, writing poetry." The American students were allowed to shop in the

Russian stores or purchase food and other items in the commissary of the US embassy. "It was not living lavishly. It was comfortable," Wortman recalled.[19]

Riha's supervisor was Dr. Boris S. Nikiforov, a haughty and arrogant Moscow State University historian who stymied his efforts to work in other libraries or in archives.[20] Fortunately, Riha had a much more sympathetic adviser named Evgenii Demitrievich Chermenski, an orthodox Marxist and "persona gratissima" in the Communist Party.[21] On a cold October day, Riha met with a group of Russian scholars to talk about his dissertation. He was researching Paul Miliukov, a Russian historian and pro-Western politician. The Russians were scornful of Riha's choice and demanded to know why he was pursuing such an unimportant person. Riha told them that he thought Miliukov was a worthy subject because of his influence on Vladimir Lenin.

The American exchange students rarely saw the Soviet historians in social gatherings, but Riha's adviser invited him to dinner one evening. He was the only exchange student to receive such an invitation and he accepted eagerly. On a chilly evening, he made his way to one of the newer housing districts on the outskirts of Moscow, where his adviser and his family lived. "He shared the apartment with another family but it was quite spacious compared to what I saw of Russian housing later, both in Moscow and smaller cities," Thomas would write. "We first went to my advisor's study, a rather, large sparsely furnished room. There were few books, aside from the large Soviet Encyclopedia, second edition. My advisor explained that he had lost his library during the siege of Leningrad where he had lived during the last war. But knowing the Moscow and Leningrad book markets and his not inconsiderable salary I remained puzzled by the fact that he had not bothered to replace such items as were available to anyone who tried."[22]

The two men visited for a while and then moved into the living room where the historian's wife served tea, cakes, and cookies. She was about to embark for a cure in Carlsbad, Czechoslovakia, and was curious about Riha's homeland. Riha happily answered her questions and the questions of her ten-year-old son, who was interested in America's subways. "I went home with a very warm feeling that I could be friends with these people," he would write.

During his months as an exchange student, Riha was allowed to travel freely through Russia. Sounding a little like a Russian himself, he writes, "Trains and buses of every description and quality took me across the Russian land in all seasons—rainy autumn when unpaved Russia is sunk in mud, icy winter when the compassionate snow beautifies the ugly little houses, and the short but so welcome spring when all the greenery seems a miracle, when the water fountains at Peterhof begin to work again, when the excursion boats ply the Neva and Moskva rivers, and when Soviet students will take you to gather lilies of the valley in the beautiful woods around Moscow some of which, alas, are off limits to the foreigners."[23]

The Lenin Library was open seven days a week. With a self-service cafeteria in the basement, it soon became Riha's home. "I confess a genuine affection for the place and its people. Nowhere else in the world was I able to satisfy my curiosity about Russian history so easily and promptly. When tired, I had the consolation of looking at the splendid gilded domes of the Kremlin churches through the windows. In the corridors and the cafeteria I could talk with Soviet citizens in all walks of life, and from all parts of the vast country. Spending one's days in the Lenin Library was an education itself."[24]

When Riha wasn't in the library, he immersed himself in the nearby bookstores, which were filled with hard-to-find volumes and rare maps. Book binding in the Soviet Union was done in a haphazard way and many of the books Riha looked at were literally falling apart. For thirty dollars, he purchased fourteen wall maps, some of which measured five feet by six feet. He also purchased two hundred books and had them shipped back to the United States. "Standing on my shelves now they are the most vivid reminder of my Soviet education," he writes.

Riha left Odessa by boat and did some more sightseeing in Europe. He departed Paris on August 20 and arrived back in the United States on August 26, 1959. (A few months later, Lee Harvey Oswald arrived in Moscow, startling the Soviets with the announcement that he wanted to defect.)

A year after Riha's return, the FBI knocked on his door at 11 Dana Street in Cambridge, Massachusetts. The agents were interested in learning more about Soviet efforts to recruit US exchange students and also in the possibility of using Riha as a double agent. Since both topics were considered sensitive, Riha's file was initially classified "secret" and a handwritten note on the cover page states, "No dissemination since this was attempt to develop possible double agent."[25]

By then, the FBI had compiled a lot of information on Thomas. They knew, for example, that in 1954 he had begun receiving through the mail "Young Communist" and "Pioneer" propaganda, which were intercepted by the Collector of Customs in New York as part of the CIA's operation, HTLINGUAL.[26] The FBI also knew that Riha had been in contact with foreign intelligence agents while he was abroad. In order to use him as a double agent, they needed to assess his loyalty and truthfulness. The first test would be whether Riha voluntarily revealed his foreign intelligence contacts during the interview:

Care will be exercised to protect the original source in this matter. No direct questions will be asked during the interview which will disclose to the subject the identity of the official or the establishment contacted, the method used in the contact or the fact that we are aware of the contact. The interview will be conducted in a manner so that the subject will volunteer the details of the contact. If this subject is cooperative, no affirmative steps will be taken during the initial interview to direct his activities, but a separate communications will be directed to the Bureau setting forth the rest of the interview and requesting authority [remaining text deleted].[27]

Thomas told FBI agents about Mr. Chrpa, but he characterized the encounters as very casual. He said the StB agent was simply trying to make a "goodwill ambassador" of him, omitting the fact that the Czechs had offered him a professorship in Bratislava and that they had offered to return the elegant flat below Prague Castle. "RIHA," writes the FBI, "advised that CHRPA never asked him to do anything of an intelligence nature."

Riha also admitted that he had met two or possibly three intelligence agents in the Soviet Union and downplayed those encounters, too. While studying in the Lenin Library, Riha said that a Mr. Mikhalkov invited him to dinner in an expensive hotel. Riha accepted the invitation, despite repeated warnings from his academic advisers that the KGB and her sister agencies were always looking to entrap students. "MIKHALKOV hired a private room in a very expensive and exclusive hotel to have dinner. RIHA said he was suspicious of him because of his wealth and therefore never warmed up to MIKHALKOV during this visit. RIHA stated that their conversation was very general and that MIKHALKOV made no requests of him whatsoever. RIHA stated this was the last time he saw MIKHALKOV."[28]

Riha also told the FBI about several Russian women he dated. One was Natasha Meyer, who ended the relationship after two months, saying she would be expelled from her library job if they continued. He then began seeing a young Russian girl named Larissa Kuchberia. "RIHA said that he was suspicious of LARISSA KUCHBERIA and therefore very cautious in his relations with her. KUCHBERIA never made any requests of him to do anything of an intelligence nature. However, he said she constantly praised Czechoslovakia and pointed out its advantages and attempted to interest RIHA in returning to his native country. RIHA told her many times he had no desire to return to Czechoslovakia."[29]

While talking to FBI agents, Riha made his relationships with his Russian friends sound cold and superficial. But that's not how he portrayed them in conversations with other US historians heading for the Soviet Union. "So many Russian students would unload their troubles on us, he [Riha] said, that we would find ourselves in the most intense atmosphere we have ever encountered," writes historian Loren Graham.[30]

Riha told the FBI that he had not been contacted by any foreign intelligence agents since his return to the United States and would contact the Bureau immediately should such a contact occur. "RIHA states that he was proud of his American citizenship and has no desire to return to his homeland for permanent residence."[31]

5 ★ CHICAGO

It was as if an invisible hand was guiding Thomas Riha's academic career. In 1960, after completing his course work at Harvard, the University of Chicago hired him as an instructor. Although it was an entry-level position, it was almost as prestigious as landing in the Ivy League. There would be teaching sabbaticals, a travel allowance for history conferences, and ample time for research and writing. If Riha did well, he might one day receive tenure. Chicago also was home to a large number of Czechs, who established restaurants, grocery stores, bakeries, banks, churches, and real estate firms.

Riha had a large office and taught in the undergraduate college, which traditionally took a backseat to the university's world-class graduate school. In 1964, he received a joint appointment,[1] which meant he could start teaching graduate students. William McNeill, then chairman of the history department, remembered Riha as a "very quiet, thoroughly nice man" who developed an innovative course on Russian civilization based upon the histories of three cities—Moscow, Kiev, and Leningrad. He also organized a student choir that performed Russian Christmas carols.[2]

On the weekends he invited fellow academics to dinner. They marveled at the hundreds of rare books that he had acquired on his travels and admired his beautiful collection of religious icons and statues. Riha had inherited most of the items from Ruth's parents.[3] The most important piece was a carved wood eight-figure Pietà valued between $6,000 and $8,000.[4] He also owned a thirteenth-century wood statue of the Madonna, a pair of fifteenth-century, carved wood panels entitled respectively *The Annunciation* and *Michael the Archangel*, a wood statue of St. Dominic, a trunk inlaid with ivory, a silver snuffbox, and several paintings.

Women, as always, were an important part of his life. "He liked to flirt a lot. He was not a ladies' man. He was awkward. I remember him flirting with a very beautiful student and he even took her out. I assume something was going on there," remembered Richard Wortman, one of his colleagues in the history department.[5] "Other people who knew him better had the impression he was not easy with women. A couple of people suspected him of being gay but I saw no evidence of that."

Jarmila came from Czechoslovakia to spend a few weeks with him. Riha was already becoming set in his ways and went to bed early, so Jarmila spent the evenings with his friends, going to the theater and other cultural events. "He lived alone and probably was not so adaptable for visitors," she recalled.[6] Riha did take her to a garden party, pointing out three women and playfully asking her opinion of each of them. "He loved women," she said.

On one occasion, Jarmila accompanied Thomas to a television station where he was interviewed by journalists from Italy, France, and Russia. "He was very kind to the Russians and after that interview, I asked him how was it possible for him to be so Soviet-minded," she said. "He was surprised by my question. But I felt I knew the Russian people better than he because in Czechoslovakia we had the Russian Occupation and Socialism."[7]

While Jarmila was visiting, Riha's mother flew in from Mexico. Jarmila thought Ruth would enjoy some traditional Czech food and cooked potato soup. Ruth was in no mood for such humble fare and dumped the soup down the sink. Jarmila, sensing how uncomfortable Thomas was, decided to go to San Antonio to visit family friends while Ruth was in Chicago. "Ruth was very strong, stronger than he was. He was afraid of complications and was very glad I offered to go to Texas. He could not speak about that with Ruth," Jarmila recalled.[8]

After two years of teaching at the University of Chicago, Riha went overseas again, spending a year at the University of Marburg in West Germany. While there, he took trips to Leningrad and Moscow. The West Germany connection would loom large one day in the mind of James Jesus Angleton, the CIA's chain-smoking counterintelligence chief who had enjoyed long, alcoholic lunches with British spy, Kim Philby. After Philby decamped to the Soviet Union in 1963, Angleton became convinced the Agency had been penetrated by a Russian mole named Sasha.[9] The one slender and incontrovertible lead Angleton had was that Sasha had spent some time in West Germany.

When Riha returned from his posting in Germany, Robert Byrnes's group at the University of Indiana put Riha's name on a list of candidates for another academic exchange with Czechoslovakia. The Czech government denied Riha entry because the United States had purportedly rejected several of their scholars.[10]

★ ★ ★

Riha's colleagues in Chicago don't remember seeing Thomas and Galya together, but Galya's daughter, Margie, said she once saw Riha's name on her mother's mailbox. When she asked her mother who he was, Galya responded, "'He's a friend. I'm keeping his mail for him. He's away.'"[11] Law enforcement officials in Colorado would speculate that Thomas and Galya had a long-standing sexual relationship, but Riha's friends think such a relationship unlikely.[12]

Galya had moved to Chicago four years before Thomas. She carried a leather pocketbook, wore blue serge dresses and crimson lipstick. She was larger and softer from her pregnancies and her complexion bloomed with health.

For Galya, driving to Chicago with her daughter, Margie, beside her and their belongings neatly stowed in the trunk, was one of the happiest moments in her life. They had detoured to St. Louis to see Galya's aunt, but had not been invited to stay overnight. "The visit with Mary had been pleasant, but very strained, I had wanted her to show some sign of caring—but none was forthcoming," Galya would write.[13]

They drove on through the summer darkness. Galya drank coffee and popped No-Doz pills to stay awake. After a couple of hours of rest, they arrived in Chicago, parked on the north side of the Loop, and began walking. "Neither of us had eaten a regular meal since leaving St. Louis," Galya writes, "so we indulged ourselves like two hungry wolves on Woolworth's hot dogs, Cokes and frozen custard cones."[14]

Galya soon found a job and an attic apartment. At night, she and Margie patched and painted and laid down carpeting. On Christmas morning, they took the Burlington Railroad to Galva, Illinois, to spend the day with relatives. Galya had brought gifts for everyone, but her relatives had nothing for her or Margie. They took the evening train back to Chicago. "It was dreary & raining when we go in at Union Station, but riding in the cab to our small apartment, seemed 100 percent friendlier & almost beautiful. I was crushed inside by the experience of the trip and the utter rejection that we had encountered. The next day was spent just cuddling together & looking at our own Xmas tree, and doing little niceties for each other, making popcorn, hot chocolate and the like."[15]

The following Monday, Galya called in sick. When she returned to work, she discovered that she didn't have any enthusiasm for her job. "Little by little I let the job I had loved slip away from me."[16]

Galya quit her job and became a recluse, measuring time by Margie's school day. "I'd sit and wait, clean up my small home, waiting as though in a trance until this one person who cared would come home at 3:30 from school."[17]

The newspapers piled up outside, the bills came due, but she couldn't shake off the strange lethargy. Inexplicably, she awoke one morning filled with energy. She soon landed a job as a combination bookkeeper and layout artist at a firm called Advertising Promotions Inc. "It couldn't be true—such a glamorous job, and the pay was a whole $150 a week—I could hardly wait to start. I was sitting on cloud ninety-nine and I thought I had finally found my nitch [sic] in life. Maybe—just maybe—I could get full time on the drawing boards—I was so elated I didn't even hear the partner who described the condition of the records and files."[18]

Galya worked long hours and Margie came to the office after school and helped her. Numerous freelance artists worked for the agency, including a graphic artist named Charles Russell Scimo, who was Sicilian and reportedly had connections to several Chicago mobsters. Scimo developed a crush on Galya and showered her with gifts—corsages, lilies, dresses from Chicago's finest clothing stores, and grocery bags filled with choice meats. At work, he showed her many commercial art techniques, including how to create overlays and screens to add texture and color to printed images. In the evening, he took her to theaters, nightclubs, and restaurants. In the middle of this whirlwind courtship, her brother Pete showed up and Galya agreed to let him stay in her apartment.

Over a glass of wine one evening, Scimo asked her to marry him. She said yes and they were married on November 26, 1958, at Chicago's City Hall. Galya wore a lace dress and carried a bouquet of flowers. Afterward they had a huge catered party at their new apartment. A couple of months later, Galya found herself pregnant again.

"While pregnant, reality leaves completely and another mental situation takes place. With Russ, I began to become frantic every time he was out of my sight. I felt his just going about routine business was rejection & that he didn't love me anymore. I wanted to be with him all the time or I was frightened even though there was a live-in housekeeper, a day woman and the children."[19]

On November 8, 1959, Galya gave birth to James David Scimo. Galya was determined to raise the child properly and relied on Margie to help her. She was still working full-time at the advertising agency, but having a hard time balancing the company's books. One morning, two partners from the advertising firm showed up at her apartment. "They were very polite and I sensed something was wrong. I was asked if there was anything I wanted to tell them and to which I replied no. Nothing else was asked & then they told me to seek employment elsewhere. I was floored—there was no additional explanation—just go elsewhere."[20]

It seems that her brother, Pete, who was in debt to several Chicago bookies, had stolen money from the firm. Galya said she wound up taking the rap. On May 27, 1960, she was arrested and charged with obtaining money by false pretense.[21] She was fingerprinted, photographed, and released on bond. "Thoroughly shaken, I collected my car and went home. I still didn't know what had happened at all. Warrants were issued for my brother, and he was no longer findable."

Two months later, Galya was sent to the Cook County House of Corrections to serve a nine-month sentence. Margie was sent to Galva, Illinois, to live with Galya's mother and Jimmy, who was only nine months old, was placed in a foster home. While she was in jail, Galya was found guilty of two additional counts of forgery and embezzlement and sentenced to one to five years at the State Reformatory for Women in Dwight, Illinois.

On a gray, drizzling morning, a sheriff's deputy transported Galya and three other female inmates to the prison. Located at the end of a long, winding driveway, the brick prison resembled a medieval fortress. The women were housed in cottages that could accommodate twenty to thirty prisoners. Each cottage included a kitchen and recreation area. Galya was assigned to the Lincoln Cottage. She worked on the prison's weekly magazine and ran the movie projector on weekends. She also took some college courses by closed-circuit television. Eighteen months later, she was released on parole and put on a bus back to Chicago.

★   ★   ★

Galya initially lived with a rabbi and his family, but Russ Scimo kept calling the house and she was asked to leave. She moved into a hotel in a high-crime neighborhood. While living there, she learned the importance of having a confident walk. "The one thing that saved me from being jumped was my walk. One evening when comming [sic] home I passed a gangway between buildings and heard a youth tell his buddy, 'Not her, that's the fuzz.' It took a few minutes to click, that my erect, long-strided walk had made the area punks think I was a lady cop—and consequently left me alone. That to me was absolute irony, for here I was married to that Sicilian gambler, just out of the joint myself, still felt that everywhere I went people would read jail bird written all over me—and the dumb, stupid street punks thought I was a cop. Well, I capitalized on walking that way even more, taking my high heels in a shoe bag to be afoot in flats, and nothing at all happened to me."22

A woman named Phyllis Kaplan invited Galya to move in with her, saying they could split the rent and groceries. Everything went smoothly at first. Then Phyllis grew possessive of Galya, becoming jealous when she talked to Russ or even kissed Margie goodnight. One night, when they were watching television together in bed, Phyllis ran her hand between Galya's legs. Galya got up abruptly and left the room.23 Soon afterward, she was admitted to the Illinois Research Hospital. She told an intake clerk she was forty-three years old (she was thirty-two) and gave her name as Gloria Ann Zakharovna. She told the medical staff that Phyllis was trying to poison her and that she was suffering from a toxic bone marrow disease.24

The physicians examined her and found no evidence of disease. However, an electroencephalogram test revealed abnormal brain wave patterns.25 Upon her discharge, she was urged to get psychological counseling. Galya went to one or two counseling sessions, then quit.

In the midst of the turmoil, she landed a freelance art job at Tanenbaum Design Associates, a firm known throughout the Midwest for its high-quality graphics. The company was owned by Leo Tanenbaum, a member of the Communist Party USA and a political cartoonist for the Chicago Star, a liberal newspaper founded by several trade unions.

The FBI had been keeping tabs on Leo for a long time. Their interest intensified in 1960, when Leo took a trip to Cuba and returned with photographs and an enthusiastic report about the utopia Fidel Castro was building. He shared his findings with 150 guests in Hyde Park in a presentation sponsored by the Fair Play for Cuba Committee, which had been established a few months earlier. Fair Play was of interest to both the FBI and CIA, and their interest increased after Lee Harvey Oswald was seen passing out Fair Play for Cuba leaflets in New Orleans in August 1963 just several months before the assassination of President John F. Kennedy.

Tanenbaum, described in FBI records as a "white male, born August 5, 1919, in Austria,"26 was one of the thousands of people whose names were on the FBI's Security Index, a roster of alleged subversives who were subject to being rounded up and placed in detention in the event of a national emergency. As J. Edgar Hoover explained, "These indexes have been arranged not only alphabetically but also geographically, so that at any time, should we enter into the conflict abroad, we would be able to go into any of these communities and identify individuals and groups who might be a source of grave danger to the security of this country."[27]

The FBI also kept a "Communist Index," which was renamed the "Reserve Index," for people it considered particularly dangerous. And in the late 1960s, it created a Rabble Rouser Index, later renamed the Agitator Index, which was composed of individuals who had a propensity for creating racial discord.[28]

An FBI informant in Leo's design studio had been reporting on him for five years. That informant—whose name is deleted from records—talked at length about Galya. "Zakharovna was constantly talking and bragging about herself and especially about her experiences during the war," the informant told the FBI.

> She claimed that she had been a spy for the Russians during World War II and had been dropped behind German lines for espionage purposes. She claimed to have been wounded and that she was receiving a disability check from the United States government because of her services to allied forces. She claimed to be an expert regarding radio and electronics and said that she had been the one responsible for designing the small radio transmitter, which was concealed in an artificial olive and for which a toothpick was used as an antenna. She also said that she had designed a transmitter in the form of a matchbook, which could be concealed in sensitive places for the purposes of overhearing and broadcasting confidential conversations. [Name deleted] was of the opinion that Zakharovna very definitely had an emotional or mental problem.[29]

Chicago was home to numerous graphic arts firms and it's not known how Galya landed a job at Tanenbaum's design studio. But a complication soon developed: Galya fell deeply in love with Leo. "He was a well known designer, reasonably good looking and extremely charming," she writes.[30] "I was in love with the man, he could do no wrong. If he would have said his middle name was Nikita Khrushchev I wouldn't have cared."

Galya soon became pregnant with her fourth child. When Rebecca Eva Tanenbaum was born, Galya listed herself on the birth certificate as "Galya Anna Zakharovna" and her birthplace as Moscow, USSR.[31]

Galya and Leo made plans to marry, but one of Leo's relatives grew suspicious of Galya and hired a private investigator to research her background. He found a "jackpot" of information on her, including her stint in the penitentiary.[32] The wedding was called off and both Leo and Galya had nervous breakdowns. "From mid-August until the time Leo walked out, I lived in some weird sort of dream world. I thought I knew what was happening, and then again I didn't. I didn't even seem to be me. I was whoever Leo wanted me to be," she writes.[33] "I was the most lost individual you would ever want to meet when Leo left, and he seemed so indifferent to it all. . . . I suddenly had no reasoning ability at all."[34]

In the midst of her despondency, Thomas Riha reentered her life. Galya gave varying accounts of how she reconnected with him. According to one story, she said that she lived next door to a woman who worked at the University of Chicago Press who was editing one of Riha's manuscripts. She arranged to meet Thomas at the editor's apartment and later ran into him on the University of Chicago campus.[35] When they realized they were neighbors—they both lived on Kimbark Avenue—he began coming over for dinner.

Galya told other people that she met Riha at Leo's design studio. Leo's firm did design books and jacket covers for the University of Chicago Press and was actually in the process of publishing the first volume of Riha's *Readings in Russian Civilization,* a compendium of articles about Russian life and history. "He was having struggles beyond and beyond. . . . I helped as much as I could," Galya would say.[36]

Although Thomas was not yet forty years old, Galya described him as the quintessential absentminded professor. "In one sense, Thomas is naïve as the grass," she would say years later when she was interviewed by Boulder journalist John Olson. "There's just twenty four hours in the day and he put his whole mind and his ideas in researching history. He wasn't particularly interested in the history that was being made right today, you know. It wasn't part of his everyday thinking at the time. He's that kind of an individual and so he went from pillar to post."[37]

When the first volume of *Readings in Russian Civilization* was published, the University of Chicago thought the book did not reveal much originality or insight. "It was a decent enough book but in Chicago they wanted something a little stronger," remembered Richard Wortman.[38] The book did nothing to counter the growing opinion that Riha was an intellectual lightweight. "He was a good teacher. 'Congenial' is the word I would use to describe him. But there was a superficial side to him. I thought he was a decent scholar who would have a successful career but not at a place like Chicago," Wortman said.

After six years, Riha's academic career had stalled. He began looking for another job. Galya was also feeling the need for a change. She had waged a bitter paternity lawsuit to force Leo to acknowledge the fact that he was the father of her youngest child, Becky, and to help pay for her upkeep. Leo denied paternity, but a judge ordered him to deposit $4,000 in a bank account for Becky's upbringing. The judge also instructed Galya to stop using Leo's last name. She complied—sort of—by putting an extra n in the first syllable of Tanenbaum.[39]

6 ★ BOULDER

In August 1967, just a few weeks before the fall semester began, Thomas Riha moved to Boulder. He landed a tenure-track job in CU's history department, which was eager to expand its Slavic studies. While CU was not nearly as prestigious as the University of Chicago, the ambiance of the small college town and its majestic surroundings made up for it. Riha bought a house that was a stone's throw from the Flatirons, ancient slabs of granite that rise out of the foothills and act as a barrier and reminder of the rugged mountains beyond. The air was resinous, the sky an infinity of blue. From his backyard, he could see red-tailed hawks gliding down from their dark perches to scoop up their prey. Bobcat slunk through the neighborhood and deer glided by.

Riha's arrival coincided with Boulder's transformation into a spiritual hub and a mecca for hippies. Hundreds of young people camped in parks and panhandled on University Hill, which was the town's equivalent of Haight-Ashbury. The smell of marijuana wafted through the streets and *Sgt. Pepper's Lonely Hearts Club Band* blared from stereos. "There was this overwhelming, deep-seated belief that if we could just release enough acid into the major water supplies then our social problems would clear and the world would be a good place to live in again," one anonymous drug dealer told the *Denver Post*.[1]

Riha unpacked his rare books and filled the bland, suburban rooms of his house with pieces from his art collection. He walked to and from the campus nearly every day, cheerfully waving off rides. Though he was a slender man, he had a distinctive way of walking, with his head flung back and a wide smile. "He had this perky face," recalled neighbor Gretchen King, lifting up the corners of her lips to demonstrate his expression. "It was almost as if he had a face lift."[2]

Riha whistled as he walked down the corridors of the history department, his cheeriness in stark contrast to his colleagues, who were locked in battles stemming from grudges and slights that went back decades. Occasionally, he had coffee with a young historian named Jim Jankowski, who had arrived in Boulder in 1966 with a PhD from the University of Michigan and specialized in Middle Eastern and Egyptian history. Riha didn't take the departmental strife too seriously and reassured the younger Jankowski that the disputes would blow over. "He was a very intelligent, reserved man who had a great deal of self-control. He was able to assess the situation pretty well and decide whether something was important or unimportant," Jankowski recalled.[3]

Boyd Hill, a professor of medieval history, discovered that he and Riha were both army veterans and had served in the same psychological warfare unit at Fort Bragg. The unit consisted of several thousand men and they didn't know each other at the time. "We laughed and joked about being in the army," Hill recalled.[4] Hill introduced Riha to the Black Bear Inn, a restaurant located fifteen miles north of Boulder in the tiny hamlet of Lyons. The restaurant served delicious dishes, such as Weiner schnitzel and Hungarian goulash, and was owned by Czech émigrée Franziska Stein and her German-born husband, Georg.

Joyce Lebra, a tall, willowy professor and the first woman in the United States to receive a PhD in Japanese history, cotaught a class with Riha. Lebra thought Riha was a refreshing change from the male chauvinists who dominated the history department. "I was the only woman in the history department for fifteen years," she recalled. "Nobody had ever heard of sexual harassment."[5]

Lebra was interested in Japan's modernization struggles and Riha was interested in those same struggles in Russia. "We talked and somehow just decided to do a class together. He was easy to work with. I didn't go to all of his lectures and he didn't go to all of mine. We gave alternate lectures on parallel topics."[6]

Riha also had friends in Denver, including Libor Brom, an associate professor at the University of Denver. Brom's background was remarkably similar to Riha's; he was Czech, spoke multiple languages, and grew up amid the cataclysms in Europe. In April 1945, the Nazis captured fifty hostages in his village and threatened to kill ten hostages for each retreating German soldier killed by a Czech guerrilla fighter. "Being first in the alphabet, I found myself in a courtyard facing two soldiers armed with machine guns, not knowing if I had one minute, ten seconds, five seconds to live," he writes.[7] As he waited, Brom thanked God for giving him the chance to die for a noble cause even though he had not yet had the opportunity to live for one. "Happiness momentarily filled my being—finally my life made some sense. Without any advance warning, the guards were ordered to take me back to jail. Eventually we were released. From that moment on I have believed in miracles."

Brom left Czechoslovakia in 1958—more than a decade after Riha. He detested communism, having experienced what he called the "poverty, misery and despair of the Soviet trap."[8] The Czech government confiscated property belonging to Brom's family and many of his relatives had been jailed. One day, a Czech intelligence official, whom he referred to as the "Inconspicuous Man," appeared in his Prague flat and offered him the position of commercial attaché at the Czech Embassy in Belgrade, Yugoslavia.[9] Brom knew the position entailed espionage, but thought he would take the offer and defect to the West. When he asked the "Inconspicuous Man" to stipulate in a contract that he would not have to kill anybody, the agent vanished.

Neither Brom nor Riha's other academic friends recall meeting Galya during Riha's first year in Boulder. Yet Galya told authorities that they lived together from September through December 1967 as man and wife, or "common law," as she put it.[10] (Leo Tanenbaum would later confirm her statement, telling a credit card company that Galya had left Chicago in 1967 and moved to Boulder with a man named Riha.)[11]

Galya said she loaned Riha $7,000 for the down payment on his Boulder house with the stipulation that the loan be repaid immediately if either decided to marry someone else.[12] Although they weren't head over heels in love with each other, the decision made sense at the time, she thought.

"I was pretty distraught because Becky's father was gone and here she was three or four years old at the time and Thomas said, 'Well look. Neither one of us are getting any younger. I don't have any children. Supposing we give it a try. That was in September of '67 and he didn't know beans from apple butter. . . . He was real green and he thought it might work out. . . . He bought himself a nice little Volkswagen and I had a big old tub of a car, which I still have, and we thought between us we didn't need anything else. We had the family car and we had the town car, which was the VW."[13]

But Galya's two children were energetic and noisy and Thomas found it impossible to work. "It was terribly distracting," Galya remembered. "I had just hopped out of a bad marriage situation and was still pretty broken up and it seemed like it was more irritation than it was gonna be smiles and I decided that, well, I'll take the kids and go back to Chicago."[14]

So Galya left, leaving Thomas to concentrate on his work. He did have a heavy load: Three history courses to teach, committee assignments, and undergraduates and graduate students to advise.[15] He wrote one or two slender papers and put the finishing touches on his Paul Miliukov book. He also took frequent trips to Canada, where he had a business relationship with Treasure Tours International, a travel agency in Montreal.

Women, as usual, were an important part of his life. He dated Elisabeth Israels Perry, a newly minted PhD in the history department who went on to have a very successful career in women's studies at St. Louis University. Perry remembered Riha as a well-groomed man who kept an immaculate house. "It wasn't a bachelor pad. It was a neatly kept, middle-class, well-appointed residence," she recalled.[16]

Riha invited her to his house for dinner one evening and served grilled steaks. "I still make my steaks the way Tom made them. He taught me how to spread mashed garlic and soy sauce on steak." Afterward, she thinks she may have spent the night with him. "There were aspects of him that were mysterious. There was a kind of 'closedness' about him. He was not terribly open in the way some people wear their heart on their sleeve. He was much more controlled, as well as controlling. He had very strong opinions on how things should be done or not done."

Elisabeth had just extricated herself from a marriage with a husband who had similar traits and wasn't interested in pursuing a relationship. "What I saw in Tom was a very domineering and controlling personality, which was a lot like my first husband," she said. "After one encounter, I decided this is not for me."

Nevertheless, Riha was an exceedingly popular teacher and his teaching load went from 83 to 176 students.[17] Sometimes he took students to Black Bear Inn for lunch or dinner. "We were new in the area and one of our first customers was Professor Riha," Franziska Stein remembered.[18] Franziska and Thomas had much in common, including the suffering and dislocation they experienced during World War II. Franziska and her husband were part of Czechoslovakia's German minority and lived in the Sudetenland. Georg was drafted into the German Army and injured twice on the Eastern Front. Later he was taken captive by the Soviets.

In a memoir, Franziska writes of being riveted by a speech that Hitler delivered in her hometown of Carlsbad. "Those in the audience, including the teenagers like myself, held their breath as this charismatic man cast his spell over us. He told us how we were delivered from years of oppression and fear," she writes. "Could we have seen through the façade paraded before us? The performance given by Hitler's entourage and that of the soldiers was scripted to the smallest detail by the propaganda ministry. They set out bait in a trap to deceive us and the world. We had not been accustomed to such things and fell for it. Whether rich or poor, who would not have wanted the economic improvement and prosperity he promised?"[19]

Thomas Riha and the Steins became good friends. Sometimes he was moody and withdrawn, but other times he was joyous and lively. Rumors circulated that he was having an affair with a student. "I cannot prove it. Maybe the student was so beautiful it was worthwhile having an affair with her," Franziska said.[20] Once he came into the restaurant with a beautiful young woman who worked for the BBC in London. They spoke to each other in Russian and seemed to be very much in love. "She was very charming, very beautiful," remembered Mrs. Stein.[21]

★   ★   ★

Riha's life was about to get more complicated; Galya was returning to Colorado. In March 1968, she sent a letter to Boulder attorney Dennis Blewitt asking him for his help in finding her a place to live. Blewitt was the hell-raising son of rancher parents from Loveland, Colorado, who dropped out of college to go to barber school. Eventually he landed a job in a barbershop in an area of downtown Denver known as Skid Row. "Whenever there was a convention in town, the cops would go through Skid Row and knock the shit out of all the winos and haul them off to jail, saying they were resisting arrest. It was 1961 and they have been doing it ever since. It was my first exposure to police brutality."[22]

Blewitt eventually tired of finger waves and shaves and returned to school at the University of Colorado in Boulder. At that time, billboards on the outskirts of Boulder carried messages like, "Impeach Earl Warren" and "Get US out of Red UN." Joseph Coors, one of the founders of the conservative Heritage Foundation and champion of Ronald Reagan, served on the board of regents. When Coors vowed to kick all the Communists off campus, Blewitt decided it was time to leave. He enrolled in law school at the Illinois Institute of Technology in Chicago, where he met Martin Luther King and organizing genius Saul Alinksy.

Blewitt worked for Leonard Karlin, a garrulous attorney active in the antiwar movement and a member of the National Lawyers Guild. (The House Committee on Un-American Activities in the early 1960s had declared the Lawyers Guild a Communist front. From 1940 to 1975, the FBI tapped the organization's phones, burglarized its offices, and planted informers at their meetings.)[23]

It was actually Leonard Karlin who referred Galya to Blewitt. "I get this letter from Galya Tannenbaum who said she was a friend of Leonard Karlin's and Leonard had given her my name and she was coming to Colorado and would I help her? Then Leonard called and wanted to see if I could help her out. That's how that started," Blewitt said in one of several interviews.[24]

In a March 18, 1968, letter to Blewitt, Galya writes, "I would like to vanish from Chicago, as quickly as possible and move to Denver. I have come through an exceptionally ugly divorce mess, have two beautiful children, a girl age 2, and a boy 8. After all was said and done, I have come out with nothing, and to complicate matters, I have been in the same trade as my now ex, and the graphic design world here is very small . . . too small for the both of us. Result, since he is very vindictive, and is much better known, I have not been able to find a decent job."[25] Galya went on to say that she had a master's degree and completed some course work toward a PhD. "So, there should be little difficulty in obtaining decent paying employment. I am a Mensa, if that is any credit."

Galya had not gone through an ugly divorce, she didn't have a master's degree, she hadn't completed work toward a PhD, and she wasn't a Mensa member. But Dennis Blewitt would not have known any of that. He found Galya a small brick bungalow on Logan Street, just south of downtown Denver. The house had three bedrooms, a bathroom, a large kitchen, a basement, and a yard—plenty of space for Galya and her two children. Blewitt paid the first month's rent of $125.[26] He also opened a bank account in Galya's name and offered to let her stay with him and his wife until she got settled.

Once Blewitt got to know Galya better, he realized that she was indeed a windbag. "There were times she called me and I put the phone down and she would talk for two hours and never know I wasn't there," he said in an interview in 2013.[27] "She was a real pain in the ass. I never figured out how she made her money, but she always had a lot of money."[28]

Blewitt was convinced Galya was a government informant and that she was keeping tabs on Leonard Karlin in Chicago and was sent to Boulder to keep watch on him. "She had all these fantastic stories," he said. "My wife and I got suspicious. We staked out her house at 248 Logan and one evening followed her downtown to the Customs Building. She drove into the garage and came out that morning at about six o'clock. The Customs Building housed the armed forces, intelligence forces, things like that."[29]

By May 1968, Galya had settled into her new home.[30] Although her house in Denver was thirty miles from Boulder, she thought nothing of driving up to

Riha's house at night on Highway 36, a road that rose steadily into the foot-hills and was hazardous during rainstorms or the heavy spring snowstorms that swept down from the mountains.

Summer was returning to the high country and the valleys were carpeted with bluebells, phlox, and daisies. Wearing sleeveless dresses and flat shoes, Galya often motored into the mountains with her kids in her big, sloshy fam-ily car. The Rockies were riddled with old mines and abandoned shacks from the gold and silver booms of the previous century. Galya often went hiking with her two children and had no problem navigating the rocky terrain.

She initially worked with Dennis Blewitt and several other businessmen to establish two development companies—Universal Land and Investment Company[31] and the Lake Valley Estates Homeowners Association.[32] She was on the board of directors of both firms and her job was to solicit funds and submit paperwork to various federal agencies. Although she seemed competent enough, her letters to potential investors were marred with mis-spellings. She was aware of her poor spelling skills and in a letter to one of her aunts, she wrote, "I can not spell well, (and really do not care as I have a good secretary), so forgive the boobs."[33]

Paul Morris, a Boulder attorney who worked with Galya for a couple of months on the land development projects, said that Galya boasted of knowing many rich and powerful people and claimed that one of her jobs was to exterminate Communists.[34] He didn't believe that she actually killed Communists, but had no reason to doubt her other claims. In the summer of 1968, she contacted the Federal Housing Authority and obtained prelim-inary approval for a $1 million loan for the Lake Valley Estates project.[35] When the FHA ultimately decided not to make the loan, Galya was fired.

Her financial situation grew precarious. She secured temporary work from Manpower, but it was not enough to support her family. Her take-home pay was $132 a week. Rent was $125 a month, utilities were $25, and the phone was $9.[36] Becky was sick often and the medical bills were astronomical. Frus-trated by the fact that she could withdraw only $60 a month from the $4,000 fund set up by the Chicago judge for Becky's upbringing, she tried to have the court order modified so she could withdraw $100 a month. "I have to pay $60.00 per week for a sitter to come in and take care of the baby, while I earn money for the family to live on. It's a tremendously big bite of earning, and the $100.00 would hardly even cover half of the sitter fees, and no funds toward the business of living at all," she told one lawyer.[37]

★ ★ ★

While Galya struggled to make ends meet, Riha was immersed in his new life. In the summer of 1968, after completing his first year of teaching, he led a group of scholars abroad for a six-week tour organized by Treasure Tours entitled "The USSR for the Historian."[38] Riha and his tour group ranged as far as Samarkand, an ancient city in Uzbekistan, which had centuries-old mosques and churches, but nothing of apparent political or military value.[39]

Max Putzel, a historian at Indiana University, was among the scholars on the tour and he was impressed by Riha's competence and knowledge. In a letter to Fred Gillies, a *Denver Post* reporter, he wrote, "His knowledge of Russian was often better than the Intourist translators, especially when specialized historical terms were involved. Some of the people in the group thought he did not 'do enough' for the group, but they forgot that Tom was the academic leader of the tour, and that the Intourist people were supposed to handle the day-to-day arrangements. I found my conversations with him during those six weeks very helpful both in getting as much as possible out of the tour and our meetings with Soviet historians, and in getting help and advice for the Russian Civilization honors course I was putting together."[40]

Following the tour, Riha apparently paid a visit to an antiquarian bookstore, which was located at 4763 Victoria Avenue in Montreal and owned by a Philip Lozinski. Born in Kiev, Russia, Lozinski was cavalry lieutenant with the Polish forces during World War II. He was captured by the Germans and sent to a prisoner-of-war camp where he escaped and joined the Maquis, the French underground. While fighting, he was once again recaptured and this time the Germans sentenced him to death. But he managed to escape once more and returned to France, where he fought with the underground until the end of the war. Afterward he moved to the United States, where he obtained a PhD in art history from Yale University.[41] The two men had a lot in common and may have chatted for a while. Then Riha ordered two books for a total of $26.70 and continued south to New York City.[42]

Riha had planned on going to Czechoslovakia while he was abroad, but the political situation there had grown volatile. Alexander Dubček, first secretary of the Communist Party of Czechoslovakia, had begun restoring many freedoms to the Czech people in a liberalization period that became known as the Prague Spring. He abolished censorship, gave citizens the right to assemble peaceably, and allowed criticism of the government. The Czechs were euphoric, but beneath the happiness was a strong sense of anxiety. "It was freedom unleashed by fear. It was not a comfortable freedom," recalled Czech filmmaker Milos Forman.[43]

The Kremlin watched Dubček's liberalization movement, worried that the thirst for freedom would spread to other Warsaw Pact countries. Finally, it had had enough. At 10:15 P.M. on August 20, 1968, the Soviet Union and its Warsaw Pact allies invaded Czechoslovakia. "They came like burglars in the night," recalled one observer. Some five hundred thousand soldiers and five thousand tanks from East Germany, Bulgaria, Hungary, Poland, and Russia crossed the border. The troops rolled through the countryside and didn't stop until they reached Prague's Wenceslas Square. Soviet paratroopers carrying Kalashnikovs seized the airport. Dubček and several aides were arrested and flown to the USSR on a military transport plane. Scores of residents protested in the streets and were killed in sporadic gun battles. One young student named Jan Palach set himself on fire to protest the crackdown. Other self-immolations followed. When the political opposition died down, Dubček was allowed to return to Czechoslovakia, but his fate was sealed. Within a year he resigned his post and was expelled from the Communist Party. The pall of communism resettled over the country for two more decades. "We were very happy before 1968. After August 1968, there was nothing," remembered Riha's niece, Jarmila.[44]

Zdenek and Jarmila had fled to Vienna during this period. Zdenek decided to continue on to the United States, but Jarmila couldn't bear to leave her homeland and returned to Prague. "I talked with Thomas by phone from Vienna and he asked me to come to America with my brother and I couldn't do it," she recalled.[45]

In the years to come, she was interrogated by the StB on more than half a dozen occasions. "These people, these agents and secret police, recognize who is afraid and who is not afraid," she said.[46] Jarmila worked for a while for a large export company in Prague that employed about a thousand people. She estimated that half the employees worked in some capacity for the StB. In exchange for information, the informants were given promotions and better places to live. "It was very, very bad because it was like in Russia. Every third citizen was an agent."

Jiri Cerveny—Zdenek and Jarmila's father—had put an ad in several Czech newspapers for Thomas saying an American professor of Czech origin was looking for an old-fashioned bride. Hundreds of young women responded. "He got something like two hundred answers and pictures of beautiful girls," recalled Zdenek. "Thomas was supposed to go to Prague at the end of August but the Russian tanks came instead."[47]

The elder Cerveny then suggested that Riha look up Hana in New York. "He told him there was a Czech girl already here and she looked very good," recalled Zdenek.

Riha sent Hana a letter and a picture of himself and they began corresponding. When Riha arrived in New York, he spent a week with Hana at her aunt and uncle's summer home on Long Island.⁴⁸ On September 1, 1968, they became officially engaged.

Riha then invited Hana to come to Colorado. She took him up on the offer, staying first at the Boulderado Hotel and then moving into a spare bedroom in his home. "He asked us if Hana could come to Boulder to take a look at how he lives, how are his friends. So, we didn't mind it, because he seemed to be nice," remembered Rose Grossman, Hana's aunt. "We said she should go and make up her mind what she wants to do. Then when she came back she said they will be married."⁴⁹

Riha seemed to be in a big hurry to get married, Hana remembered. "Everything was so fast," she said. "But I don't think he loved me. I don't think he loved me."⁵⁰

★ ★ ★

The wedding took place on October 13, 1968, a perfect autumn day, the sky brimming with blue and the leaves of the aspen trees spinning like gold coins on the hills. Riha's mother had asked Thomas to postpone the wedding a few months so she could attend, but he decided to go ahead without her.⁵¹

Riha wore a dark suit and his graying hair was smoothed back. Hana wore a lace veil and a white wedding gown. Jim Jankowski, the young Egyptologist whom Riha had befriended, thought Hana made a stunning bride. "She was a very, very pretty woman," he recalled.⁵² Anne Fisher, who also attended the wedding, said Riha seemed more like a father figure than an anxious young groom. "We thought it might have been an arranged marriage."⁵³

After the ceremony, the guests pelted the couple with rice and they headed to a reception at the Black Bear Inn in Lyons. Franziska Stein had prepared a lavish feast: Russian eggs, consommé with liver dumplings, pork roasts, veal roasts, potatoes, steamed cabbage, apple and poppy seed strudels, kolacky, brandy, cognac, and slivovitz.⁵⁴

As the guests were about to sit down at the table, Galya barged in. "She appeared out of the blue," remembered Franziska, still puzzled decades later by her sudden appearance.⁵⁵ It was the first time that most of Riha's acquaintances had ever seen Galya. "Somebody came and whispered in Tom's ear and he went off and didn't come back for an hour," remembered Anne Fisher.⁵⁶

Thomas and Galya sat down at the bar and conversed animatedly. The food grew cold and conversation lagged. When one of the guests entreated Riha to return to the wedding feast, he lashed out, saying he was engaged in important business. After Galya left, Riha told the puzzled guests that she was a colonel in military intelligence and was helping to expedite Zdenek Cerveny's entry into the United States.

Galya claimed that Riha had insisted that she come to the restaurant. "And I said, 'Look, I don't want to come to the reception.' And he said, 'Will you come and pick up the material and talk to me about it, at least?' So I met him on the other side of the Black Bear Inn and I wouldn't join the reception because I was a little miffed at the whole business of him getting married in the first place."[57]

But Galya didn't stay miffed for long. Only two weeks after they were married, Thomas began to treat Hana with contempt.[58] As for Hana, she discovered there were two Thomas Rihas—the charming flirt whom academic colleagues knew and the cold, distant man she lived with. "Charming, yes. He could make you believe he was the most charming man in the world but under the closed door it was a different story."[59]

Thomas wanted the dishes washed, the floors swept, the laundry done, and dinner ready when he came home from work. But he complained to friends that the house was a mess, with bed linens unchanged and dirty clothes shoved back into bureau drawers.

Hana said his complaints were baseless. "I was spic and span," she said.[60]

Hana had found plenty wrong with Thomas, too. She discovered he was more than just thrifty; he was a miser. "He was very, very stingy. Oh yes!"[61] Thomas refused to shell out thirty dollars for a bouquet of flowers on their wedding day and when they were alone together on the night of their wedding, he asked Hana to sign a life insurance policy and a will.[62] Stunned by the request, she said, "We just got married. What are you talking about—last will and insurance?"[63]

Thomas gave Hana five dollars a week in spending money and sometimes he didn't even give her that. He forbade her from hanging paintings on the walls because he said the nail holes would reduce the resale value of his house. He put a lock on the phone so she couldn't make long-distance calls to her aunt and uncle in Brooklyn, stopped stocking the refrigerator with food, and even went so far as to hide the salt from her. "The only time we went somewhere together is when friends invited us for dinner, but as far as going out and spending money—never, ever. He wouldn't even buy me slippers."[64]

Hana also saw no evidence of the "omnivorous sexual appetite" for women that Riha was said to possess. "I was twenty-three, twenty-four, and I would know if a man had a sexual appetite, believe me."[65]

Hana said she was also sure that Riha was not having an affair with Galya.[66] "She was not for real. That little bun on her head. She was like a little old lady."[67] Still, Hana could see that Galya did have some kind of hold over Thomas. "Who was she? She was a nobody. She had something over him that he was afraid of."[68]

Galya, who saw herself as Thomas's ally in the growing domestic strife, said Thomas often called her to blow off steam. "Hana was lazy. She wouldn't cook, she didn't know how to cook. She drank a lot, she wouldn't wash a dish and get it clean, and it bothered the hell out of him. She wouldn't even pick up her own dirty stinking laundry, her personal laundry, and put it in the wash and get it clean. She'd put the dirty clothes back in the drawer, and it used to make him just burn. She wouldn't pull a sheet off a bed. He was forced to do the sheet changing. He did the house cleaning. And she was sitting there like she was to be taken care of, and he was beside himself."[69]

Hana said Galya's characterization of her domestic life was inaccurate. "I cooked. I cleaned. I did everything. Even Thomas said, 'You cook so well you could open your own restaurant.'"[70]

Riha began spending more time in his office. In the evenings, he went to dinner parties at the homes of friends, a bottle of wine and poetry book in hand. He seemed to be so much on the prowl that Galya dubbed him "Tom Cat."[71]

A month after the wedding, on November 16, 1968, Zdenek Cerveny arrived at the Denver bus station.[72] Thomas was teaching classes and asked Galya to pick him up and drive him to Boulder. "I didn't know what to think about her," Cerveny said of Galya.[73]

At Christmas, Hana flew back to New York to visit her aunt and uncle. Riha joined her there and shoehorned in a visit with Vera Dunham, a Russian expert and former employee for the Office of Strategic Services, America's wartime intelligence agency.[74] From New York, Riha left for another history conference, this time in Washington, DC.

On February 10, 1969—after four months of marriage—Riha filed a petition to have the marriage annulled, claiming that he entered into the marriage under duress and that Hana was guilty of "extreme and repeated cruelty."[75] (The petition does not contain specifics about the allegations.)

The day after the divorce papers were filed, Riha had an appraiser named Ernest Tross come to his house and evaluate his art collection. The appraiser spent several hours looking over the pieces, concluding the entire collection was worth $13,000, which was equivalent to about $75,000 in today's dollars.[76] The most important piece was the Pietà, which showed Christ lying in the lap of Mary surrounded by several followers after he died on the cross. Tross estimated the carving was done around 1525.

Galya knew that the divorce was coming, but didn't warn Hana. "I didn't let her know it, because I'm not that kind of a guy," she would say. "I felt for Hana in a way, that she was a woman in all this mess, but she had made all this mess herself. She was going on with the pretense that oh, 'I'm Mrs. Riha, and everything else,' and I knew that they weren't even sleeping in the same room anymore."[77]

Boulder attorney Gerald Caplan, who represented Hana, sent out interrogatories probing Riha's finances. Colorado was a community property state and normally assets were divided equally between husband and wife. But their marriage had been so brief that Thomas felt that Hana wasn't entitled to anything. He wasn't wealthy by any means, but he did own his house, a 1967 Volkswagen, hundreds of rare books, and his art collection.

While the divorce proceeding was under way, Thomas managed to keep up with his university work. In an odd conversation with Carol Word, he talked about espionage and mentioned that an agent's useful life was about ten years if "you do your stuff and are lucky."[78]

His bank statements, property records, and other documents went missing from his home. Riha thought Hana had taken them. On March 4, Riha's savings bank in Denver issued a $2,685 check made out to Mr. or Mrs. Riha.[79] The back of the check shows it was endorsed by Hana Riha and paid to Galya Tannenbaum. Upon depositing the check, Galya subsequently turned around and paid her landlady $700 in back rent.[80]

Joyce Lebra invited Riha for dinner on Friday, March 7, 1969, the night that Galya took Hana for the long car ride. He brought with him a bottle of sake. Joyce and Thomas were good friends and often talked about marriage while coteaching their course, "Comparative Modernization of Japan and Russia." Lebra had guessed in January 1969 that all was not well.

"Tom, I have an intuition about you," Joyce ventured.

"What is it?" Riha responded.

"You're getting a divorce," she guessed.

"That's right, but don't tell anyone yet," he responded, adding, "The immigration authorities are coming to take my wife away at night soon, because she is here without a visa."

"Tom," she said, "people just don't get taken away at night."

"Apparently that's the way they work," he responded. [81]

Thomas had arranged for Hana to stay with a Czech family while the divorce was under way. Instead, Hana stayed away from the house all day, returning home about nine or ten o'clock at night. "Things went from bad to worse," recalled Galya. "The tension got so incredible it wasn't even funny."[82]

PART II ★

"ALIVE AND WELL"

7 ★ NEIGHBORHOOD WATCH

After Thomas Riha left Jan Sorensen's birthday party at around midnight on March 15, 1969, his exact whereabouts are unknown. A notation in his calendar shows he was planning to attend a history symposium in Denver the following morning—a Saturday—but he never showed up.[1] Carol Word called his home five or six times that day to confirm that he would be attending a family dinner on Sunday, but the telephone calls went unanswered.[2]

The following week, Donald Fanger received a letter in the mail from Riha dated March 15, 1969. Riha could have written the letter and posted it before Jan Sorensen's party or he could have written it sometime afterward. The letter is lighthearted and optimistic and contains none of the anxiety that Jan Sorensen had detected. His book on Paul Miliukov had just been published and he complained about a lackluster review in *Library Journal*. He shrugged off the reviewer's remarks, saying that he would survive the review, as well as his divorce:

If my beloved wife has her way I shall not have the seven dollars to read PORTNOY'S COMPLAINT. Her lawyer has already launched a full-scale campaign to ruin me financially, and all this for less than four months of marriage. My wife has actually stolen from my files copies of my income tax returns, titles to house and car, and my savings account to boot. She moved out a week ago after a scandalous scene involving the police, whom she summoned. But it all backfired, her room was found to contain several empty liquor bottles, and smelled of ether. The police report was that she had been "on a bad trip." So I am exonerated before the neighbors. And best of all, I have it on unimpeachable authority that she will be deported in very short order. In fact she was subject to deportation when I met her, and this is why the big hurry and pressure put on me for the wedding. She is guilty of four violations of immigration law, including fraud—a firm she said would employ her as a secretary when I met her does not in fact exist. She has not paid her 1967 income taxes. The list of her sins is long, and so will be my life without her. Since our divorce hearing comes up only in May she will by then be deported, and it will be an uncontested divorce. I have seen her Czechoslovak passport, which is valid only for return to Prague and is stamped "not to be readmitted to the USA." Her goose is cooked. That all this was not exactly soothing on the nerves of your faithful Admiral goes without saying, but I shall survive to tell my grandchildren.[3]

Patricia Faulkner, who was forty-eight years old, with thick brown hair, unruly bangs, and the residue of a tomboy in her face, lived in an old rambling farmhouse directly across the street from Thomas Riha. She had plenty to keep her busy—she had four kids, played the stock market, swam, skied, bred Irish setters, and co-owned a photo studio with her husband—but she was intrigued by reports of the mysterious "colonel" and decided to keep a log of what was going on at Riha's house.[4]

From her upstairs windows, she could readily see into Thomas's front and backyard. She also had a sweeping view of the intersection of Sixth Street and College Avenue. Whenever she talked about the case on the telephone, she would invariably receive another call a few minutes later, which consisted of a few seconds of silence followed by a soft click. She became so unsettled that she stopped discussing the case on her home telephone. Her log begins:

Monday, March 17—I began to feel fairly uneasy about Tom's dark house. I wasn't really sure whether he was gone but I found myself thinking back to the last time I had seen him. . . . I did recall that on Sat. 3/15 I had seen the "Colonel's" child playing out in Tom's back yard and at the time, I assumed he was at home. But then I thought of how quiet it was over there on Sunday.—So even though I saw the "Colonel's" car out front on Mon. afternoon, just as it had been many other days the week before, I felt sure that Tom wasn't there.[5]

★ ★ ★

Tues. 3/18—During the morning it occurred to me that I should make a definite effort to see if the "colonel" entered the house alone with a key.—At about 2:30 P.M. she drove up, got out of her car, let her small daughter out, then went straight to the mailbox, took the mail out, looked it over, tucked it under one arm & reached into her coat pocket, pulled out a key (all in plain sight) & walked to the front door & let herself in. She remained about an hour. That evening, after dark I noticed one police car parked by Tom's front walk. I went to a different window for a better view & just saw one man (civilian) and one policeman walk down College Ave. past Tom's house turning the corner at the front on 6th Street & they got into the car & drove up 6th Street (south). I didn't know what to make of it but was more concerned & decided to be observant.—About ¾ of an hour later two police cars & one station wagon pulled up in front of the house. This time there were 3 policemen, two other men & one woman. The woman remained in the station wagon & the rest started to check all around the house with flash lights. (I watched from my front porch. My daughter was at the upstairs window with it opened.) No one entered the house but they looked in every window. They also checked the shed, bomb shelter & car. I decided to see if they were aware of the "colonel's" entering the house so I went over.

The woman in the station wagon was Marie Wood, a secretary in the dean's office. The other civilians included Riha's divorce lawyer, Richard Hopkins, and several university administrators. After talking to Patricia Faulkner, Mrs. Wood got out of the car, walked to the back of the house, and returned to the vehicle with Hopkins. Patricia Faulkner was eager to talk to him about Galya: "From the little I had seen of the 'Colonel' & from what I had overheard on the night of the 8th & from what I had gathered from a few conversations with Tom, I thought she came on as a real crack pot, and somehow sinister—'Nutty.' He right away agreed. Then as we were walking out of the house onto the porch I expanded my thought and added that from what I had heard on the 8th, I would also say that she seemed to me to be really sadistic. He emphatically agreed." On Wednesday, March 19, Mrs. Faulkner phoned Richard Hopkins's office to ask if Tom had been located and to provide information on where some of his friends could be reached. His secretary said he was at the university and would return the call. Hopkins never called back.

What Faulkner didn't know was that Hopkins had received a telegram that day that appeared to have been sent by Thomas. In the message, Thomas asked Hopkins to "please subdue the panic" over his departure. He added that while his friends may have thought he should have consulted them before leaving, he didn't think their permission was necessary.[6] In the weeks to come, Hopkins would receive other letters signed by Riha with Canadian postmarks on the envelopes.

On Thursday, March 20, a yellow Cadillac convertible pulled up to the curb in front of Riha's house. Four young men in their twenties were in the car. Two got out. One was holding a clipboard. They rang the doorbell. When they received no answer, they piled back into the vehicle and drove away. In other developments that day, Wheeler Realty, a Boulder real estate firm, received a letter signed by Thomas Riha, asking the firm to put his house on the market and emphasizing that Galya should be repaid the $7,000 she loaned him to buy the house.[7] On Saturday, March 22, Faulkner decided to contact the Boulder district attorney Stan Johnson:

> His wife said to phone back in an hour—then five minutes after I hung up I received a silent phone call. I then went to a friend's house on the other side of town & phoned Stan Johnson to see if anything was being done from his office. He asked a number of questions & our conversation ended with my feeling that at least he had an awareness of the problem and it would be looked into. He suggested I phone the police if the neighbors wanted some kind of surveillance. I did and gathered that they were in a state of wonderment about the whole affair. The corporal said I should come down & speak to a detective & wondered what people should be protected from. This is the problem! So I let it go and did not speak with a detective.

Joyce Lebra had also grown increasingly worried about Riha. She, too, had been receiving the same kind of phone calls as Mrs. Faulkner—a few seconds of silence followed by a soft click. She contacted numerous law enforcement officials, including the Boulder police chief, the Boulder DA, the Denver branch of the FBI, and the INS. They all assured her Thomas was okay and had left town for personal reasons.[8] Lebra then asked Fritz Hoffman, the chairman of the history department, and William Briggs, the dean of arts and sciences, to make inquiries. They, too, received the same bland assurances: Tom was fine, he was still in the country, and no international intelligence was involved.

Lebra thought the university administrators seemed strangely indifferent toward the case, an attitude that could have stemmed in part from an unresolved salary dispute.[9] Riha had been promised an annual salary of $12,500 only to arrive in Boulder and find that his pay had been scaled back to $11,000. Incensed, he had begun to look into federal grant applications that funded the Slavic Center, alleging that administrators were fudging some of their data.

Libor Brom was also puzzled by Riha's sudden disappearance. People living in communist countries disappeared every day, but he thought such events didn't happen in the United States. He contacted John Todd, the regional director of the INS, who told him that Riha was alive. A month later, when Brom recontacted him, Todd changed his story, warning Brom he should "not be interested" in the Riha affair.[10] Brom also contacted Merrill Smith, an FBI agent in Boulder, who said Riha was alive and had left Colorado for personal reasons.[11]

Ruth Ann Cook, Riha's lovely and demanding mother, began corresponding with Brom. "What on earth has happened? I wrote him on the 15th of March—my birthday. Now I understand he disappeared on that date," she wrote. "If you are in touch with him—influence him to stand up to whatever has come his way—police protection is available if he is threatened and a good lawyer can always help. Certainly there are solutions to every problem; running away hardly solves anything."[12]

Brom wrote back to Ruth, telling her he had little information on Riha's disappearance. "During the past six months, Thomas has taken us three times by surprise: 1) When he got engaged on his way from Russia via New York; 2) When he hurriedly concluded a marriage with this utterly incompatible youthful Czech; and 3) When he enrolled upon the divorcing process by suddenly disappearing from the scene. We have not heard from him since. . . . The FBI has assured me that he is OK. Through FBI I have left a message that he should contact his ailing mother in Germany." He added, "Should you wish that I make some steps for you to locate him through my connections going beyond FBI etc., let me know." (His "connections" may have been a reference to the CIA.)[13]

Ruth wrote several more letters to Libor Brom. In a May 6, 1969, letter, she questioned the FBI's involvement in the case and once again expressed puzzlement over her son's behavior. "Wholly inexplicable is for me Tom's action in abandoning position, home and work. I grieve very much for him and pray that his life should get settled."[14]

Professor Stephen Fischer-Galati, a flamboyant academic with an abiding distrust of authority, took over Riha's classes for the rest of the semester. At first, Fischer-Galati thought Riha might have "lost his mind" because of the divorce and his feud with the university. Then he began to suspect that something darker was afoot.[15]

Fischer-Galati had escaped from Romania with his wealthy family at the beginning of World War II. His father was a renowned physician, his mother a lovely creature who was so docile that she asked for permission to use the bathroom. "If she wanted anything, she would ring a bell cord," his wife, Anne, recalled.[16] Fischer-Galati refused to eat dark bread and always left food on his plate to show he was not a starving peasant.

He founded the *East European Quarterly* and wrote dozens of books and magazine articles. He knew of the alliances that the CIA forged with taxpayer money and how its tentacles spread through universities, respected nonprofits like the Ford Foundation, and innumerable smaller philanthropies and front companies. Anne Fisher said her husband didn't work for the CIA, but relished the idea that other people thought that he did.

Joyce Lebra, meanwhile, continued to pester law enforcement officials. The Boulder police and the campus police said they couldn't take action unless a missing person report was filed by the next of kin. Lebra pointed out that Riha's estranged wife and nephew were unlikely to file such a report because they were new to the United States and unfamiliar with police procedures. She asked if she and several of Riha's colleagues could file a missing person report instead. The Boulder police acquiesced and on April 4, Joyce rounded up Patricia Faulkner, Boyd Hill, Mr. and Mrs. Wilson, Mr. and Mrs. Hanson, and several other people.

Patrolman Donald Alps was dispatched to Lebra's home. Joyce Lebra and Boyd Hill sensed the policeman wasn't really interested in the case. "He had a brief one-page form and asked perfunctory questions such as 'When did you last see Riha?' 'What was he wearing?' He asked no questions other than those that were on the form and seemed very unconcerned about our anxiety for Tom. Later in the day I talked with him over the phone and was told that the police were not concerned about him [Thomas], as they knew where he was and he was alright," Lebra would write.[17]

But Alps wasn't telling Joyce everything. In a one-page memo to his supervisor, Capt. Willard Spier, he recounted what happened next: "On my return to the station I informed my supervisors that the report was on Professor Riha as I had heard the name mentioned around the station, etc. This time the report was taken into Capt. [Lowell] Friesen. He in turn notified me that we would not take a report on Riha again and the report was torn up. He stated that we had notification (unknown to this officer how) that Riha was in New York and that he was well and there of his own accord. At this time I personally phoned Miss Lebra and informed her of this. This was my last contact with the investigation."[18]

Although the local newspapers had not yet picked up on the Riha case, one of Lebra's friends had been asked about his disappearance by a military official at a cocktail party in Washington, DC. Joyce finally contacted CU President Joseph Smiley and asked him to look into the case, pointing out that the university had some responsibility toward the missing professor.

Smiley, who had served in the navy during World War II, told Lebra that he would contact some of his "wartime connections" and get back to her.[19]

Round-faced and courtly, Joseph Smiley was a civilized man who found himself besieged by student activists throughout his career. In 1963, the University of Colorado had hired him away from the University of Texas at Austin, hoping he could calm student unrest in Boulder, but the confrontations and demonstrations had only grown more strident. About the time that Thomas Riha disappeared, Smiley was in the process of resigning his post to become president of the University of Texas at El Paso. There he hoped to slip into quiet retirement as a French professor, but he would first be burned in effigy by angry students who wanted UTEP to hire more Mexican American teachers and offer more courses about Mexicans and Native Americans living on the border.[20]

President Smiley made several inquiries and called Joyce Lebra back. "He got the same story that we were getting from the police and the FBI: Tom is all right, he is in this country, there is no international intelligence involved," Lebra would write.[21]

Smiley refused to divulge who gave him the "alive and well" assurances. One rumor circulating among the academics was that Smiley had called former President Lyndon B. Johnson, whom he knew from his UT days. "They had some relationship and Johnson told Smiley not to worry about it, that Riha was okay and not to concern himself with it," recalled Boyd Hill.[22]

Instead of quieting speculation about Thomas's disappearance, Smiley's "alive and well" reassurances only spurred more interest in the case. After all, it was not every day that a respected professor of Russian history simply vanished from his home, his table set for breakfast, and the contents of his briefcase scattered across his desk.

The Boulder police had jurisdiction to investigate the case, but aside from their visits to Riha's home in the week following his disappearance, they did nothing. By contrast, the FBI and CIA were busy behind the scenes. Meanwhile, the trail for Professor Riha would grow cold and the murderer—if indeed he had been murdered—would be free to tidy up loose ends.

8 ★ COUNTRY COUSINS AND SOCIALITES

In the 1960s, the University of Colorado in Boulder was one of the most radical campuses in the country, ranking just behind Berkeley, Columbia, Stanford, Harvard, Cornell, the University of Michigan, and the University of Wisconsin. The demonstrations in Boulder were mostly peaceful, but not always, and two years earlier, twenty members of Students for a Democratic Society succeeded in driving a CIA recruiter off campus.[1] In March 1969, the month that Riha disappeared, students hurled chairs, bottles, and lit cigarettes at a speaker from San Francisco State who had become an overnight hero to the people President Nixon referred to as the "silent majority."[2] Criminal charges were filed against eight students and two SDS members were expelled from the university. Three days later, hundreds of students clashed with the police and marched to the district attorney's office demanding amnesty for those involved in the riots.

Both the CIA and FBI had agents stationed in Boulder who reported to officials in Denver. Michael M. Todorovich (pronounced toe-door-yo-vich) was the CIA's Denver field chief and Scott Werner was the FBI's special agent in charge of the Denver office. Both were experienced agents, courageous under enemy fire, ambitious, loyal, and not adverse to stretching the truth or dissembling when it was in the interest of their agency or their country. Todorovich, like others in the CIA, referred to his FBI counterparts as "country cousins." FBI officials referred to CIA men as "socialites" because of their Ivy League backgrounds and connections to prominent people. Todorovich and Werner were aligned against enemies of the state, but in time they would find themselves engaged in a bitter dispute over the Riha case.

Todorovich was a balding man with shrewd dark eyes who had come to view the world with lofty amusement. When Riha disappeared, Todorovich was in his late fifties and spent his days writing long, ruminative memos about local events to the domestic contact chief back at Langley. Todorovich was the son of a Montana coal miner who had emigrated from Yugoslavia to the United States at the turn of the century. He didn't come from the Ivy Leagues, but his athletic and academic accomplishments were remarkable. He was a skilled linguist and fluent in seven languages, including Russian, Czech, Polish, Serbo-Croatian, Spanish, and Italian. In the 1930s, he won a football scholarship to Gonzaga University, a Jesuit-run institution in Washington state that insisted its athletes also excel in its rigorous scholastics program.[3]

Recruited by naval intelligence during World War II, Todorovich landed by submarine in Yugoslavia, where he fought alongside members of the Resistance who were trying to rid the Balkans of the Nazis. He thought that the future Slavic dictator Josip Broz Tito was a son of a bitch and had looked him in the eye and said just that. While stationed in the Mediterranean, he had wept unashamedly as he carried more than fifty dead orphans from a building that had been accidentally struck by a Nazi bomber. Later he was dispatched to Murmansk, a desolate port in the Russian Antarctic and destination for convoy ships carrying American supplies to the Russian Front. Hoping to disrupt the supply line, the Nazis had bombed the port repeatedly. The craters and twisted debris added to the gloomy, end-of-the-world atmosphere. One day, when he was surreptitiously trying to photograph an ice-breaking ship, he felt the muzzle of a Kalashnikov at the back of his neck. "Misha, dovate foto apparat," the sentry said, ordering him to turn over his camera.[4] Todorovich told the Russian he would likely provoke an international incident if he pulled the trigger and the soldier sensibly lowered his weapon.

Surrounding Murmansk were Stalin's labor camps—the Russian Gulag—where malnourished prisoners worked in subzero temperatures. The inmates often unloaded the ships and were marched into the port at dawn singing the Internationale. "We called them the 'Happy Workers,'" Todorovich would write in a memoir.[5] When the sentries weren't around, Todorovich tried to talk to the prisoners. They were doctors, farmers, factory workers, and teachers. "Most were simply awakened in the early morning hours by NKVD officials with no warning," Todorovich wrote. "Their families, wives or husbands were brushed aside and not apprised of the circumstances underlying the arrests." Then they were shipped off to the Gulag, where they died by the thousands from malnutrition and exposure. In Murmansk, the prisoners carried no lunch pails and labored for eight to ten hours with nothing to eat and only tea or water to drink. They often pilfered food and clothing, but Todorovich instructed the navy guards to ignore the thefts.

After Todorovich was discharged from the navy, he began working on a master's degree at the University of Montana. Eventually he accepted a teaching job at the University of California in Berkeley. On his way to meet his supervisor, he stopped at a Berkeley bookstore and noticed many of the periodicals and journals seemed "extra left-wing" and subsidized by Communists. His impression of Berkeley worsened as he walked across the university grounds and saw a scruffy, bearded speaker espousing the teachings of Marx, Engels, Lenin, and Stalin. Thinking back to those emaciated ghosts in Murmansk, Todorovich was appalled. When he met his Berkeley supervisor and realized that he also seemed soft on communism, Todorovich concluded the job was not for him. That evening he shared his conclusion with his wife, who was waiting for him in a motel with their worldly possessions piled on top of a Plymouth.

Todorovich obtained a teaching job at Napa Community College and started commuting to Stanford University to continue his graduate studies. He began speaking out against the Soviet Union, vowing to dedicate his career to exposing what life was really like in the USSR. "Life as it 'really was,'" he would write, "rather than the speculative philosophical dissertations delivered by naïve professors, journalists, politicians, and contriving extra left-wing Soviet encouraged lecturers, teachers, orators, and finally by carefully covered and concealed NKVD agents posing as diplomats in the United Nations and the various foreign embassies in the Western Hemisphere."[6]

In November 1946, an unidentified man telephoned Todorovich and asked to meet him at a San Francisco hotel. Todorovich suspected the caller was from the CIA and when they met, he was astounded to discover how deeply his background had been researched. Todorovich wasn't sure he wanted to work for the CIA, but decided to "give it a whirl" for a year. He remained for the next twenty-five years. Unlike his adventurous wartime years, Todorovich found himself yoked to a desk, first in Honolulu and then in Cincinnati. In 1963, the CIA asked him if he would be interested in heading the CIA's Domestic Contact Office in Denver. Todorovich liked the idea of returning to the West and accepted the job. By 1969, he had established a network of high-level informants—politicians, academics, and law enforcement types— who kept him updated about events in Colorado.

(The Church Committee would conclude that the CIA's "passive" receipt of information from agents working in these Domestic Contact Offices was simply one step removed from covert collection efforts.[7] For example, in 1969, the field offices were specifically instructed to collect domestic intelligence from black militants, radical youth groups, the underground press, and deserter/draft resistance movements.)

Scott Werner, the FBI's special agent in charge in Denver, was Todorovich's equal in every way. "He was a big, handsome man with a full head of distinguished snow-white hair and matching mustache, one of the few men in Hoover's FBI permitted to wear one, probably because he looked so well in it one would take him for a central casting senator rather than an FBI official," wrote G. Gordon Liddy, who worked in the FBI's Denver office in the 1960s and went on to become one of the most infamous of the Watergate burglars.[8]

Born in Quincy, Massachusetts, Werner earned his law degree from San Francisco State. He joined the FBI in 1941, moving between headquarters and field offices in San Francisco, Portland, Honolulu, Omaha, San Antonio, and Denver.[9] He was a popular speaker at law enforcement gatherings and in 1948, Hoover sent Werner and two other agents to Hollywood to serve as technical advisors for *The Street with No Name* and *House on 92nd Street*. The movies depicted the FBI in such a flattering light that Hoover gave the three men special commendations.

Every Tuesday morning, Werner held a mandatory staff meeting. In his autobiography, Liddy writes that he thought the meetings were a waste of time because Werner usually did nothing but complain about people taking his parking spot. "I don't care what you have to do, let the air out of their tires—anything—just keep them out of my parking space!" he raged.

When a big black Cadillac slid into Werner's spot one day, Liddy went over and began letting the air out of the tires. The returning passenger caught him and screamed, "Just who are you and what the hell do you think you're doing?"

"I'm Special Agent Liddy of the FBI and I'm letting the air out of your tires," responded Liddy.

"I don't believe this!"

"Believe it," said Liddy, as he let the second tire go flat.[10]

One of Werner's most sensational cases was the February 9, 1960, kidnapping and murder of Adolf Coors III, chairman of the Coors brewery in Golden, Colorado. On February 9, 1960, Coors's station wagon was found near a remote bridge. Blood was spattered on a railing and a pair of glasses belonging to the Coors chairman found nearby. The focus of the hunt soon narrowed on Joseph Corbett, a thirty-one-year-old convicted murderer who had walked out of a California prison five years earlier. FBI men fanned out across the United States and Canada, eventually locating Corbett in a motel in Vancouver, British Columbia. When they knocked on the door, Corbett cracked it open and they pushed their way inside. "Okay, I give up," he said.

After serving nearly two decades in prison for the Coors murder, Corbett was paroled and lived as a recluse in a one-bedroom apartment off Federal Boulevard in southwest Denver. In 2009, after apparently contracting cancer, he put a gun to his head and killed himself.

Werner also oversaw the investigation of a November 19, 1968, bombing of a Continental Airlines plane flying from Los Angeles to Denver.[11] The aircraft's landing wheels were extended and the seatbelt lights had just come on when an explosion occurred in a lavatory. A flight attendant slammed shut the door, keeping the smoke and fumes out of the passenger cabin. The plane landed safely. Werner's team arrested a man named Lawrence B. Havelock, who was born in Czechoslovakia and had immigrated to the United States decades earlier. Havelock had served twenty years in the air force and retired to a 150-acre ranch west of Colorado Springs.[12]

According to the *Manila Times,* Havelock was the "sole survivor" of an air force cargo plane that crashed in 1963 in the central highlands of Mindanao in the Philippines allegedly carrying the stolen loot of Madame Nhu, the beautiful sister-in-law of South Vietnam's President Ngo Dinh Diem. Havelock reportedly struggled to Cagayan de Oro, where he was treated at a hospital for exposure and minor injuries. Later he was repatriated and then mysteriously given a general discharge from the US Air Force. Several years after his discharge, Havelock returned to Mindanao to find the crashed plane. He was unsuccessful and returned to the United States, broke and in debt.[13]

At his arraignment for allegedly starting the fire aboard the aircraft, he wept openly, saying he had returned to Colorado to see Steve McNichols, a good friend and the former Colorado governor.[14] Havelock repeatedly proclaimed his innocence, but he was convicted in a bench trial and sent to Leavenworth prison.

★ ★ ★

Both the FBI and the CIA feigned ignorance when asked about the Thomas Riha case. But heavily redacted CIA and FBI records show that the agencies over the years had acquired a lot of background information about Thomas. The first mention of his disappearance in their files occurs on April 5, 1969, when Professor Fischer-Galati wrote to Michael Todorovich apprising him of the situation:

> As you may know, one of our colleagues Professor Thomas Riha has been missing from Boulder since mid-March. His unexplained absence was reported by university officials to local and federal authorities but it would ap-

pear that the only information regarding Mr. Riha has been secured through his lawyer. That information, to the effect that Mr. Riha has decided to return to Czechoslovakia, which he left over 20 years ago, seems somewhat suspicious. I am calling this matter to your attention since, should there be any basis to the university's version of the case, we are concerned with questions of direct interest to you. The matter is, of course, of direct interest to us as it is most unusual for members of university faculties to disappear without a trace in the middle of the semester.[15]

Michael Todorovich forwarded Fischer-Galati's correspondence to Langley, along with a very accurate account of Riha's whereabouts since he had arrived in the United States. Riha, he wrote, had come to his personal attention in the fall of 1968 when he made inquiries on behalf of US citizens stuck in Czechoslovakia at the time of the Soviet crackdown. "His name was mentioned to us as a possibility, since he was in Europe at the time and had planned to visit Prague. No one locally heard from him while he was in Europe, but he did return at the start of the school year. We made several attempts to contact him, but never succeeded in doing so. Finally as the weeks went by, any information he might have had became less timely. Also the CU History Department is a rather touchy group. Since we could get no sure indication from his colleagues that he would be receptive to a CIA approach we finally let the matter drop."[16] Todorovich closed his memo by saying that he planned to do nothing about the case, other than to acknowledge Fischer-Galati's letter.

Todorovich hoped the interest in the Riha case would blow over, but the story was just beginning to develop legs. The following day, April 8, 1969, he received a call from a CIA operative in Boulder. The operative, whose name has been redacted from CIA records, had been in touch with CU's president, Joseph Smiley, who was quite "perturbed" over Riha's absence.[17] Todorovich told the Boulder agent to inform Smiley that the CIA knew nothing about Riha and that they had no involvement with him.

Afterward Todorovich called an agent in the Denver FBI office and was told "Riha was in a safe haven known only to his attorney and that they were not concerned over his disappearance."[18] Shortly after that, Todorovich got another call from the Boulder CIA man. Todorovich instructed him "to soft-pedal it with Smiley and in no way involve the Agency."[19] But Smiley was persistent and Todorovich himself finally made a few inquiries. In a letter to headquarters, he wrote: "We have received a series of communications from the president of the University of Colorado seeking our help re the disappearance of Thomas Riha. To oblige our good contact we undertook some inquiries and have found that the missing Riha is in Brooklyn, quite safe, and that he apparently left Boulder, job, and wife, as the result of a domestic problem. Please forget that we ever mentioned the matter, it is of no concern to our job."[20] It's not clear who told Todorovich that Riha was in Brooklyn. It could have been an FBI agent, another individual within the CIA, an official from the Boulder or Denver police departments, or one of Riha's friends or relatives. Curiously, Todorovich accepted the notion that someone of Riha's stature—a man who had a job, owned a house, and had a network of friends in Boulder—would abruptly leave because of a "domestic problem."

Soon the *Colorado Daily,* the student newspaper at the University of Colorado, began investigating the story. Over a five-day period, one of its reporters interviewed nearly everyone connected with the case. Galya told the journalist she had received numerous letters from Riha postmarked Chicago and Montreal. Hana, who was back in Brooklyn, said she hadn't heard from Riha since the night of the ether incident. Richard Hopkins, Riha's divorce lawyer, mentioned the telegram from Riha. William Briggs, dean of the College of Arts and Science, said Riha had been put on leave without pay. And President Smiley said he had been informed Riha was safe, adding that he was unable to learn the circumstances surrounding his disappearance.

On April 9, the reporter called directory assistance in Montreal and an operator said they had an unlisted number for Thomas Riha. When he called back three days later, the operator told him they only had an unlisted number for an O. Riha.[21] The journalist also contacted CIA headquarters and the FBI's Scott Werner. Werner told him it was the FBI's policy not to comment on an investigation and that Werner's statement should not be construed as an admission that a case was—or wasn't—under investigation.

When the story was published on April 14, 1969, exactly a month after Riha's disappearance, the first paragraph linked Riha to the CIA: "The month-long absence of Russian History Professor Thomas Riha is shrouded in mystery—including a report from an official of the Central Intelligence Agency (CIA) that Riha is 'safe' but his whereabouts cannot be divulged."[22]

Stephen Fischer-Galati, meanwhile, continued to fret about the case. Two days after he penned the letter to the CIA, he wrote to Nathan Lenvin in the Department of Justice's Foreign Agents Registration Section. After sketching out the salient facts, Fischer-Galati said university administrators told him Riha had decided to return to Prague. "He is allegedly awaiting permission from Prague in New York at this time. Should that be indeed the case, there is evidence to assume that his action is not voluntary. Moreover, certain actions taken by the administration may actually contribute to his apparent decision.

In any event, it is incumbent upon me to notify you of these events to prevent either the involuntary return to Czechoslovakia of an American specialist on Russian affairs or the voluntary 'professional suicide' that he may commit under trying circumstances."[23]

Nathan Lenvin had died several months earlier, so the Justice Department forwarded the letter to FBI headquarters. Sam Papich, the Bureau's longtime liaison to the CIA, was assigned to do some follow-up. Papich, a balding, mild-looking man, was also the son of Yugoslav immigrants and also spoke Serbo-Croatian. He graduated from Northwestern University in 1936 with an engineering degree and joined the FBI in 1941, about the same time as William Sullivan, Scott Werner, and W. Mark Felt.[24]

According to a formerly secret FBI memo written the day after the student newspaper published its story, Papich contacted the CIA's Jane Roman, a close friend of Papich and another old hand in the espionage business. Roman, who reported to James Jesus Angleton, had spent her career in the CIA's counterintelligence division and was part of a cell within the CIA that monitored the activities of Lee Harvey Oswald when he was in Mexico City prior to the JFK assassination.

Jane Roman told Sam Papich that Riha was "very definitely" not being used by the CIA. "The subject has not left the United States. The story or rumor that he may have gone to Czechoslovakia is without foundation. Riha has been having difficulties from his wife, and he recently 'ran away from her,'" she advised.[25] Roman didn't reveal how she learned of Riha's domestic difficulties and like Michael Todorovich, she accepted without question the notion that Riha had abandoned his home, his job, and his friends to get away from Hana.

While Papich was checking with the CIA, the FBI's criminal division quietly opened an impersonation investigation into Galya. Impersonation was a minor crime at best and documents and interviews suggest the investigation was equally focused on Thomas Riha.[26]

The FBI's impersonation inquiry was conducted in start-and-stop fashion over the spring and into the fall of 1969. During the first phase, which began in mid-April 1969, FBI agents talked to just two witnesses: the Boulder Police Department's Capt. Willard Spier and Hana's friend, Veva Nye. (Although their names are redacted in the FBI documents, their identities can readily be deduced from surrounding information.)

Captain Spier was interviewed on April 14. He said that the Boulder Police Department didn't open an investigation into Riha's disappearance because it involved a civil dispute between Thomas, Hana, and Galya.

Veva Nye could shed no additional light on Riha's disappearance, instead describing Riha's disappointment in his young wife. "She recalled numerous complaints by Riha that his wife had no interest in his work, that she was a poor housekeeper, spent too much of his money and did not seem to 'shape up' to what he expected in a wife."[27]

After completing the two interviews, the FBI took the impersonation case to James Treece, the US attorney in Denver. Treece told the FBI to drop the case because Galya hadn't enriched herself and no crime appeared to have been committed. The FBI did halt the inquiry—but not before the agents paid a visit to 248 Logan Street to give Galya a severe warning about pretending to be an INS agent. Galya apologized profusely:

She stated she had never impersonated an officer of the U. S. Immigration and Naturalization Service or implied to anyone that she was in any way connected with this agency. She stated that she assists immigrants on many occasions by filling out forms and in other ways by helping them become adjusted to life in the United States. Tannenbaum was admonished for giving the impression in the past that she was connected with the U. S. Bureau of Immigration and Naturalization. Mrs. Tannenbaum stated she did not wish any confusion to arise from any of her acts and was sorry if any such confusion did result. She stated she would make every effort in the future to see that no misrepresentation was made by her which would cause anyone to believe that she was in any way connected with any Federal agency or actively associated with the Immigration Service.[28]

9 ★ GUS

Galya had seen three other men walk out of her life and Thomas's departure felt uncomfortably like abandonment. But she forgave him, blaming his behavior on his traumatic experiences during World War II. "Look, this guy, in his very young years of life, had a horrible experience and was very adept and became extremely skillful at making himself invisible," she told journalist John Olson. "This is nothing new for him to do. If he wants to become invisible someplace, it's the easiest thing in the world. He's the most experienced guy there is who would know exactly what you had to do to vanish because his life was so dependent upon it."[1]

Galya took charge of Riha's estate, telling people he had asked her to help him dispose of his assets. His mail was forwarded to her Logan Street address and she said he had left her some blank checks and credit cards for miscellaneous expenses.[2] She kept his location a secret, even from Zdenek, who questioned her frequently about his whereabouts.[3]

She gave Loretto Heights College, a small Catholic college in Denver, an exquisite collection of hand-painted Easter eggs, which she said was part of a Ukrainian art collection. It was a surprising gesture; just a few months earlier, she had sought a job in the school's public relations department and had been rejected. She also donated to the college roughly one thousand books belonging to Riha, along with maps, charts, and other paraphernalia. She told the head librarian that the book collection was exceedingly valuable and contained materials that had been smuggled illegally out of Russian archives. Among the collection was a twenty-four-volume set of Lenin's collected works, which had been printed in English in Moscow.

The librarian discovered an unexpected treasure between the pages of one of the books—a 1947 letter from playwright George Bernard Shaw to Thomas Riha and a companion named Igor Scholtz. The two young men were studying together in England and they had asked Shaw if they could visit him in his home. The playwright responded, "It is not possible for me to entertain my hundreds and thousands of readers at my house. Unless you have the most urgent business to put before me, I must deny you the fun of seeing the animal in his cage."[4]

In letters to Wheeler Realty signed "Thomas Riha," Thomas continued to insist that Galya be repaid the $7,000 she had loaned him to buy the Boulder house. The letters often ended with disparaging comments about his wife. "While I do not wish to go into details as to my situation, I will state that it is very serious, and my wife is an extreemely [sic] dangerous person," he advised Wheeler Realty in an April 20, 1969, letter.[5]

A woman named Gisela Hertrich entered into a contract to buy the Riha house for $27,940.[6] But the property was tied up in the divorce proceeding and the divorce itself had been delayed because Riha had fired his attorney, Richard Hopkins, for not promptly returning his phone calls. "My recent efforts to dial him direct have found in [sic] always unavailable, and since I do not wish to disclose my immediate whereabouts, I did not leave a message for a return call," a letter containing Riha's signature states.[7]

Galya sold Riha's 1967 Volkswagen to Anthony Stone, an assistant high school principal in Denver who saw an ad for the car in the *Denver Post.* "Leatherette interior, sunroof, ski rack, and back up lights. Flawless cond.," the ad read.[8] The car was parked at a filling station on Colorado Boulevard, one of Denver's busy north-south arteries. After test-driving the vehicle, Stone went to Galya's house to negotiate a price. Galya identified herself as Mrs. Riha and had a notarized transfer of title to the car, which contained Riha's signature.[9]

Stone made out a $1,250 check to Thomas Riha and returned to the gas station to pick up the vehicle. Galya endorsed the check and deposited it into her bank account, explaining later that she wanted to keep Hana from getting the money.[10] When Zdenek asked her about the car, she said that she shipped it to Thomas in Canada.

In a letter mailed to the University of Chicago, Thomas Riha asked that his royalty checks for *Readings in Russian Civilization* be expedited. The University of Chicago issued two checks to Thomas—one for $2,100 and a second for $126.34 and—mailed them to Galya's address.[11]

Administrators at the University of Colorado sent Riha two registered letters,[12] saying that they would fire him if they did not receive a timely explanation for his disappearance.[13] One letter was mailed to Brooklyn and the other to Galya's address. The Brooklyn letter came back as undeliverable, but the other apparently reached Riha, who replied that he definitely would be returning in time for the fall semester. The letter had a Canadian postmark and was hand-delivered by Galya to William Briggs, the arts and sciences dean.[14]

To get away from the stress, Galya often took frequent trips into the mountains. Her four-door Chevrolet needed frequent repairs and she took it to an auto shop on Denver's Colfax Avenue. She was known around the shop as the "Brig" because she boasted that she was about to be promoted to a brigadier general. "She comes in and she orders all these things—a brand new set of tires—a lot of nonsense that nobody in their right mind would put on a car," attendant Otis Sword would say. "Her old car would come in just totaled clear out, shocks beat off of it, springs broke, bumper systems drug off."[15] Sword often notarized documents for her and was certain he had seen Thomas and Galya together on one occasion prior to the professor's March 15, 1969, disappearance.

Through the spring and early summer, Galya's house was crowded with family members and friends who stayed up late watching television. Her mother, Margaret Forest, came for a visit. Her daughter and her newborn took the train from Chicago. Even Thomas dropped in from time to time, Galya told people. She got temporary jobs through Manpower, but money was tight and she fell back on her old habit of writing hot checks for food and other household necessities.

She took pills to get to sleep and pills to wake up.[16] "She ate pills instead of dinner," Zdenek Cerveny recalled.[17] After Thomas vanished, Galya included Zdenek in many of her activities. She invited him over for dinner and included him on day excursions to the mountains and on trips as far away as New Mexico. She even offered to "adopt" him, saying it was a way in which he could become a US citizen more quickly.[18] "She took over my life, kind of, when my uncle disappeared," he recalled. "I remember driving down to Albuquerque. Poor Becky wanted to go to the bathroom and Galya wouldn't stop. Becky peed in her pants and she beat her for that. I said, 'Why didn't you stop?' She said, 'Not in this country. You can't let people pee along the highway.' She would order a big meal and if Becky didn't want to eat it, she would get chastised again. She loved Becky, I think, but her way of loving was problematic."[19]

Galya made a new friend named Barbara Egbert, a lovely woman in her early fifties who had just gone through a divorce. Barbara, in turn, had introduced Galya to Gustav Ingwersen, an inventor, artist, and outdoor enthusiast who, at the age of seventy-eight, was still climbing mountains. Gus looked a decade younger than his chronological age, but his medical records showed he suffered from arteriosclerosis and was at risk of having a heart attack.[20]

Gus had dropped out of high school at the age of sixteen and went into business for himself as a tool and die maker, eventually establishing his own company.[21] After thirty years, he sold the business and devoted the rest of his life to his inventions and his artwork. According to the *Rocky Mountain News,* Gus held numerous patents. During the global rubber shortage of World War II, he developed his own synthetic rubber. He also designed seamless pipes for the Hoover Dam, gas masks for the military, plates for navy ships, and teeth and eyes for big-game trophies.

Gus also invented a machine that could extrude plastic, which could then be molded into plastic pipes. Although plastic piping is ubiquitous today, that wasn't the case when Gus developed his idea. He also partnered with a gynecologist to develop a diaphragm and tampon applicator, but didn't receive any recognition or money from those inventions either. "My grandfather was a pioneer in the plastics industry," said his grandson, Pete Ingwersen. "He could have been a millionaire, but he couldn't see the long-term use of his inventions."[22]

In the 1930s, Gus also leased a gold mine west of Denver called the Lucky Find. One winter, he gave a grubstake to a man with the understanding that they would split the profits from any gold that was found. The man dug out thousands of dollars' worth of gold, sold it to the Denver Mint, and disappeared. "He was taken advantage of his whole life," Pete Ingwersen said.[23]

Gus lived in a brick bungalow on Forest Street in central Denver. He never threw anything away and his house was filled with tools and chemicals. In the basement, where there was hardly room to walk, he had stored over a pound of nitroglycerin.[24] In the backyard there were several twenty-five-gallon containers of acid that had been filled to the top and sealed. The garage, too, was brimming with stuff he had accumulated in his forty-five years as an inventor. In the southeast corner stood a fiberglass vat that was about five feet long, two and a half feet wide, and four feet deep.[25] It was filled to the halfway point with sulfuric acid and copper sulfate. The sulfuric acid was clear and the copper sulfate had solidified in the bottom.

Gus's kitchen was also cluttered. When he wanted to eat, he simply pushed aside his bottles and tools to make room for his food. "The whole kitchen table was filled with chemicals," remembered Denver police detective Tom Lohr.[26]

Ingwersen had three grown sons—Robert, Thomas, and Donald—and numerous grandchildren. But his wife had died several years earlier and he had grown close to Galya and her two children. Becky liked to watch television with him and Jimmy was fascinated by Gus's collection of rocks and fossils. "I became more than just fond of Gus, love in a way, but not the kind of love that would exist between a man and a woman," Galya would write. "I would do just about anything for Gus and worried about him quite a bit. I thought of him as family, with all the rights and privileges of a close member of the family."[27]

Gus and Galya motored into the mountains to explore the abandoned mines left from the gold and silver booms of the previous century. Gus also had once leased the Stanley Mine above Idaho Springs, a small town west of Denver, and the famed Matchless Mine, which was located in Leadville and originally was owned by Sen. Horace A. W. Tabor and his wife, Baby Doe, a pale Victorian beauty who died in extreme poverty.[28]

Together, Gus and Galya developed a plan to build prefabricated homes that could be dropped by helicopters onto remote mountain sites. Galya would design the houses and Gus, with his extensive knowledge of plastics, would take care of the construction. They also developed a prototype for a portable rock crusher. Galya said she loaned Gus money for the project and he, in turn, gave her a note on his house.[29] "Everything was okay, 100 percent all right, and always approved by one another. I do not recall a lot of discussion, we were so close that one heck of a lot was conveyed with just a glance, a raise of the eyebrow, or the most casual comment."[30]

Gus had been thinking about drawing up a will and on June 5, 1969, he called his niece and asked her a question about it.[31] Two days later, he proposed to a woman named Irene Theis, whom he had known since the early 1940s.[32] Irene turned him down, but the rejection didn't appear to trouble Ingwersen. The next day he left for a plastics convention in New York.

Galya gave him a ride to the airport. On June 15, a Sunday, she picked him up and drove him back home. It was Father's Day and to celebrate, Galya had baked Gus some nut bread.[33] When they walked in his house, they discovered it had been left in disarray by the house sitter. Galya put the cake on the table and helped Gus clean up the bungalow.

Later that evening, he went to her Logan Street house for dinner, leaving some papers. On Monday morning, June 16, Gus's sister-in-law, Gertrude Bromley, telephoned him. She asked him how he was feeling and he responded that he "never felt better in his life."[34]

On Tuesday evening, Gus was supposed to have dinner at Galya's, but he never showed up. The following morning, Galya telephoned Bonnie Ingwersen—Pete's mother, who lived in Boulder—and suggested that a family member check up on him.[35] Bonnie contacted Donald Ingwersen, Gus's youngest son, who lived in Denver and worked at Midland Savings and Loan. Donald, in turn, telephoned a neighbor named Barney Gross and asked him to look in on his father.[36]

Barney crossed the yard and went up onto Gus's porch and knocked on the front door. When no one answered, he let himself in with the spare key. Gus was lying on the couch in the living room.[37] When Barney drew closer, he realized Gus was dead. His arms were folded across his chest and he was clad in a white shirt and tie, gray trousers, and black shoes. He normally wore a garnet ring, but it was missing from his finger.[38] He also may have been holding a handkerchief in his hand.[39] Barney Gross returned to the phone and relayed the news to the son.

It was about 6 P.M. on Wednesday, June 18, 1969.

Donald Ingwersen notified the police and then got in his car and drove over to his father's house. By the time he arrived, several policemen and an official from the Coroner's Office were there. He told them that his father was being treated for heart disease and that he had spent three days in St. Luke's in mid-May to have a tumor under his left arm removed.[40] The coroner concluded Gus had died of natural causes and authorized the release of the body to a local mortuary.

Afterward, Donald went around the house tidying up. He saw a partially eaten piece of nut bread lying on the table and tried to stuff it down the kitchen drain. But the cake was too hard and he dropped it into a blue breakfast bowl and put the bowl back on the table.[41] Then he went home to call his two other brothers.

The following day, June 19, a young boy dashed into Probate Court in downtown Denver, slapped an envelope on the counter, and bolted.[42] The envelope contained Gus's last will and testament, which was dated June 5, 1969. The two witnesses were listed as Zdenek Cerveny and Esther Foote, a substitute teacher who lived in Colorado Springs. A probate clerk logged in the will and assigned it the case number, 706. Half an hour later, an unidentified woman called to inquire if the will had been delivered. One of the clerks told her it had.[43]

As these events were unfolding, Ingwersen's sons were searching Gus's house for a will. When they couldn't find it, they contacted Probate Court and learned a new will had just been filed. They piled into a vehicle and drove downtown. A clerk retrieved the will and the family members sat down to read it.

In the will, Gus castigated his three sons for abandoning him and praised Galya and her two children. "I wish to state that I have given long deliberate thought to the relationship that has existed between myself and my sons and their famlies [sic], and because they have displayed no visable [sic] care or concern for me in my lonliness [sic] and age, I have come to these decisions."⁴⁴

Gus willed his automobile to his house sitter, Dale Crippen; a watercolor painting to Barbara Egbert; his books, chemicals, and laboratory equipment to Loretto Heights College. To Jimmy Tannenbaum, "who always had a kiss for 'Uncle Gus,'" Ingwersen willed a dinosaur bone, his mineral specimens, and fifty shares of Global Marine Inc. stock. To Rebecca Tannenbaum, he also willed fifty shares of Global Marine stock, a small red chair, and his color television, which "she liked to watch with me so much." To Galya, in exchange for "all the time and kindness she freely gave me thinking I had nothing," Ingwersen willed his drawing table, a cuckoo clock, and one hundred shares of Travelers Corp stock.

The rest of his property was divided up between his three sons and his grandchildren. After reading the will, the Ingwersen family sat in puzzled silence. They didn't recognize Galya Tannenbaum's name or the names of the two people who reportedly witnessed Gus signing his will. They were also mystified that their father would give each of the Tannenbaum children fifty shares of Global Marine stock. Gus and his sons knew the stock was worthless and not a "fitting gift" for anyone.⁴⁵ They also noticed numerous spelling errors in the will—"famlies," "visable,""lonliness," "specimins," and "grandaughters."

On Friday, June 20, Donald Ingwersen asked Denver police detective Phillip Villalovos to meet him at his father's home on Forest Street. Villalovos had been a detective in the juvenile division before transferring to Denver's homicide bureau. He was about forty years old and an experienced investigator. "This was not my first homicide investigation," he said in an interview.⁴⁶

Donald Ingwersen ushered Detective Villalovos into the kitchen and pointed out the blue bowl containing the nut bread, some sugar-like crystals scattered across the plastic tablecloth, and a small vial of potassium cyanide.⁴⁷

The son told the detective that his father was careful when handling chemicals, but he was worried nevertheless that he may have inadvertently ingested some cyanide. Villalovos summoned technicians from the Denver Crime Lab, who bagged the nut bread, the vial of potassium cyanide, and the crystals. They also took possession of the will and five cancelled checks, which were made out to Galya and totaled about $385.⁴⁸

The Ingwersens called the funeral home and asked that Gus's partially embalmed body be transferred to the Coroner's Office, which was located in an antiquated building on the Denver General Hospital campus. Dr. George Ogura, a brilliant forensic pathologist, gathered his instruments together and prepared to do the autopsy.

Dr. Ogura compared human bodies to clay and said it was his job to solve the riddle of a person's death, whether it was from disease or an obscure chemical.[49] Dr. Ogura was known at Denver General for his rigorous Friday afternoon "organ recitals," in which he gathered physicians and surgeons and quizzed them about the causes of their patients' deaths. If their diagnoses were incorrect, he would explain the actual cause of death based on his examination of the bodies. Dr. Ogura, who was Japanese, graduated from the University of Colorado medical school in 1942, a time when anti-Japanese fervor was at fever pitch and many Japanese had been rounded up and placed in detention camps. It was a "terrible era," he acknowledged in an interview, but said he preferred not to think about it. "When you harp, or dwell on unpleasantries, your whole life becomes destroyed so I shoved it to the back of my mind." Dr. Ogura said he didn't remember the Ingwersen case because he always left his cases at the office. "Otherwise I would have gone batty."[50]

Gus's autopsy report, however, is still on file in the Denver Medical Examiner's Office. According to that report, Dr. Ogura first inspected Gus's entire body, noting the embalming incisions and an irregular reddish-gray discoloration in his lower extremities. Then he began removing the organs. The heart was strong and firm, but the valves were thin, the wall of the left ventricle abnormally thick, and the coronary vessels filled with plaque.

When he finished examining the heart, he moved on to the gastrointestinal tract. If Gus had ingested potassium cyanide, Dr. Ogura said he would have expected to see evidence there. "Cyanide's a corrosive and it will burn the stomach," he said.[51] In the stomach folds, according to the autopsy report, Dr. Ogura found a four-inch patch of discoloration that was akin to a burn.

When Dr. Ogura was finished, he sent various tissues and fluids to a lab for analysis. When he got the results back and had reviewed all the physical evidence, he concluded that the primary cause of Gus's death was potassium cyanide poisoning. Arteriosclerosis was the secondary cause.[52]

The bottle and granules taken from Gus's table and sent to the Crime Lab also tested positive for potassium cyanide. But there was no potassium cyanide in the cake that Galya had baked for Gus, according to police reports.[53]

Cyanide is toxic even in minute quantities and causes death by preventing cells from producing the energy needed to keep the body alive. Victims who ingest or inhale lethal amounts feel like they are being strangled or suffocated. Nausea, confusion, and disorientation set in, followed by writhing and gasping, then unconsciousness and death. Death row inmates killed by a gaseous form of cyanide have been known to have suffered excruciating deaths. As a consequence, many states have banned the use of cyanide in executions because it can be construed as cruel and unusual punishment.

Despite the death throes Gus must have gone through, his clothes weren't disheveled nor was his body contorted. He looked peaceful, as if he had just dozed off for a nap.

On June 21, Detective Villalovos went to Donald Ingwersen's home in southeast Denver to return the will and the cancelled checks. While there, Donald Ingwersen informed him of other developments in the case. He said Galya had gone to the mortuary the day before to view Gus's body, but had been told it wasn't ready. She then drove out to Stapleton Airport, where Bonnie Ingwersen and other relatives were waiting for the flight of another family member. Galya had Bonnie paged over the intercom and the entire family went to the location where she was waiting. When Galya asked Bonnie why the viewing had been delayed, a frisson of anger rippled through the family. "A remark was made to her by one of the brothers to the effect that she really made out on the will. She replied that she should have as she paid in a lot of money on a business venture with Mr. Ingwersen," Villalovos would write.[54]

Following the funeral, Galya contacted Robert Ingwersen, another son, and asked him to look for a gold wedding band she had left with Gus. The ring, she explained, belonged to a friend. Gus was supposed to remove the inscription, polish the ring, and return it to her along with a second ring he was working on.[55] Gus often repaired jewelry for friends and Robert didn't think anything of the request. He hunted for the ring throughout the house, but couldn't find it.

The Denver police, meanwhile, contacted the FBI to find out if Galya had a criminal record. The FBI's records division in Washington, DC, couldn't find anything under her name. She also had no criminal record on file with the Denver Police Department. In fact, the only person mentioned in the will who apparently did have a criminal record was Dale Crippen, who had housesat for Gus while he was at the plastics convention. Suspicious that he was being set up, Crippen told police that Galya had called him a couple of days before the will was filed and wanted to know how to spell Crippen's last name. He also told police he didn't remember spilling anything while he was housesitting for Gus.[56]

On July 8, 1969, Detective Villalovos drove to Galya's home at 248 Logan Street. Galya ushered him into her house, asking him if he would like a cup of coffee and a piece of cake. The detective refused. "When I go to interview suspects, I don't normally eat cake and drink coffee with them."[57]

Despite Galya's hospitality, Villalovos's suspicions were aroused. She seemed like a con artist to him, weighing her words carefully. "She did not respond immediately like most people. It was like she was thinking of an answer," he said in a 2020 interview.[58]

Galya described to the detective her relationship with Gus. She said they had done several business deals together and that she had loaned him $10,000 to pay off a mortgage.[59] An installment note and deed of trust securing the loan from Galya to Gus was drawn up on June 12, about the time Gus departed for New York City.[60]

Detective Villalovos asked Galya if she recalled giving Gus some pastry. "She stated that on Father's Day she did give him some nut cake which she had baked from a Betty Crocker or Jewell cake mix."[61]

Galya denied any knowledge of the will or that it was her son who delivered the document to Probate Court. She also had an alibi: she said she and her children were in Leadville, Colorado, paying a ticket on the day the unidentified boy delivered the will to Probate Court.[62]

When police contacted Zdenek Cerveny, he confirmed that he had witnessed Gus signing his will. The detectives couldn't reach the other witness, Esther Foote, the substitute teacher who lived in Colorado Springs.

The Ingwersen family, convinced the will was fraudulent, hired a lawyer to begin the process of having the document set aside. When Galya learned of the effort, she became frustrated and angry. She wrote to Boulder attorney Dennis Blewitt begging him for help. "I knew Gus's feelings about the people involved. He often said he felt they were unadulterated treachery and they were at odds with each other," she wrote.[63]

She also complained about the delays in the sale of Riha's house. "I do not know what it is with Thomas R—but I'm about the only one really being hurt by this house affair—and I am literally *desperate* for cash right now. We plainly just won't eat if some of these things don't get straightened out. I can go a lot of strain but really I have reached my capacity and am about to go absolutely nuts with worry."[64]

Galya asked Blewitt to stop by her house the next time he was in Denver so she could discuss the issues with him—"NOT on the phone, *which obviously has ears.*"[65] In a follow-up letter a few days later, Galya again mentioned that she thought his telephone was being tapped. "I still would like to talk to you without having unknown persons listening in on the phone. You must have something really 'hot' in your kettle to get so easily bugged," she writes.[66]

Despite her money woes, on July 30, 1969, Galya chartered a four-seater Cessna owned by Judson Flying Service in Longmont, Colorado, to take Zdenek and an out-of-town guest to San Antonio, Texas. Galya sat up front with the pilot, Robert Gaines, and Zdenek and his friend sat in the back. On the way to Texas, the pilot let her fly the Cessna, instructing her in the basics of straight-level flying and turns. When they touched down in San Antonio, Zdenek and his friend departed and Galya flew back to Denver with the pilot.

She paid him with a $330 check that had been presigned by Thomas Riha. A few days later, the check bounced. Zdenek eventually repaid the pilot $220. "He said he didn't want to make money off me, so that's all he took," he said.[67]

Two months later, the closing on Riha's house took place. One of the attorneys was a Boulder lawyer named Neil King, an ardent conservationist who was well known in legal circles. King's father had been dean of the University of Colorado's law school for twenty-three years. King himself had served as Boulder's city attorney and had won a landmark zoning case that marked the beginning of an intense effort to assemble open space around the city.

Galya received a check for $1,392 at the closing, which represented a percentage of the $7,000 she claimed to have loaned to Thomas, as well as interest and fees.[68] Sometime after that, Neil King said his file on Galya disappeared from his Boulder office. "Our offices were downtown at Fourteenth and Pearl. Our office was always locked. We were in what was formerly the Penny's building. We had the whole ground floor. Our file room had banks of files. That file, which was fairly thick, was just gone. It disappeared. I never saw it again. What happened to it, I have no idea."[69]

Gus's family, meanwhile, decided to put his house on the market. Getting it ready was a gargantuan task and meant paying someone to dispose of the chemicals. While cleaning the kitchen, Don Ingwersen found the wedding band Galya had been looking for behind a canister. The inscription read, "Hana to Tomás 13 Oct. '68."

When Det. Tom Lohr learned that Riha's wedding band had been found in Gus's house, he got permission from Don to search Gus's house and yard for Thomas Riha's body. He began by inspecting the basement, where he saw no evidence of recent repairs to the floor or walls. There was also no sign of digging in the backyard. Lohr then turned his attention to the huge vat of acid in the garage. Don Ingwersen, who was knowledgeable in chemistry, said that if a body had been placed in the solution, the only thing left would be metal, such as gold crowns. "Flesh, bones, etc. would be completely eliminated," he told Lohr.[70] Ingwersen added that it was his feeling that nothing had been placed in the vat for some time.

Toward the end of the visit, Don Ingwersen told Detective Lohr about a couple of other strange things. After his father died, he spotted his dad's Leica camera in the dining room. Seven pictures had been taken and he made a mental note to have the film developed. Next to the camera were two claim slips for film being developed at a photo store on East Colfax Avenue. He put the claim slips in his pocket. That night, he had the front door lock changed. When he returned to his father's house the following day to retrieve the Leica, it was gone. He asked other family members about the camera, but none of them had taken it. When Don Ingwersen called the photo shop to ask about the film, he was told that a woman who claimed to be a family member had already picked it up.

Don then contacted his brother, Robert, in Boulder and asked him to look at the last photo slides known to have been taken by his father. Robert did so and found six slides missing from the middle of the roll. The slide just before the missing group showed his father and Galya Tannenbaum standing on top of Loveland Pass, which has an elevation of nearly twelve thousand feet and is located on the Continental Divide sixty miles west of Denver.

Don also told Detective Lohr about an aunt's chilling vision. "Don stated he has an old aunt that is weird. She claims to be clairvoyant. She has had a dream numerous times where she sees the body of Thomas Riha. He is bundled up tightly in plastic or rubber and is near a north wall of stone. He is covered by wet cement. Not fresh, but cement with water over the top of it. Don says this aunt is a little goofy, but all his life a good percentage of her visions come true."[71]

10 ★ BARBARA

Barbara Egbert seemed to have it all—a loving husband, three rambunctious boys, and a beautiful home. She was five feet two inches tall, with grayish-blue eyes and long brown hair with gray strands running through it.[1] She was a graduate of Swarthmore College and had studied ballet in New York City. Her limbs and torso were still supple and she glided through rooms. She was a marvelous cook and occasionally enjoyed a glass of sherry.[2] Despite her good fortune, she was plagued by a sense of dissatisfaction. "You marry . . . you raise a family . . . not enuf," she writes.[3]

Barbara and her husband, John, packed their belongings and moved to California. But California did not quiet the restlessness within her, so they moved again. Over time, their marriage began to disintegrate. Barbara tried to leave him, but said she kept "chickening out." She was worried about her boys and worried about what other people would think. The couple separated, reconciled, and separated again. One day she called it quits for good. "I lived a hell on earth for every year of my so-called married life," she writes. "I was a magnificent martyr but a very foolish woman."[4] Barbara gave her husband custody of her three teenage boys because she could not financially support them and felt they were at an age when they needed to be with their father.

At the age of fifty-one, she found herself living alone. She received fifty-nine dollars a week in unemployment benefits and earned forty dollars a month as manager at a small apartment complex on Race Street in Capitol Hill, an old Denver neighborhood filled with crumbling, nineteenth-century mansions that had been converted into apartment houses. She purchased her clothing at a secondhand store in Cherry Creek called the Encore Shop and was in the process of distributing her résumé to advertising agencies around town in the hopes she could land a job as a part-time copy editor.

Her duties as apartment manager were light and consisted mainly of keeping peace between tenants and making sure the younger residents kept the volume on their stereos turned down. Her first-floor garden apartment consisted of one large room, a bathroom, a galley-style kitchen, and a patio. Despite her reduced circumstances, she was excited by the future. "We will all be so surprised and delighted with what life has doled out to us . . . that we will literally be jumping from star to star with the most magnificent spiritual and material glee we could ever imagine," she wrote to an old friend.[5]

Part of her newfound happiness stemmed from her discovery of the Metaphysical Research Society, which was located in a beautifully restored mansion on a hill overlooking Denver's historic Seventh Avenue. The mansion's rooms were large and filled with Victorian accents, including decorative plasterwork, indoor fountains, stained-glass windows, gilt-painted trim, and paintings on the walls and ceilings. A huge chandelier hung in the foyer and an oak staircase rose up through the main levels of the house. Screened-in porches were located on the west side.

In the meeting room of the Metaphysical Research Society, rows of straight-backed chairs faced a small podium where the teachers delivered their lectures. Presiding over the facility was a commanding teacher named Trenton Tully, who wore a long white robe and a gold brocade belt around his waist. "He had a head of thick, straight black, perfectly groomed hair; flawless, wrinkle-free skin; dark brown eyes with thick eyebrows; and full lips on a symmetrical oval face," writes author Sonia Choquette. She thought Tully was a "very young" forty-five, but would later learn he was closer to sixty-five.[6] Tully was articulate and charismatic and could speak for hours on the nature of God and the universe, blending the teachings of Buddha, Jesus, and Mohammed with occult disciplines such as astrology and numerology and the healing power contained in crystals and certain light waves. "He said so much in those two hours that my brain hurt from being so full. I'd never met anyone so knowledgeable in all the things I craved," Choquette writes.

The Metaphysical Research Society was affiliated with the Brotherhood of the White Temple and the Shamballa Ashram in Sedalia, a small town about an hour's drive south of Denver. The ashram was founded by Dr. Maurice Doreal in the 1950s and included a church, outbuildings, and a scattering of homes.[7] (The Brotherhood of the White Temple still exists. The church itself is nestled among pine trees along a rural dirt road. The small white building resembles any other country church, but instead of a cross above the front door, there is a small blue square that contains a pentagram flanked by two Egyptian ankhs, which symbolize life.)

Doreal's real name was Claude D. Dodgin and he was born in 1902 in Oklahoma. In the early 1950s, thinking an atomic attack was imminent, Dodgin and his followers moved to Sedalia, where he thought the lead in the surrounding foothills would protect them from radioactive fallout.[8] Doreal's philosophy was a canny mixture of Eastern and Western religion and science fiction. He was short and pudgy, with thinning dark hair, and resembled not so much a religious avatar as an encyclopedia salesman. He claimed he had no need to study mathematics, chemistry, or any other subject because he remembered his past lives completely and already knew everything. His wisdom, he said, had been further enhanced when he astral-traveled to a place beneath Tibet, where he communed with enlightened beings.

Trenton Tully toned down the more far-out aspects of Doreal's philosophy and focused instead on New Age topics like the barriers to achieving one's goals; the toxicity of anger; the power of love and forgiveness; the nature of time and space, and the ability to experience past lives.

Gus Ingwersen also was a member of the Metaphysical Society. One evening, he had fainted in the lecture room and Barbara had given him a ride home. "I do not believe she ever went back because Gus was very lively and B. didn't want any kind of an involvement," Maryann Hendee, a friend of Barbara's and a nurse in Denver's Public Health Department, would write.[9]

Galya sometimes accompanied Barbara or Gus to the meetings, scrawling large, nearly unintelligible sentences in a notepad. Secretly, she thought religion was for "idiots," but could adapt her personality to whomever she happened to be with. When she was with Barbara, she played the role of a sophisticated matron who enjoyed slumming with the bohemian characters who populated Denver's Capitol Hill neighborhood. She also went out of her way to do favors for people, creating a sense of obligation in the recipients. At the time, she was trying to line up job interviews for Barbara, who felt smothered by Galya's attention. "I will get my own job," Barbara fumed.[10]

Barbara's parents visited her over the Labor Day weekend and she had shown them the old brick mansion that housed the Metaphysical Society and introduced them to Trenton Tully. They also met Galya, who had grown close to Barbara in the weeks and months following Gus's death.

For her birthday, Barbara's parents had given her an eighteen-karat gold Omega watch with a sapphire crystal. She wrote them a September 10, 1969, thank-you letter, adding, "Galya is coming over for dinner tonight and bringing a steak and some mushrooms. She said she is tired of buying steak and feeding it to the kids who won't eat it and the neighbor's dog ends up with most of it. They much prefer ground meat, it seems . . . which is the way with children. So she is going to feed them and then bring the steak over here so we can both enjoy it."[11]

On September 11, Barbara visited with Maryann Hendee. When Maryann confided to Barbara that she was lonely, Barbara seemed surprised.

"I've never been lonely in my life," Barbara told her.[12]

"Well, you have your problems and I have mine," Maryann said.

Galya, however, thought Barbara was despondent and grew worried about her when she didn't show up for dinner on the evening of September 12, a Friday. She telephoned Barbara's ex-husband, John Egbert, and urged him to check up on her.[13]

John Egbert didn't know what to make of Galya, but he did know that Barbara believed Galya was a colonel in military intelligence.[14] The following morning, September 13, a Saturday, he began telephoning his ex-wife's apartment. On the first try, he received no answer. On subsequent attempts, he got a busy signal. He continued to call throughout the day. Finally, he called the owner of the apartment complex and asked him to look in on Barbara. The owner went to Barbara's apartment and knocked on her door. Hearing no movement, he used his pass key to enter. He saw Barbara lying on an oval rug in the middle of the living room and knew immediately that she was dead. He returned to his apartment and called the police.

At 7 P.M., detectives Charles McCormick and Jack Isenhart arrived. They stood in the entrance to the apartment, looking over the scene. There was no sign of forced entry, no sign of a struggle. The death, they thought, looked like an obvious suicide.

Barbara was clad in a blue floral pantsuit and lying face up on an oval rug. Her body was cold to the touch and there was a bluish discoloration around her lips and fingernails.[15] Her head was resting on two throw pillows, one red and the other blue. Two more pillows lay to the right of her head and a large green pillow lay to the left. Her right hand was palm up and level with her face and her left hand was resting on her stomach. Clutched in the left hand were dried rose petals. More rose petals were scattered over her body and the rug, but there were no petals beneath her body.

Her shoes were sitting in front of a chair and her eyeglasses and wrist-watch were on a nearby table. On another table were framed photographs of her sons and a photograph of a man in ornate religious garb, who was likely Trenton Tully. A large blue candle was burning and incense was smoldering in a small, gold-colored Buddha statue.

Two typewritten notes were also lying on one of the tables. One was Barbara's will and the other was a suicide note. In the suicide note, Barbara begins by saying she had decided to "stop this life existance [sic] and be available to try another."[16] She continues: "For the past year or more, I have tried repeatedly to find employment without success. Always I have been concidered [sic], but, in the end, not good enough, and someone else would be chosen for employment but not me. I have taken jobs which made me misserable [sic] for short times, just to eat, and even they are unavailable now . . . I cannot stand anymore, and so I choose to leave this existance, [sic] and start over in a new incarnation, with hope it will be better.[17]

Her will was very brief. She asked that her bills be paid, her books donated to the Metaphysical Research Society, and everything else divided up between her husband and sons.[18] She also willed a collage to Galya and thanked her for "her consistant [sic] help and loans."

After reading the two documents, the detectives moved on to the kitchen, where they found an empty wine glass containing a whitish residue and some white powder in a plastic prescription bottle. Two jugs of wine, one empty and one full, were sitting on the floor next to her typewriter. They ordered the body taken to the morgue and bagged the wine glass and the prescription bottle as evidence.

As the two investigators prepared to depart the scene, Detective McCormick took one last look around. Something about the death scene felt wrong to him. The burning candle and incense, the rose petals, the artfully arranged photos resembled a stage set. More importantly, it was also the first time he had ever seen a typed suicide note. Most victims were usually too distraught to do that.

Dr. George Ogura once again performed the postmortem, beginning with an examination of Barbara's body. He noticed her face, neck, and shoulders were an unusual shade of reddish purple. As he removed the organs, he saw that the lower lobes of the lungs had a similar discoloration and were filled with gray mucus. He found no burned areas in the stomach, but did recover a plastic-like material that suggested partially digested capsules. Dr. Ogura sent the capsules, as well as samples of Barbara's blood and gastric juices, to a lab for analysis.

He was surprised when he got the lab results back. Barbara had an extremely high concentration of sodium cyanide in her blood. Sodium cyanide is slower acting than the potassium cyanide found in Gus's body but just as deadly.

The capsules were vestiges of Darvon, a widely prescribed painkiller in the 1960s, which was pulled from the market in 2010.[19] Dr. Ogura concluded that Barbara died of "acute cyanide poisoning."[20] He speculated that the Darvon probably had been ingested a short time before the cyanide.

Two days after Barbara's death, Galya sat down and wrote a sympathy letter to Barbara's three sons. She could have easily been talking about herself. "Barbara was very confused," she began:

> She often felt horribly alone and rather than face a hurt within herself she created a world all her own. She is not the only person who has done this, many people have in varying degrees. Some survive, and sometimes things become so depressing, that the unreal world consumes them.
>
> People who are so afraid of life that they find it necessary to "create" their own world need a lot of love and patience, *more* generally than most other individuals are *able* to give, particularly because in their hurt, they do things which makes it even harder for their families to reach them . . .
>
> You would not condemn, or be angry with a person with a broken leg, and please do not be angry with Barbara who was ever so ill emotionally and mentally that in desperation she reached out to a false philosophy. . . .
>
> A friend
> Galya[21]

Barbara's relatives and friends were shocked to learn that Barbara had committed suicide. Her sister, Constance Hall, flew to Denver from New Jersey. She called Galya and told her she wanted to talk with her. Galya refused at first, but finally relented. At about 10:15 P.M. on the evening of September 14, Constance and her husband arrived at Galya's house. Constance thought that Barbara had died from an overdose of pills and asked Galya if she knew where her sister could have gotten the pills.

"It wasn't pills," Galya said.

"If it wasn't pills, what was it?" Constance asked.

Galya did not respond.[22]

At that point, Denver pathologist George Ogura was still investigating the cause of Barbara's death and no one knew what she had died from.

Barbara's parents gave Denver detectives a copy of the letter that Barbara had written three days before her death. It was upbeat and chatty and mentioned the fact that she was distributing copies of her résumé about town. Her father, Clinton Smith, told police that the will and suicide note didn't resemble Barbara's writing.

"My daughter was a good speller, therefore we wondered who wrote the suicide note. I point out the misspelled words, 'usless,' 'concidered,' 'misserable,' and 'Me' instead of 'My,'" he wrote. "It may be repetition to say in our visit with our daughter August 31 to September 2, there was no indication of distress, moroseness or depression. She bought a pair of shoes on September 2. She had not sold her clothing." [23]

Clinton Smith wondered if his daughter had been murdered because she knew Galya had forged Gus's will. "Did Barbara know something about the forging even though not a party to it? I suggest questions which might cause Tannenbaum to reveal something. I understand that when angered she is apt to tell things."[24]

Maryann Hendee was also in contact with the Denver police. She told investigators that she had had dinner with Barbara just two days before her alleged suicide and that she didn't seem despondent. In a letter to Barbara's parents, she added, "I KNEW SHE WAS HAPPY, THE HAPPIEST IN ALL HER LIFE AND NEVER, NEVER SUICIDAL."[25]

Galya was again summoned to Denver's homicide bureau. Detectives Phillip Villalovos, Jack Isenhart, and Charles McCormick were present for the interview.

McCormick remembers the interview well. He thought Galya an imposing woman who spoke in a loud voice and was glad to be in the company of other homicide detectives. "She was exactly what she looked like: Uptight, big, overpowering physically. She would knock you down with what she had to say. But she was not impolite. She fit the profile of somebody who would be the commander of an intelligence wing. Her manner of dress was very plain. She wore plain shoes. There was nothing ostentatious about her," he recalled in an interview in 2020.[26]

Settling her bulk into a chair, Galya began talking about Barbara's many problems. She said that religious differences—not John Egbert's temper tantrums—led to the couple's divorce. John was a Mormon and had persuaded Barbara to join the church, but she abandoned it when she discovered the Metaphysical Research Society. Galya went on to say that Barbara had begun to think she was the incarnation of some ancient Egyptian queen and went around showing people a picture in a book, exclaiming, "'This looks like me!' 'This looks like me!'"[27]

Barbara, she added, was passionately in love with Trenton Tully, the charismatic teacher at the Metaphysical Research Society. She was also having "visions" in which she was seeing the founder of the Brotherhood of the White Temple, Maurice Doreal. "This is why Mrs. Tannenbaum called Mr. Egbert stating she thought he better check on his ex-wife as she appeared to be going off the 'deep end' on this metaphysicism," one of the homicide detectives wrote.[28]

Galya also insisted that Barbara was upset over losing custody of her sons. "She tried to pretend that all was well, she was free, etc., but the act didn't come off very convincing. She was really troubled by the loss of her children." Galya added that Barbara was desperate for money and had not held a job since mid-July.

Toward the end of the interview, one of the detectives asked Galya if she had access to cyanide. She said that she did. Her husband, who was a photographer, used cyanide to develop his photographs. Gus, with whom she claimed to have lived with for a while, also used a cyanide mixture to extract gold from ore. (Galya had no photographer husband nor had she ever lived with Gus.)

Galya left the police station, confident that she had answered questions in a way that would deflect suspicion. But the police were still actively investigating Gus's and Barbara's deaths.

The Ingwersen family hired handwriting analyst Ben Garcia to examine Gus's will, the $10,000 installment note, the deed of trust, as well as the checks made out to Galya. Garcia concluded that Gus's signatures were forged on the documents and checks.[29] He also determined that a typewriter seized from Galya's home was used to type the Ingwersen will.[30]

The Denver police asked Garcia to examine Barbara's will and suicide note. Garcia concluded that the signature on the two documents had been traced and that the typewriter used to type the documents belonged to Galya.[31]

The Denver detectives decided it was time to take a trip to Boulder to talk to their counterparts at the Boulder Police Department. By then, Thomas Riha had been gone for seven months.

To Det. Charlie McCormick, the case felt like it was spinning out of control. Witnesses needed to be questioned and leads needed to be followed up. But multiple jurisdictions were involved and no one was coordinating the investigation. "It was confusing as to who was doing what and why," McCormick remembered. "There were lots of cooks in the kitchen, but no chefs to take charge."[32]

To add to the confusion, the FBI and CIA were skulking on the periphery of the cases, stoking rumors. "The fact that the CIA and FBI were involved made it worse," McCormick said. "They were very hard to deal with."[33] Added Det. Tom Lohr, "The FBI was stonewalling everything."[34]

11 ★ "BAG OF SNAKES"

On the morning of September 22, 1969, Denver police detectives Phillip Villalovos and Tom Lohr knocked on the office door of Capt. Willard Spier, head of the Boulder Police Department's detective bureau. Spier was fifty-one years old, cagey and smart, with probing eyes and wavy brown hair. He was still athletic and powerful looking, but time and his desk job were working against him.

When the Denver cops asked him about Thomas Riha, Spier was vague. Yes, he said, he had heard that the professor "was missing under peculiar circumstances."[1] But he added, "No official pickup or complaint had been filed by anyone with the Boulder Police Department." Spier didn't mention the missing-person report that Joyce Lebra and other faculty members tried to file on April 4, 1969, nor did he reveal that Capt. Lowell Friesen had torn up the report.

After forty-five minutes, Spier stood up, indicating the interview was over. He ushered the two detectives out of his office, suggesting that as long as they were in Boulder, they might want to visit with attorney Gerald Caplan.

Caplan was more open, talking freely about what he knew of the case and lending the Denver detectives the eight depositions that he had taken immediately following the ether incident. He told them to come back in two days and he would have Hana and her aunt, Rose Grossman, available for interviews.

Afterward the two detectives drove back to Denver, stopping in at the office of FBI agent Ray Mathias in the Federal Building at 19th and Stout Streets. Mathias was evasive, saying that the FBI had received some "impersonation" complaints about Galya Tannenbaum, but the complainants had refused prosecution.[2]

In fact, records show the FBI had actually reopened its impersonation case against Galya after one of Gus's relatives contacted the Denver FBI office and said that Galya had been holding herself out as a colonel in army intelligence and claimed she was about to be promoted to brigadier general.[3] Esther Foote, the Colorado Springs substitute teacher whose signature appeared on the Ingwersen will, also contacted the FBI and told them that Galya was impersonating an army intelligence officer and carried a briefcase with the word *Army* on it.

It was the second time since Thomas's disappearance that the FBI had investigated Galya for impersonation. Once again, FBI officials brought their information to the US Attorney's Office in Denver. Once again, the case was turned down because Galya had not obtained anything of value. Curiously, an assistant US attorney specifically instructed the FBI agents that Galya should not be "re-contacted."[4]

On the morning of September 24, the Denver detectives returned to Boulder to interview Hana. She was working in a bank in New York, but had flown back to Colorado for her divorce hearing. (The divorce decree was signed on September 30, 1969, and the judge ordered the still-missing Thomas Riha to pay Hana a lump sum of $5,000.)[5]

Hana launched into her long, confusing story, beginning in October 1968 when Galya barged into her wedding reception at the Black Bear Inn. She talked about the white pill that Galya tried to shove down her throat during the car ride, the ether incident, and Galya's incessant demands that she sign unspecified immigration papers. She also mentioned a carton of orange juice and a hunk of salami that Galya had stowed in Riha's refrigerator.[6] She said Thomas drank some of the orange juice and afterward became pale and dizzy. There was one more thing: Hana said that Galya had tried to persuade her to withdraw $3,000 from a checking account and give it to her for safekeeping, but she had refused.

The two interviews took about an hour. After Hana and her aunt had departed, the Denver detectives stuck around to talk with Gerald Caplan and his law partner, Donald Brotzman, a Republican and a Boulder congressman. "Mr. Caplan at this time brought forth an important subject, the correct spelling of 'consideration,'" the detectives wrote.[7] Caplan pointed out that "consider" was misspelled as "concider" in documents purportedly written by Hana. And when the Denver police went back and reviewed their records, they discovered documents allegedly written by Thomas Riha and Barbara Egbert also contained the same misspellings.

Galya grew panic-stricken when she learned that the Denver cops had been in Boulder and called the Denver Police Department repeatedly. Finally, a detective called her back. She talked at length about Thomas Riha, saying she had known him since he was seventeen and that he had left Boulder to get away from Hana. "A running battle commenced during which Rea [sic] tried to have Hana deported. The immigration people apparently wanted to deport her, but were powerless to do so as long as she was married to an American. According to Mrs. T., Rea tried every way possible to get away from Hana, but was unsuccessful. He, again according to her, reverted to type, & ran."[8]

Galya added that Hana was a Communist spy and had powerful contacts behind the Iron Curtain. "Mrs. T says Rea is definitely, definitely alive and has not been murdered. He is alive and living in Montreal."[9]

Galya's ramblings were unconvincing. The criminal investigation began in earnest, moving along several tracks. Galya was now a prime suspect in the disappearance and probable death of Thomas Riha and the cyanide poisonings of Gustav Ingwersen and Barbara Egbert. Hoping to get Galya off the streets and behind bars as quickly as possible, police focused on the lesser forgery charges.

In Boulder, police officials began pursuing the $330 hot check that Galya passed to Judson Flying Service for the trip to San Antonio and the alleged forgery of documents associated with the sale of the Riha house. In Denver, police began to build a forgery case around the Ingwersen will and a second forgery case involving the sale of Riha's Volkswagen.

A breakthrough occurred when the detectives finally made contact with Esther Foote. Esther had tutored Galya's children in the summer of 1969 and Galya had paid her with a $350 check written on Thomas Riha's bank account. When the check bounced, Foote contacted the FBI, hoping mail fraud charges could be filed against Galya.

Esther told Denver police that Galya had asked her to sign Gus's will several days after Gus died. Foote said she intended to sign—and told Zdenek that she was going to sign—but decided against it after she checked with a friend, who told her it was illegal.[10] Foote continued:

I am a reader of the cards and I had an add [sic] in the Denver Post and Galia [sic] Tannenbaum called me and I went over and read for her but I didn't charge her. I didn't particularly trust her. She told me she was a colonel in Intelligence in the Army and told me she had killed people before. At the time I believed her. After I had met her she asked me to tutor her children, we decided on the price of $350.00 a month. I only tutered [sic] her children one month. All this time we had gone to some movies and also played Wegee [sic] board One time when we were playing the Wegee [sic] board she told me she felt the spirit of Thomas Rhia [sic], that Thomas Rhia was also a member of the CIA and that he had been sent on a mission and had gotten killed. If you believe in this type of thing it was a bad spirit. I don't really believe in it, but she also said she had the couch downstairs that belonged to him. The Wegee board said Gilia [sic] was not even human!"[11]

When police asked Esther how Galya killed people, she replied, "I guess she shot them, she didn't say."[12] Galya, she added, claimed to know washing machine magnate Robert Maytag, former Colorado governor Steve McNichols, and the sitting governor of Colorado, John Love.[13] Galya told Foote that in addition to Jimmy and Becky, she had six more children and they were all attending Columbia University.[14] The detectives dutifully wrote down the information and asked Foote if she would agree to give them a sworn affidavit stating that it was not her signature on Gus's will. Foote agreed.

When Galya learned of Foote's conversation with police, she went to a private investigator named Everett Jones and asked for his help in discrediting Foote. "Galya wanted Jones to prove that Esther Foote was insane and a whore so she could not testify in the Ingwersen forgery case, and it would be thrown out of court. Galya told Jones that she knew Ingwersen and that the only thing she got out of the will was a color T. V. set and a small red chair. She also added that one of Gus's sons, Donald Ingwersen, had poisoned his own father because he didn't like him."[15]

Galya also had a problem with the other witness to Gus's will: Zdenek Cerveny. When Zdenek learned that both Gus and Barbara may have been poisoned, he went to the Denver police and recanted his story about witnessing Gus sign his will. He told police that Galya had persuaded him to sign as a witness, saying that Gus had really wanted her to have something after he died. "The police didn't prosecute me because they believed my version that she conned me," he said in a 2014 interview.[16]

On October 27, 1969, seven and a half months after Thomas Riha disappeared, Galya was charged with forging Gus's will and booked into Denver County Jail, which was located atop the Denver Police Department headquarters at Thirteenth and Champa Streets. At the booking desk, a dirty plywood edifice, she was ordered to empty her pockets. Then she was fingerprinted, photographed, and sent to a large holding cell filled with other female prisoners. The steel bunks were painted green and covered with thin mattresses. A toilet and shower stood in a corner. Galya, who was extremely neat and orderly, was revolted. She jumped to her feet whenever the sound of the buzzer announced a new arrival, hoping that she was going to be bailed out. The jail was so noisy that she couldn't sleep.[17]

While she was behind bars, detectives descended upon her house at 248 Logan Street and executed the first of several search warrants. They were looking for chemicals and other artifacts that might have been used to disguise or alter documents. In the basement they seized a powder-like substance that was later found to be cyanide.[18]

Galya needed a lawyer and contacted former Colorado governor Steve McNichols, who referred her to Dan Hoffman, a brilliant attorney who had participated in Martin Luther King's 1965 civil rights march from Selma to Montgomery, Alabama, and had served as an adviser to Robert Kennedy during his 1968 presidential campaign.[19] Thinking Tannenbaum's case was a relatively simple forgery, he referred her to John Kokish, a young, dark-haired attorney who had worked his way through law school as a reporter at the *Denver Post*.

Galya was one of Kokish's first clients. "I took the case for a five-hundred-dollar retainer. That was okay money in those days. I never got any more money but became infatuated with the case," Kokish recalled in a 2012 interview in his Castle Rock office.[20] With Kokish's help, Galya was released from jail after posting a $1,500 bond.

Zdenek Cerveny, meanwhile, went to the Boulder Police Department and filed a one-page missing-person complaint about Thomas Riha. Then he sat down for a recorded interview with Capt. Willard Spier and Lt. Ralph Ruzicka, a warmhearted cop who had a way of getting people to open up. Ruzicka, which means "little rose" in Czech, was thirty-five years old, with disheveled brown hair, vivid blue eyes, and an ex-footballer's frame. Originally from Milwaukee, Wisconsin, Ruzicka attended Marquette University, married his high school sweetheart, and in 1960 moved to Colorado to join the Boulder Police Department. He would remain with the Boulder PD for a decade before transferring to the Colorado Bureau of Investigation, where he would work narcotics, organized crime, and homicides.

Although Cerveny's command of English was good, he had been in the United States for less than a year and occasionally dropped articles and used incorrect verb tenses when trying to explain complicated issues. The secretary who later transcribed the recording of the interview apparently had a difficult time understanding what he was saying and left numerous blanks in the transcript, which gives the interview a disjointed and confused feeling. The transcriber used the initials—WS, RR, and ZC—to identify who was speaking. The following are some excerpts:

RR: What can you tell us about Thomas Riha as an individual? What type of person is he?

ZC: I didn't know him very well. He left Czechoslovakia in '47 when I was nine years old. He lived with us, with my father, mother and my sister. After the war he went to college in other part of the country and in '47 his father and my grandfather paid for him some college in England. But something happened. My uncle was deported or something like that and he went to the United States . . .

RR: Would you label him in our society now, as a right wing . . . ?

ZC: He was liberal in his thinking.

RR: What did he talk about? Did you notice anything that might be out of the ordinary, like he's trying to hide something? Did he seem odd in any way?

ZC: I didn't get the impression that he is concerned or upset with anything other than his marriage.

WS: Do you have any idea where he met this Tannenbaum lady?

ZC: She is insisting that they met before in Chicago, but all people that I know, including my uncle, told me that the first time they met it was in connection with my arrival in the United States as he was looking for someone with power to help me earlier to the United States.

RR: What do you think happened to your uncle?

ZC: I don't know. She told me that—at first she was saying that it was simply in connection with the divorce, that he left because it would simplify the whole proceeding for him and save his property. And then when I got impatient and I asked for a letter from him or something to know what he is really doing and what is his will, she started another story that he is working for CIA or some other government agency and that nobody is supposed to start an investigation about him and that he is all right . . .

WS: Do you have any idea—did your uncle ever tell you why he and his wife weren't getting along or the reason for the divorce?

ZC: No, it was too fast marriage and my father was for a visit last year and he came in December and his first question was, 'What do I think about Thomas's marriage?' and I told him at that time that I don't think it will last, as there was too big difference between those two—it was too fast. They didn't know each other.

RR: Do you think Tannenbaum and Mr. Riha were intimate or anything like that?

ZC: She is insisting they were, but I don't know anything about it.

RR: Do you think your uncle's dead?

ZC: Oh no. I hope he is not.

RR: That has never entered your mind?

ZC: It did because many people are afraid that he is dead. All his friends, from time to time, ask me if I am sure he is not dead. I still believe he is not.

RR: Who are the—the will that was forged—that gentleman?

ZC: It was an old gentleman, who was German, I think. I met him the first time through Tannenbaum. She says that she knows a very experienced engineer and if I like it she will introduce me to him so I said I do and it was sometime in May or June . . . I saw him a number of times, mostly in her house or in her presence, and I was told he was very ill and supposed to undergo some operation but that they didn't find him in condition to survive the operation . . .

RR: What was the cause of death?

ZC: I was told that he was poisoned.

RR: What was your reaction when you found out that he was poisoned?

ZC: I was no more willing to keep it up with Tannenbaum.

RR: Well, we have an older gentleman that had some type of a medical problem and it turns out that he died of poisoning. We have Miss or Mrs. Eckberg [*sic*], who allegedly committed suicide, who was actually poisoned. We have Mrs. Tannenbaum involved in every one of them. We have your uncle missing over 7 months. All indications are that the letters that are allegedly from him are forged. No one can substantiate that they actually saw him in Toronto or New York or anywhere after he left Boulder. The possibility is getting stronger that he is not alive. Now let's assume that this is correct. Could Mrs. Tannenbaum somehow dispose of a body? Would she be physically able to do this?"

ZC: She is very strong and my uncle was lighter than I am.

In the next section of the tape, Cerveny tells police that an unnamed friend of Riha's contacted officials in Washington in May 1969 and was told Riha was okay and living in Toronto. But when the friend inquired again in the fall about the case, he was told to stay away from it.

RR: Well, I don't want to ask you his name. What I would appreciate is if you could contact him again and ask him if he would meet with me and you somewhere, anytime, and if he would just talk to me. What I'm interested in actually is who the hell told him that your uncle was fine because I can then check that out . . . What we're interested in is finding your uncle.

ZC: He told me the name of an FBI officer there in Boulder—Mr. Smith—who is supposedly informed about all this.

RR: How long ago was it that you talked to him about—or he sent you to *Smith?*

ZC: It was yesterday.

WS: Just yesterday?

ZC: Yes.

RR: This situation here is what we call a "bag of snakes," if you understand our terminology.

ZC: I feel that way for a long time now.

RR: All indications are that from the physical evidence at hand, he did not leave of his own free will.

ZC: Yes, that's clear.

RR: I'll talk to Mr. Smith tomorrow, and see if I can get any more out of him.

ZC: I don't know if he [Riha] was or wasn't involved with CIA or some other agency, but logically I should admit it was what Tannenbaum was telling all the time. Because he was very familiar with Russian condition. He speaks fluently without any accent Russian, he speaks Czech, he speaks English, French and German, so in that business he would be valuable.

WS: She has been reported to carry a gun. Do you ever see her carrying a gun?

ZC: Every time, all the time, even in bed she has a gun. She told me that she is supposed to because she was working and I was stupid enough to believe it. She has several guns at home.

WS: Did she carry different guns or just one kind?

ZC: She told me that she has some small firearm in her purse and she was carrying a 9 mm Walther in shoulder holster all the time and I know she has a .357 Smith and Wesson.

Cerveny also told police about a curious phone call. One day, he called Mrs. Stein at the Black Bear Inn from a pay phone at the Samsonite plant where he worked. Afterward the operator called Mrs. Stein and requested the name and address of the caller. "I don't think it's a usual thing," Zdenek said.

RR: That's where you work—in Samsonite Corporation?

ZC: Yes, it's in the cafeteria. There are two coin phones I use in all my private calls.

WS: Well, it's unusual, that's for sure, but there's no plausible way they could have any kind of . . .

ZC: I asked Denver police about that and they told me that they are not doing it. I wouldn't mind if it was the police.

RR: Well, they couldn't do it.[21]

But William Sullivan and his operatives in the FBI's domestic intelligence division could have been doing it. By 1969, Sullivan was no longer the wide-eyed innocent who had joined the Bureau on the eve of World War II, but an experienced agent who didn't hesitate to use the FBI's "technicals" to gather evidence on domestic subversives or foreign intelligence operatives.

Under Sullivan's tenure, the Bureau undertook some 2,370 COINTEL-PRO, or counterintelligence operations. The majority of the targets were Communists, mobsters, and Ku Klux Klansmen, as well as members of the "New Left" and "Black Hate" groups of the 1960s.[22]

FBI agents wrote anonymous letters to employers in order to get the targets of their investigations fired; penned poisonous letters to spouses in an effort to destroy marriages; obtained tax returns and persuaded the IRS to do audits; sowed dissension and suspicion in political groups by labeling certain members as "government informants," which led to expulsions and sometimes violent attacks; disrupted demonstrations; wrote propaganda articles and planted them in "friendly" news outlets; and leaked derogatory information to news organizations.

FBI agents also tapped telephones, planted listening devices, and burglarized the homes and offices of targets. The Bureau kept the information from lawmakers, the courts, and the media by using a sophisticated form of "plausible deniability." For example, if an FBI agent in the field wanted to do a black bag job, which was named after the small black satchel that the burglar carried, his supervisor and the agent-in-charge wrote a detailed memorandum to the appropriate assistant director at headquarters. The request was subsequently reviewed by either Clyde Tolson or J. Edgar Hoover. If approved, it was filed in the assistant director's office under a "Do Not File" file. In the field, the agent-in-charge wrote a memo describing the approval and locked it away in his safe. The following year, when W. Mark Felt or one of his inspectors came through, the memo was destroyed.[23]

Intrigued by the elaborate process, US Sen. Richard Schweiker, of Pennsylvania, a member of the Church Committee, several years later asked the FBI's Charles Brennan why the memo wasn't simply taken from the normal file and destroyed.

"There would have been a record of it," Brennan responded.

"In other words, each file of the FBI is serialized, and as new information is put in, a serial number is assigned. So is it not correct that if it had been filed in the normal procedure and then removed, there would have been a gap, as far as the number is concerned. Is that correct?"

"Yes, sir," Brennan responded.

"How did the field offices know about the 'Do Not File' procedure and the destruct mechanism?" the senator asked.

"Well, frankly, I don't know how they knew. Apparently, it was a very highly 'need-to-know' type of operation," replied Brennan.

"I gather that one purpose was, if a black bag job went afoul, and somebody got hauled before the court, the Bureau, or someone in the Bureau could make a statement to a court, or any other person investigating, to the effect that we searched our files and records, and there is nothing to indicate we did such and such?" Schweiker asked.

"I think so, Senator," responded Brennan.

"Yet, in fact, it would be nearly total deception," Schweiker responded.[24]

Zdenek Cerveny said that he and his friends were so convinced their telephones were being tapped that they would read Czech books to each other so that whoever was listening would have to hire not only transcribers, but also translators.

Galya was certain that Dennis Blewitt's phone was tapped and Galya's daughter in Chicago also thought someone was listening to her telephone conversations. "I always felt our phone was tapped. Every time I picked up the phone you could hear something start like it was making a recording."[25]

The telephones of Patricia Faulkner and Joyce Lebra also were also likely tapped because the silent calls that they received occurred within minutes after they had concluded a telephone conversation about Thomas Riha.

William Sullivan, whose name and initials appear on numerous FBI documents related to the Riha case, could have not only tapped telephones, but he and his agents might also have been responsible for sowing misinformation.

For example, Detective Ruzicka was able to wheedle from Zdenek the telephone number for his anonymous friend. When Ruzicka called him, the anonymous man said he was told Riha was okay. "This from a high government official," Ruzicka would write.[26]

Ruzicka also contacted FBI Agent Merrill Smith, who had interviewed Galya at her home at 248 Logan Street. In a memorandum to the Boulder District Attorney's Office, Ruzicka writes that he was initially told by Agent Smith that Riha was alive:

> Agent Smith stated he would contact me as soon as he verified what he thought he had overheard. I also asked Agent Smith if I should bother looking for the body of Professor Riha and Agent Smith stated no, it would be a waste of time. This led me to believe that the F.B.I. had some knowledge of Mr. Riha's activities and whereabouts. On November 5, 1969, Mrs. Judy Else [a secretary] received a telephone call from Agent Smith, who wanted to speak with Lt. Ruzicka, but since he was out of the office, Agent Smith relayed the following

information to Mrs. Else, which is as follows: "Files indicate that another government agency advised Riha left Boulder to get away from his wife, and that he has not left the country. This is strictly off the record, do not quote me."[27]

The message from the FBI's Merrill Smith accomplished several important things. First, it discouraged Ralph Ruzicka from further investigating the Riha disappearance, which could be interpreted as obstruction of justice. Second, it shifted the blame for the "alive and well" rumor to the CIA. Third, it protected Agent Smith's identity and prevented Ralph Ruzicka from vetting the information with other officials in the FBI and the CIA.

It was a response worthy of William Sullivan himself.

12 ★ MAKING MUD

Snow was accumulating in the high country and the sky was sagging and gray, portending the bitter winter ahead. The storm door of Thomas Riha's house stood ajar and a thin layer of snow covered the picnic table where he had once served his steaks. During November and December 1969, Galya was free on bail and many of the people she had befriended now wanted police protection.

Hearing his car honking in the middle of the night, Zdenek Cerveny thought Galya had come to kill him and dove out his bathroom window into the snow, only to discover the front seat of his Fiat had fallen forward on the steering wheel and was pushing against the horn. The front door of his house was locked and he couldn't get back in, so he took a piece of wood covering the crawl space, propped it against the wall, and climbed back through the bathtub window. "I sat in the bathtub for half an hour defrosting myself. I was scared for my life. I knew she had a gun."[1]

Somehow, Galya landed a job as a manager of the Soda Lakes Country Club, a small privately owned club in the foothills southwest of Denver. She had big plans for the club and did a good job keeping the books and updating the liquor license. Soon, though, she began dipping into the cash register, pocketing a few dollars so she could stop at the grocery store on the way home and pick up food for her children.

The local police and the old hands in the intelligence game thought they were finally free of the Riha story and its sticky tentacles. But in early December, Fred Gillies, a *Denver Post* reporter, began looking into the case. When officials realized how dogged Gillies was, they may have remembered the axiom: "When your opponents are stuck in the mud, it's hard for them to charge the hill. Therefore, when necessary, make mud."

Then in his late forties, Fred had the pale angular face of an ascetic and lived in a 1903 brick house in Capitol Hill, which was only a few minutes by car from the homes of Galya Tannenbaum, Gus Ingwersen, and Barbara Egbert. His shelves overflowed with books, a stereo took up the south side of the living room, and a stained-glass window at the landing of the stairs cast a warm glow over the interior.

Many beat reporters unwound from deadline pressure by trading jokes or swapping stories at the end of the day, but Gillies was a reserved man and kept to himself. He wore freshly laundered white shirts, perfectly knotted ties, and pressed khakis. His hair was brown and short and he had a mustache that wandered indecisively over his upper lip.

Writing did not seem to come easily to him. He wrote and rewrote, cut and pasted, until he was satisfied—or until an editor demanded that he turn in his copy. After his stories had been filed, he updated his notes and began methodically working the phones, following up on news tips, or checking with officials on stories he was monitoring. He had a network of reliable sources and the people he interviewed trusted him.

Born in Boston, Massachusetts, Gillies had enlisted in the US Army Air Forces during World War II. He was assigned to the 154th Weather Reconnaissance Squadron, which flew sorties over North Africa and monitored the movements of the Third Reich's Erwin Rommel, the cunning general known as the Desert Fox. After Germany surrendered North Africa, in 1943, the Squadron was reassigned to the European Theater and conducted hundreds of observation missions over Italy, Germany, France, Hungary, Romania, and Greece.

The squadron drew praise from numerous generals, including Dwight D. Eisenhower. When Gillies mustered out of the armed forces, he was awarded a Bronze Star and wrote a history entitled "The Story of a Squadron," which was privately published in 1946. Afterward, he was admitted to Harvard, where he graduated cum laude in 1950. He tried his hand at playwriting, but didn't have much luck and moved west, working at several small newspapers in Colorado before landing a job in 1968 at the *Post*.

He would remain at the *Post* for the next two decades, reporting on the twists and turns of the Thomas Riha case over a ten-year period. "There was so much espionage," he said during an interview in his hospital room in the fall of 2013, a few weeks before he died.[2]

After his death, a nephew found a large box of documents on the Riha case in Fred's house. Inside were spiral notebooks filled with innumerable interviews by Fred, as well as letters, newspaper clippings, responses from the FBI and CIA to his Freedom of Information Act requests, and a calendar chronicling day-by-day events leading up to Riha's disappearance and events that occurred for months afterward.

Gillies was a meticulous reporter and reading his notes is almost like being present for those long-ago interviews. Nearly all of the interviews are dated, the writing is legible, and the quotes that he jotted down are reproduced faithfully in newspaper stories. When Gillies agreed to accept information off the record, he honored that commitment and marked off the words carefully in his notebooks.

Throughout the month of December 1969, Gillies interviewed Riha's neighbors, his colleagues at the university, Boulder attorneys, and the police. Soon he had pieced together the bizarre ether incident, Riha's marriage to Hana, and details about Galya Tannenbaum.

Capt. Willard Spier of the Boulder Police Department did his best to keep Gillies from digging too deeply. He insisted in an interview on December 3, 1969, that Riha "was just a fellow who dropped out of sight."[3] On December 4, Gillies reinterviewed Spier and jotted down the following quotes:

- No reason to dig into this junk—no one come forward to say someone taking all of Riha's property.
- Don't know why the great interest in R. People drop out of sight every day.
- My understand that R disapp of his own accord—& there is no use wasting time looking for him just on a missing person—
- FBI enter in when T. said she had something to do with military or immigration departments. We doubt it. This gal has been around plenty & I don't where. She's nothing but a con artist and picks up money wherever and from whoever she can. Not know whether she had any hold over T.
- *Confidential:* After Cerveny's missing persons rept, investigation was active until we know what was going on—thru FBI—that he was alive & all right. FBI knows great deal more about Riha than we do or Denver PD. Have no interest in T until it's proved there was foul play in relation to Riha or she's forging papers in Riha's name & taking property.[4]

Gillies then turned his attention to Lt. Ralph Ruzicka, who was frustrated by all the innuendo and mystery. "We've been told not to worry, but when we talk to friends and associates we hear facts that don't stand up logically and we get worried again," he told Gillies. The detective added, "The nephew says someone informed him not to be worried about the safety of his uncle. Who the hell are these people? The impression we're getting is that someone does know what's going on."[5]

Eventually Gillies contacted Lt. Glen Reichert in the Denver Police Department's Intelligence Bureau who agreed to talk to him off the record.

Gillies dutifully wrote in his notepad, "DON'T QUOTE," and jotted down the following:

- "We've been told by respected source—that R. is alive & well, not in this country." "Satisfied with this, don't question it."[6]

Finally, Gillies interviewed Denver Police Chief George Seaton, who also agreed to talk to him as long as it was off the record. OFF RECORD is underscored twice in Gillies's notebook. The Denver police chief said two agencies told them that Riha was:

- "alive & well. They know this positive. Written him off as possible murder victim. R & T—they're prob up in Canada."[7]

The misinformation and outright lies from both the Denver and Boulder police departments are astonishing, especially given the fact that the cops knew Riha and two other people had likely been murdered and that Galya was the prime suspect in all three deaths. But Gillies was too experienced to accept their statements at face value and continued with his reporting. On December 28, 1969, the *Post* published a front-page piece on the missing professor. The story captured the bizarre twists and turns of the case, the stonewalling by local and federal authorities, and the numerous unanswered questions. It was a huge scoop and the editors at the rival *Rocky Mountain News* rushed to catch up. The *Rocky* sent a reporter to Chicago and Gillies flew to New York City to interview Hana.

The CIA's Michael Todorovich sent a copy of the *Denver Post*'s blockbuster to Langley, calling the story an "over-flogged horse," and jubilant that Gillies had not made more of the CIA's involvement.[8] "It would seem now that the agency is no longer on the hook—at least at the present. Perhaps Immigration and Naturalization Service and the Justice Department will find Fred Gillies repeatedly pushing them for information."[9]

But Todorovich's relief was short-lived. The following day he got a call from Anthony Ripley, a *New York Times* correspondent based in Denver. Todorovich told Ripley the "sum total" of what he knew was contained in the *Denver Post* article.[10]

While Gillies was researching his story, Ruth Ann Cook, Riha's mother, was begging the FBI's Scott Werner for help in locating her son. Her life had not been easy since her second husband, Howard Cook Jr., had committed suicide. She had remarried for a third time, but the marriage was short-lived and ended in divorce. She returned to Europe in 1964, teaching French in a girl's preparatory school in Fulda, West Germany. There she met a wealthy businessman and they made plans to marry.[11] But in 1968, she had become ill with breast cancer and was forced to relinquish her teaching position and postpone her wedding plans. She had undergone two surgeries and her prognosis was grim.

Werner's responses to Ruth were cold and bureaucratic. "Please be advised that the Federal Bureau of Investigation has no jurisdiction in matters of this nature and we are not able to conduct an active investigation concerning your son's disappearance."[12]

But Ruth would not relent. "I beg of you to tell me what I should do to help my son—who as the rumor goes—worked for the *CIA* of which I have no knowledge and to tell me also where he is or whether he has met foul play at the hands of this Mrs. Tannenbaum who apparently is well armed and always carries a gun. I *implore* you to help me and advise me of my son's whereabouts."[13] In another letter, she added, "I am very sick, Mr. Werner, with double pleurisy and have lost—since I wrote you—due to my sickness one eye sight—having only barely recovered after cancer. I wish I could talk to you and ask your advice in this grievous matter."[14]

Werner softened a little, saying that the FBI could place a missing-person notice in the FBI's Identification Division. Ruth considered the offer, then rejected it. Her refusal may have been related to an anonymous message she had received around Christmas 1969 suggesting that Thomas was alive and living in Czechoslovakia. "Don't worry about him and don't say anything about this," she had confided to Riha's friend, Libor Brom.[15] In a letter written afterward to her brother, Pavel, she said Thomas "must have taken the wrong turn."[16] She died in West Germany on February 21, 1970, before she was able to explain what she meant by Thomas's "wrong turn."

A week or so after Fred's story was published, Donald Brotzman, the lawyer and congressman who worked with Gerald Caplan in Boulder, sent a letter to US Attorney General John Mitchell inquiring into the baffling case. "It seems to me that the interest of the nation in general and the credibility of the FBI in particular is not well served by the proliferations of a belief that Professor Riha is the victim of some kind of international intrigue, if such is not the case," he wrote.[17]

Brotzman added that in late 1969 he had asked both the CIA and FBI about the case. "I learned from the Central Intelligence Agency that at one point last year it made some preliminary inquiries, determined that no transactions within its jurisdiction were involved, and turned over whatever files were generated to the FBI. CIA also informed me that it understands, unofficially, that the FBI did look into the matter further and that the Bureau may well know the whereabouts of Professor Riha and the circumstances behind his unusual disappearance."[18]

The attorney general forwarded Brotzman's letter to the FBI. Hoover himself responded, reiterating almost verbatim what Scott Werner had told Ruth. "The FBI has conducted no investigation concerning the disappearance of Dr. Thomas Riha since there is no indication of violation of any federal law within our jurisdiction. We have no knowledge concerning Dr. Riha's whereabouts."[19]

The FBI responses were especially disingenuous because it had amassed a staggering amount of data on Thomas Riha through its stop-and-start impersonation investigation into Galya Tannenbaum. The FBI had reopened the impersonation case against Galya for the third time in mid-December 1969. Agents again contacted Capt. Willard Spier in the Boulder Police Department, as well as Gerald Caplan and Richard Hopkins, Riha's attorney. Hopkins told the two FBI agents that he had talked to Tannenbaum four or five times on the telephone before Riha's disappearance and could hear Riha talking in the background. "He described Tannenbaum as persuasive, domineering, very defensive once anyone questions confidence in her, a rambler and finally, a neurotic. By neurotic, he advised, she has delusions of grandeur of importance, of her own ability and of official capacities. He advised it was his opinion that if Tannenbaum were ever taken to court and was pushed, she could plead insanity with no difficulty."[20]

The following month, FBI officials interviewed Zdenek Cerveny, Franziska Stein, Hana, attorney David Regosin, and numerous other witnesses. They took their findings to the US Attorney's Office in Denver, which again turned down the case, saying that Galya's actions didn't rise to a "prosecutable violation" because she had received nothing of monetary value from her misrepresentations.[21] Nonetheless, federal authorities could have uncovered other "prosecutable violations" had they wanted, including:

1. Possible mail fraud charges against Galya for sending Esther Foote a $350 check through the mail that was written on Thomas Riha's bank account.
2. Fraud charges against Galya for persuading the Denver Art Museum to issue a letter justifying a tax credit to her daughter for some of Riha's donated art. (An IRS intelligence agent told Fred Gillies the transaction did constitute tax fraud. "This is unique. In my twenty five years I've never seen anything like this.")[22]

3. Fraud charges in connection with the filing of Thomas Riha's 1968 federal tax return. That return was filed between March 15 and March 17, 1969. Yet, Hana claimed to have seen the unfinished forms in Riha's study sometime after those dates. The IRS refused to say who had signed the tax return and whether it had issued a refund.[23]

On December 31, 1969, Galya burglarized the Arvada home of Betty Jo Helton, taking a briefcase with Mrs. Helton's checkbook and other items. Two days later, she appeared at the drive-in window of a bank and cashed a $1,000 check containing Mrs. Helton's signature. A few hours later, she attempted to cash a $2,000 check inside the same bank, but fled when she saw a bank teller go to another part of the bank to consult officials.

Galya began keeping a diary of her activities. "Have this to say," she wrote, "I do not know what sort of black cloud has been hanging over my head, but I NEED HELP."[24]

13 ★ SIGHTINGS

Boulder detectives Ralph Ruzicka and his partner, Robert Diezi, were far behind in their investigation when Fred Gillies broke his first story. Soon the tips poured in. Earl Morrelli, the Denver mechanic, told them Galya had brought her car in to be repaired in late March.[1] The front end was badly damaged and the underside was caked with red mud. Galya explained that she had been chasing a soldier who had gone AWOL ten miles west of Central City.

Next, they received a call from Bill Fowler, the manager of a resort in Eldorado Springs, a small community located about eight miles south of Boulder. Fowler told them that Galya often went hiking in Rattlesnake Gulch, a mile west of the resort. The resort manager and the two detectives hiked up into the gulch, where they found a bone in the ruins of a burned-out hotel and were shown a dump area covered in red clay. "Bill says March '69 was a rainy period. Might coincide with front end damage to Mrs. T car & red mud," one of the detectives mused.[2]

On January 12, 1970, the two detectives interviewed Boulder attorneys Richard Hopkins and Dennis Blewitt. Hopkins showed them a telegram and letter he had purportedly received from Riha, saying he was convinced they were forgeries. "He stated he met Riha and his observations indicate an intelligent and meticulous individual who spoke perfect English. The letter he received from Riha in Toronto could not have been sent or written by Riha because the language in the letter was not the language Riha would use."[3]

Dennis Blewitt proved less cooperative. "Blewitt wants assurance that whatever he says will be confidential & not revealed to anyone. Since he represented both individuals he has a conflict & does not feel he can give us everything he knows."[4] Blewitt did tell the investigators he received a $100 check from Riha on March 10 and a $300 check sometime after the professor disappeared. The latter check bounced.[5]

When the cops asked Blewitt where they could find Riha's body, he suggested they look around Caribou, an old silver mining town in Boulder County. "He related that he & Tannenbaum had traveled to Caribou on a number of occasions looking in old abandoned mines & he thinks Riha is up there."[6]

Suspecting Blewitt knew more, the detectives told him they would be at his office on the evening of January 14. When they arrived, Blewitt confided that Riha had come to see him before his disappearance because he wanted advice on how to hide his assets from Hana. "Dennis thinks Galya double-crossed T & killed him. Thinks T put everything in Mrs. T name to cover assets. Riha told Dennis he met Mrs. T in Chicago, said they were friends for a long time."[7]

Blewitt showed the detectives his file on Galya, which included the letters she wrote to him in the late summer of 1969, as well as correspondence from Thomas Riha. Blewitt warned the two policemen that if they wanted copies, they'd have to subpoena them. Galya, he added, had given him a bottle of potassium cyanide. He threw it away when he realized how deadly it was.

The detectives also contacted Boulder attorney Neil King, who told them that Galya boasted at the house closing of having a Lear jet standing by at Stapleton Airport to take the documents to Riha in Canada for signature. She returned with them the following day. When asked why a Denver notary had witnessed Riha's signature, Galya said Tom happened to be in Denver. "Neil thought Mrs. T. & Riha were shacking in Denver and thought no more about it," one of the detectives wrote.[8]

An anonymous woman called the Boulder Police Department and suggested that police search for Riha's body around St. Mary's Lake, which was located at an elevation of ten thousand feet in the Arapahoe National Forest.[9] The manager of the St. Mary's Glacier Lodge then called and told them that sometime prior to June 1969, Galya had stayed at the lodge and that her visit was underwritten by a real estate company selling cabins in the area. Galya purchased six lots with a check. The check bounced. The manager suggested that if Galya did kill Riha, the "six lots would be an ideal location for disposal of the body."[10]

An Illinois man chided the Boulder cops for their failure to contact a professor named Gerard Croiset at the University of Utrecht in Holland. "Croiset is a sensitive who has located many missing persons in Europe and the United States. It is not necessary for him to come to this country to do his work. He is also a psychometrist so if you can send him some object that belonged to Professor Riha and something that belongs to Mrs. Tennenbaum [*sic*] he can give you even more information."[11] A local clairvoyant also called to say Riha had ingested potassium cyanide and his body was at the bottom of a mine shaft.[12]

Law enforcement officers in rural Colorado contacted the Boulder PD to see if Riha was a match for human remains found in their counties. Officials in Leadville had recovered the body of a man on Independence Pass[13] who was wearing a light parka and black loafers and had seven dollars in one of his pockets. His left arm and part of his rib cage were missing, but officials were able to reconstruct a dental chart from what was left of the mouth. When Riha's dentist saw the chart, he said the body couldn't be Riha's because the man on Independence Pass had three molars and Riha had none.[14] The Douglas County Sheriff's Department found the partial remains of a man with a mouth plate on his upper teeth.[15] Riha was once again ruled out because he didn't have a mouth plate.

The Boulder detectives interviewed Jan Sorensen, Stephen Fischer-Galati, Franziska Stein, Joyce Lebra, and others. Jan Sorenson, who was one of the last to see Riha on the night he disappeared, said Galya had given her a pair of colonel bars.[16] Sorensen said she had more to tell the cops, but the records don't indicate whether any follow-up interviews were done. Professor Fischer-Galati said Riha was part owner of Treasure Tours, the travel agency based in Montreal. He added, "Riha has split personality, had contact with Russians, when Riha disappeared, defense minister of Czechoslovakia came to Canada."[17]

Police didn't bother to interview Joyce Lebra because they thought she was only interested "in raising hell."[18] In a letter to the *Boulder Camera,* Lebra had questioned the inaction of law-enforcement agencies and pointed out that she and five others had tried to file a missing-person report back in April 1969. She writes:

> FBI authorities now deny any knowledge of the case, despite the fact that Dean Briggs, myself, attorneys for Riha and his wife, and others called the FBI at the time. I am told, on second-hand authority, that the police were also responsible for keeping news of the matter out of the Boulder papers for several weeks. By these actions the above-mentioned authorities have allowed an experienced forger and possible murderer the freedom to continue her activities in Denver following Riha's disappearance. This situation does not exactly foster a sense of confidence in law-enforcement and citizen safety in Colorado. In fact, it is reminiscent of Nazi Germany.[19]

Tammy Johnson, a young woman who worked for naval intelligence, contacted the Boulder Police Department, saying that she and her mother overheard a subpoena server named Ben Lesser saying that he had seen Riha in Galya's house sometime after Thanksgiving in 1969. She urged Lesser to contact the Boulder police, but he refused because he had received a citation.[20] Eventually he did talk to the Boulder cops. He said he had been to Galya's house to serve legal papers three times—on July 24, August 31, and October 27.[21] Lesser was sure he had seen Riha on the August 31 visit. A man he believed to be Thomas Riha opened the door and said, "Julia baby, someone to see you."[22] He was wearing a brown suit and was holding a green glass in his hand. "Lesser described the man as European and not American, possible 5–10, hair was brown or black, Dark comp. 160 to 180 lbs." The Boulder detectives then conducted a photo lineup with Lesser, who correctly identified Riha's image in five out of seven instances.[23]

Otto Stockmar, a seventy-six-year-old man who had served in the navy during World War I, thought he had seen a couple matching the description of Thomas and Galya in the mountains in late summer of 1969. Stockmar spent most of his time taking care of his invalid wife, but whenever he had some free time, he went hiking in the wild and beautiful forest around Idaho Springs, which was strewn with old mining sites and abandoned cabins. Hikers, he said, were scarce as "hen's teeth," but on a day in late August 1969, he encountered a couple on a boulder-strewn path that wound up into the mountains from Highway 103.[24] The elderly man climbed up onto a white rock and greeted them:

> He was dressed in a dark business suit, low-cut oxfords and without a hat. He appeared to be about 50 years old with slight streaks of grey hair showing and hazel eyes. I also kept an eye on the woman. She kept watching me. She was bareheaded, blonde, and wore a pretty, orange-colored dress and low-cut sneakers. She held a black bag in front of her. It was about 8" wide and 8" deep. She held it with one hand while the other was stuck into the bag holding something. She never smiled nor said a word but watched me intently as I conversed with the man. He appeared to be suspicious and scared for some reason and as he looked me square in the eye, there was a questioning expression there which I later thought was meant to tell me more but which he dared not to do as the woman kept strict watch.[25]

On January 20, 1970, Galya gave a two-hour interview to Boulder journalist John R. Olson. She was a frustrating subject, digressing often into mundane asides. Olson repeatedly tried to steer the conversation back to Riha. "Let's go back to how you first got to know Thomas Riha. That's what I'm interested in. I'm interested in Thomas Riha."[26]

Galya told Olson that Thomas worked for the CIA. "Yes, I'll say that. The CIA is known for using professors and students in much of what they do. In fact, 90 percent of their activity is not done by their agents, but by people like Tom Riha, who go abroad a lot, and who have access to various things and that they simply ask them to do thus and so."[27]

Thomas, she said, feared Hana's family in Czechoslovakia, who had powerful connections to the StB. He worried that his relatives still living in the country could be harmed. "And lo and behold, the week before he took off, he did get a letter that one of his relatives had been arrested."[28]

"Do you know what his relative was arrested for?" asked Olson.

"It was political, strictly political. And he was subsequently released after Thomas was through his divorce."

On January 22, 1970, Galya was arraigned in Denver District Court on charges that she forged Gus Ingwersen's will. She pleaded innocent by reason of insanity. The judge ordered her to undergo psychiatric tests and afterward she was released.

At noon on the following day, a phalanx of law enforcement officials from Boulder and Denver descended on Galya's house at 248 Logan Street and re-arrested her for forging Thomas Riha's name on the $330 check to Judson Flying Service and for forging his name on documents related to the sale of Riha's house. Among those present were Denver Police Department Capt. Art Dill and investigator Walt Nelson for the Denver district attorney, as well as detectives Ralph Ruzicka and Robert Diezi and Capt. Willard Spier. A second search warrant was also executed. Papers, books, a typewriter, as well as Thomas Riha's driver's license, passport, and inoculation book were seized.[29] A gram of white powder was also confiscated that was later found to be sodium cyanide.[30]

Afterward, detectives Ruzicka and Diezi escorted Galya to Boulder for arraignment. "From Denver to Boulder, Mrs. Tannenbaum was interviewed, but not advised of her rights for fear that she may keep her mouth shut."[31] Later that night, at the police department, they conducted a formal interview with her:

RR: Would you give us names of people who have allegedly seen him besides you. You're the only one who has allegedly seen him.

GT: I will say this, when he [Riha] comes in I will immediately get hold of [Denver Police Capt. Art] Dill.

RR: Well, what if he doesn't show for a while?

GT: That's not very likely.

RR: And these other charges, let's say you're convicted on the forgery charge.

GT: If it comes to a matter of conviction on the forgery charge, then I think I would take somebody out to where I think you could find him. There isn't any phone.

RR: Would you tell us where that is?

GT: Yes. It's between Montreal and Toronto. It's a summer—it's what you would call a mountain-type—

RR: How the devil did he get there without identification?

GT: He has identification. He has a Canadian driver's license. He has other identification. He's got one of these great big gismos that fold out.

RR: All we're concerned with is finding his warm body.

GT: I'll put you in contact with the man to get myself out of this botched-up mess.

RR: What about all this colonel stuff?

GT: Tom always called me that when I started helping with the book.

RR: Did Thomas have a, well, a little abnormal sex life, or was it pretty well satisfied?

GT: His sex life? I guess it was for about anybody his age.

[In a bantering and almost flirtatious way, Detective Ruzicka and Galya Tannenbaum continued to toss around the idea of taking a trip to Canada together to meet Riha. Then Galya asked for a Kleenex. She may have begun crying.]

RR: Do you want something to drink, tea or something?

GT: Where did the kids go?

RR: Ah, the Denver police took them to, well John [Kokish] knows, John arranged it all. And the cats are being taken care of by another fellow.

GT: Where are they?

RR: They're in the house, in the basement, he'll feed them once a day or whatever is necessary.[32]

A few days later, FBI agents Merrill Smith and J. Hale McMenamin paid a visit to Galya at the Boulder County Jail. The two agents informed her that she was under investigation—not for impersonation this time—but for possible violation of the federal extortion statute, a charge that may have stemmed from the way she complained about the rejection of the FHA loan.[33] The two FBI agents orally advised Galya of her rights. She waived them and began talking.

She rambled on about her marriages, her children, and her love affair with Thomas Riha. She also denied trying to pass herself off as a federal agent. "She stated that [deleted] has many times in the past jokingly referred to her as 'Sarge' and 'Colonel' when he thought she was being too demanding of him, and as a result of this tendency on his part other people began calling her by these names, with the whole matter actually being interpreted by her as a joke."[34]

Galya said that Gerald Caplan, Hana's attorney, was confused when he told the FBI that Galya had claimed to be from military intelligence. She said she was actually referring to a magazine called *M-Intelligence,* which focused on Mensas. Galya added that she had an IQ of 139 and that she herself was a Mensa member.

As the two agents continued their questions, Galya grew angry, saying "she was tired of being made a fool of by the false allegations that she had been impersonating military and government persons, and did not desire to discuss the matter further."[35]

A few moments later, she went back on the record. She told the two agents that she had met Thomas at Stapleton Airport in August 1969, but he had refused to tell her where he was living. She received a letter from him in November 1969 and he called her from a pay phone in an undisclosed location over the holidays to wish her Merry Christmas.

Galya managed to scrape together a $1,000 bond and was released about five o'clock on the evening of January 28.[36] A week later, on February 4, she was arraigned on the forged check charge in connection with Judson Flying Service and entered a plea of not guilty by reason of insanity. Afterward, a judge ordered her confined to the Colorado Psychiatric Hospital for a thirty-day evaluation period.[37]

She was evicted from her bungalow and her landlady rented the house to new tenants—a couple of "long-haired hipsters"—who put a peace sign in the front window.[38] Obsessed by the story, Fred Gillies got permission to dig up a five-foot section of newly laid concrete in the basement. He dug for a day and a half—with the new tenants occasionally pitching in. He found a bone that looked like part of a pelvis with a "saw cut" on one end and submitted it to officials at the Colorado Bureau of Investigation. The CBI ran some tests and concluded it was part of a dog's skeleton.[39]

When the *Rocky Mountain News* learned of Fred's endeavors, a reporter quipped, "There is an old saying in the newspaper game that if a reporter wants a story badly enough, he'll go out and dig for it. Reporter Fred Gillies of the *Denver Post* has done just that in his relentless quest for facts."[40]

PART III ★

THE BUTTERFLY EFFECT

14 ★ "H" BOMB

Fed up with the questions surrounding Thomas Riha's disappearance and Denver's two unexplained cyanide deaths, Denver District Attorney Mike McKevitt waded into the investigation. Like the Boulder police, McKevitt and his chief investigator, Walt Nelson, soon found themselves swamped with leads. "The plot thickens day by day," McKevitt told the *Rocky Mountain News*. "But it's hard to tell what has substance and what doesn't. It's a constant, shifting process."[1]

McKevitt knew a few things about intelligence himself, having served as an air force combat intelligence officer during the Korean War.[2] He was short and round, with incipient jowls, thin Irish lips, and a prominent nose. Born in Spokane, Washington, he attended high school in Sacramento, California, earned his undergraduate degree at the University of Idaho, and received his law degree from the University of Denver. Although he was a Republican politician in an overwhelmingly Democratic city, he was a popular figure and in 1971, he would be elected to the US House of Representatives. He held office for just two years before he was defeated by liberal Democrat Patricia Schroeder, who would keep the seat for the next twenty-five years.

During the investigation, McKevitt received numerous letters, including one from Robert Schwind, who had been posted with Riha at Fort Bragg. Schwind began his letter by describing Riha as a charming and witty man, respectful of the opinions of others, and an enjoyable companion in the tight confines of the barracks. But there was another side to him:

> He was also a person of omnivorous sexual appetite which, even for GIs—hardly a puritan group—was considered extraordinary. In the time that I knew him, his interests in females ranged from young to old, white to black, married to unmarried. He justified his conduct on the grounds that man is by nature not monogamous but polygamous. On occasions when we went to

town, he would soon separate himself from the group and head for the cathouses in the Negro section of town. . . . I had always thought that Tom would
die from apoplexy or heart attack brought on in a fit of orgasmic frenzy. That
he might have been done in by some outraged femme fatale like the Colonel
would be regrettable but hardly a surprise to those who knew him nor incon-
sistent with his style of life.[3]

Schwind, who now lives in Georgia, confirmed in a 2014 interview that he
had indeed written the letter. He added that Thomas would return from the
cathouses to boast of his sexual exploits. "He didn't make any attempt to
hide it from us. He bragged about it. That is what is so offensive. If he just
went out and did something and didn't tell us about it, that would be one
thing. But he boasted. He was really a vile person. He was not someone you
would want as a friend, or to invite home for dinner."[4]

Other witnesses also mentioned Riha's sexual exploits. "McKevitt clearly
disapproved of Riha's life style," Washington author David Wise would write.
"He saw him as a ladies' man with continental manners who took advantage
of professors' wives. He would pretend an interest in them only to get them
in bed. He would play the piano and read poetry to them by candlelight. It
was not, McKevitt said, the way Americans lived."[5]

McKevitt often tape-recorded the people who called his office. One surviving transcript is from Riha's friend, Donald Fanger. Galya was out on bail at
the time and Fanger told McKevitt that he was worried that she might run.

McKevitt said he was worried, too. "I was quite disturbed. I called the
judge about it, and the [Boulder] D. A. but nothing could be done. . . . But
she's supposed to go back. In fact, we have another case we're getting ready
to file against her now."

"But there's no way of keeping tabs on her so she doesn't leave the area?"
Fanger asked.

"No, there really isn't."

"Oh, for God's sake," Fanger responded.

Fanger thought it was time for CU's former president Joseph Smiley to
check with his anonymous source to make certain that Thomas was indeed
alive and well. "Somebody ought to tell Smiley, look you may have been the
victim of a hoax, and you may be an accomplice in the hoax by protecting
that confidence," he said.

"I plan to do that this week," responded McKevitt.

"Good, because if he can do that, he can announce that he is sure and he
has checked. If he can't, he ought to announce publicly the other thing."[6]

Thomas Riha, an assistant professor of Russian history at the University of Colorado in Boulder, married Hana Hruskova on October 13, 1968, in a church ceremony in Boulder, Colorado. (Courtesy Hana Riha)

Left to right: Thomas Riha, Hana Hruskova, Jan Sorensen, and Libor Brom. Sorensen was one of Riha's graduate students, and Libor Brom was a friend of Riha's who taught at the University of Denver. They served as witnesses to his marriage. (Courtesy Hana Riha)

Above: Galya Tannenbaum is booked into jail in Denver on October 27, 1969, on forgery charges in connection with the will of Gustav Ingwersen, an inventor and businessman. Gus was a friend of Galya's and died of cyanide poisoning in mid-June 1969. Barbara Egbert, another friend of Galya's, died of cyanide poisoning a few months later. (Carnegie Branch Library for Local History/ *Boulder Daily Camera*)

Right: Galya Tannenbaum (*left*) confers with her attorney, John Kokish, outside a Boulder County courtroom on January 27, 1970. (Denver Public Library/*Rocky Mountain News* collection)

Thomas Riha spoke five languages fluently, including Russian and English. He immigrated to the United States in 1947, receiving his undergraduate and master's degrees in history from the University of California in Berkeley and his doctorate from Harvard. (Courtesy Zdenek Cerveny and Jarmila Zakova)

This carved wood relief of the Pieta dates to 1525 and was the most valuable piece in Thomas Riha's art collection. It hung over his fireplace in his Boulder home. (Courtesy Fred Gillies collection)

Ruth Ann Cook, Thomas Riha's mother, was teaching in a girl's school in Germany when her son disappeared. She begged the FBI for help in finding Thomas, but the FBI said it wasn't investigating the case. (Courtesy Fred Gillies collection)

A page from a family photo album shows Thomas Riha; his mother, Ruth; and his father, Viktor; outside their Prague home in 1931. (Courtesy Zdenek Cerveny and Jarmila Zakova)

Zdenek Cerveny, Thomas Riha's nephew, stands outside the flat where Thomas Riha lived as a small boy. The flat, which had Renaissance paintings on the ceilings, is located on the stone steps that lead to Prague Castle and overlooks the Vlata River and the city of Prague. (Eileen Welsome)

Thomas Riha had a difficult relationship with his beautiful and dominating mother, Ruth. (Courtesy Zdenek Cerveny and Jarmila Zakova)

Above: Thomas Riha's nephew, Zdenek Cerveny, and niece, Jarmila Zakova, in 2016 in Prague. They are Riha's only surviving relatives and are convinced their uncle is dead. (Eileen Welsome)

Right: Galya Tannenbaum lived in this house at 248 Logan Street with her two children. Police executed multiple search warrants of her house, looking for forgery tools and other evidence. They found numerous documents belonging to Thomas Riha as well as cyanide. (Courtesy Fred Gillies collection)

Fred Gillies, an investigative reporter at the *Denver Post,* dug up a portion of Galya's basement at 248 Logan Street in the spring of 1970, thinking Riha's body might be there. Assisting him were two tenants who moved into the house after Galya was evicted. Fred found a piece of bone that looked like part of a pelvis, but the Colorado Bureau of Investigation concluded it was part of a dog's skeleton. (Courtesy Fred Gillies collection)

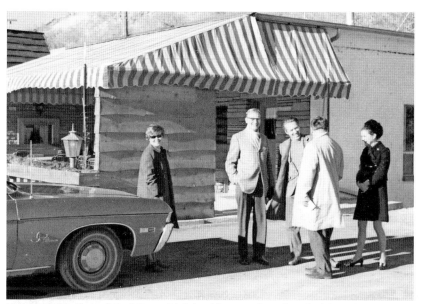

Thomas Riha (*center*) and Hana (*right*) with several unidentified friends outside the Black Bear Inn, where their wedding dinner was held. (Courtesy Fred Gillies collection)

Right: Gustav Ingwersen was an inventor, artist, and businessman who was found dead on his couch in mid-June 1969. Authorities at first thought it was a natural death, but the Denver medical examiner found Gus had died from cyanide poisoning. Galya was charged with forging his will, but no charges were filed against her in connection with Gus's death. (Courtesy Pete Ingwersen)

Below: Many people believe Thomas Riha's body was dumped in one of the hundreds of gold and silver mines that can be found throughout the Rocky Mountains. Former Denver Police Department detective Charlie McCormick stands outside the Ohio mine. (Courtesy Silvia Pettem)

McKevitt's chief investigator, Walt Nelson, also felt the time had come for Smiley to divulge the source of his "alive and well" information. "We should send a letter to Dr. Smiley this week in El Paso to the effect that we received confirmation from military intelligence and the FBI that Riha is not known to their personal knowledge, and ask Dr. Smiley if he would verify once again, what his source is because it is holding up our investigation and having an adverse effect," he wrote.[7]

The pressure continued to build on Smiley to reveal his source. On February 3, 1970, he called the Denver CIA office and asked for advice. By then, Smiley knew that three people—including one of his own former faculty members—may have been murdered. Yet he told Michael Todorovich he was still willing to stonewall the investigation. In a progress report to Langley, Todorovich wrote:

> We have assured him that this is the ideal reply from our point of view, that we very much appreciate his limited answers to the press, and it was indicated that we hope he will continue to maintain this position. Professor Smiley remains as friendly as ever and assures us that he is not bothered or perturbed by the inquiries made of him and assures us that he will continue to maintain his present stance if we desire. We have assured Dr. Smiley that we are not insensitive to his present predicament and have assured him that if pressure becomes "unbearable" we will take some (unidentified) action to assist him. Smiley who has had wartime intelligence experience, assures us that he is in complete understanding and in sympathy with our position and notes that he will continue to hold his ground. . . . We feel personally reassured that President Smiley is bearing up well under the unfortunate publicity being given this matter. We are assured, and we believe, that he will not budge from his present position and that he continues to maintain the friendliest of attitudes toward our agency.[8]

He closed with the following: "This has been a very strange trip for virtually everyone—government agencies, boards of trustees, detectives, investigators, et al. No one really knows what has transpired other than those directly involved with Thomas Riha, whoever they may be."[9]

Mike McKevitt sent Smiley a telegram demanding to know the source of his "alive and well" response. The DA hinted that if Smiley didn't voluntarily provide the name, he could be forced to divulge his source through a grand jury proceeding. Smiley then went back to his CIA handlers, saying he was still willing to keep quiet "even telling the District Attorney that he still would not breach a confidence."[10]

But officials at Langley were alarmed. Todorovich was instructed to tell Smiley "to make no immediate reply to the District Attorney's wire. He is to be told that Washington has the matter under advisement and a solution to the problem is being sought and a decision will be passed to him shortly."[11]

CIA officials then huddled with their general counsel in Washington and concluded that the only option was to have Michael Todorovich go to McKevitt's office and admit that the CIA was the source of Smiley's "alive and well" remarks. But Todorovich was also instructed to tell McKevitt that the CIA had obtained the "alive and well" information from the FBI.

Once he had his marching orders, Todorovich called the FBI's Scott Werner and invited him to accompany him to the meeting. After all, he said, it was a Boulder FBI agent who had passed along the "alive and well" information to Todorovich's CIA man in Boulder.[12]

Werner exploded in rage. He called Todorovich a "liar" and insisted that no FBI agent would have said anything of the sort because the FBI had not investigated Riha's disappearance.[13]

Todorovich held his ground, saying a Denver FBI agent had told him the same thing. Furious, Werner demanded the Boulder agent's name. Todorovich refused to reveal it. In a letter to FBI headquarters, Werner describes what happened next:

> I very emphatically told TODOROVICH that until he gave me the name of the Agent who supposedly gave him and [name deleted] this information, that I would not believe that he or [name deleted] had been given any information such as this by any Agent of this Bureau and this was based on the fact that no Agent would have any reason whatsoever to make such a statement since we had not conducted any investigation in this matter nor did we have any information concerning RIHA, and therefore, we would not be in a position to make such a statement as to whether or not RIHA was all right. I then also pointed out to Mr. TODOROVICH that if he gave the information to Mr. MCKEVITT and advised Mr. MCKEVITT the information had come from an FBI agent and if Mr. MCKEVITT contacted me I would certainly advise him that the information did not come from anyone in the FBI for the same reasons as set forth above.[14]

Werner's fiery response drew praise from Hoover. "I am most pleased to commend you for the aggressive fashion in which you handled certain information relating to a matter of extreme importance to the FBI," he writes.[15]

Todorovich then went to see Mike McKevitt by himself. He had researched McKevitt's background thoroughly and had discovered that he had played football with McKevitt's father at Gonzaga University. When they met, Todorovich mentioned the connection and the two men developed an immediate rapport.[16] After chatting for a while, Todorovich explained that there had been a "misunderstanding" between the CIA and FBI and that digging deeper would only damage the relationship between the two agencies.

Eventually the two men worked out a solution: If Joseph Smiley were willing to admit his "alive and well" comment had been the result of a misunderstanding, then McKevitt would issue a public statement to that effect and everybody would be off the hook.

After Smiley agreed to the plan, McKevitt drew up a press release, stating "the statement made by Dr. Smiley [in April 1969] was the result of a misunderstanding and an honest mistake as to the actual facts." McKevitt refused to provide further clarification to reporters.[17]

Todorovich was pleased with the outcome and heaped praise on Mike McKevitt. "This is certainly a time when an 'uncouth barbaric involvement'— football—did aid materially in obtaining support from an unexpected football fan, one who in my opinion has aided in providing all with an ideal 'out.'"[18]

He added, "Another engagement such as this (one in which your local representative was totally unwitting, 'as who said what to whom' and for that matter cannot be certain at present as to what was said to anyone) will add grey hairs in those very few scattered sectors where there were none before the bell rang for this bout."

Todorovich went on to say that the FBI ought to be grateful to the CIA for not being dragged into the mess. "It would not surprise me if our 'country cousins' had not received their information from the same source all others apparently accepted—the statements of Galya Tannenbaum."[19]

He closed with the following: "I'm facing the East with my scatter rug, visiting the Synagogue and Christian Churches—Salem Aleikum or Thanks to God. (Hopefully this is it.)"

★ ★ ★

Michael Todorovich had seriously misjudged the charged political circumstances surrounding the case. J. Edgar Hoover was incensed and ordered Sam Papich to go to CIA headquarters and demand the name of the FBI agent (or agents) who had passed the information to Michael Todorovich.

Richard Helms, Hoover's counterpart, was lunching at the White House when Papich arrived at Langley. Upon returning to his office, he found Papich and James Jesus Angleton, the Agency's counterintelligence chief, waiting for him in his outer chamber.

Helms liked Papich, writing that Papich's warm relationship with Angleton had solved many problems between the two agencies. "Jim looked so glum and Sam so forlorn that I resisted the temptation to make a reference to 'Death in the Afternoon' and summoned them inside."[20]

Papich sketched out Hoover's complaint. Helms said he understood the gravity of the situation and would order Michael Todorovich to return to Washington for questioning. Once he had all the facts, he'd report back to Hoover.[21]

Richard Helms was accustomed to putting out bureaucratic brush fires. As a young man, he aspired to be a newspaper reporter and had met Hitler in Germany while working for United Press International. He thought Hitler an unattractive man, with active salivary glands that caused the blurring of words and a lower row of teeth that were capped with gold and possibly false. "As Hitler stood talking with the handful of correspondents, his knees moved back and forth nervously. His arms and shoulders as well as his hands were involved in every gesture."[22] When the war broke out, Helms was recruited to churn out "black propaganda" for the Office of Strategic Services. He found espionage more exciting than journalism and made it his life's work.

Like everyone in Washington, Helms treated Hoover gingerly, but he didn't particularly like him. In a 2003 memoir, Helms gratuitously brought up rumors of Hoover's alleged cross-dressing and then dismissed them, saying he saw no evidence of that behavior.

Even sitting presidents feared Hoover, he would write. "President Nixon actually asked me how Hoover might be eased out of office. I understood his problem but did not offer any advice. The bottom line was always attributed to President Johnson: 'In the long run, I'd rather have Edgar on the inside pissing out, than on the outside hosing me down.'"[23]

Helms did order Michael Todorovich back to Washington. Although the city's grand monuments never failed to stir the old patriot, Todorovich steadfastly refused to divulge the name of the FBI agent, or agents, saying it was a "matter of personal honor."[24]

On February 26, 1970, Helms sat down and crafted a conciliatory letter to J. Edgar Hoover: "With regard to Mr. [name deleted] I have no reason to doubt that he acted honestly. I believe that he has reported to me in good faith. He is sincerely interested in preserving a sound working relationship between the CIA and FBI. Nevertheless, because a situation of this sort adversely affects the relationship between the two agencies, I am taking administrative action in this matter with regard to Mr. [name deleted].[25]

Hoover bristled at Helms's claim that Todorovich had acted honestly and wrote in the margins of Helms's letter: "I do not agree. [Name deleted] violated the third agency rule & refused to identify the alleged FBI agent who was the source of the information."[26]

Helms closed his letter by saying, "Mr. Hoover, I wish to state that this Agency can only really perform its duties in the furtherance of the national security when it has the closest coordination and teamwork with the Federal Bureau of Investigation. . . . I trust that we can coordinate closely any future developments or actions in these cases in order to prevent the airing in public of conflicts or differences between the two agencies. Furthermore, it is necessary that we continue to conduct our business in an atmosphere of mutual respect."[27]

But Hoover was in no mood for reconciliation. At the bottom of the letter, he wrote, "This is not satisfactory. I want our Denver Office to have absolutely no contacts with CIA. I want direct liaison here with CIA to be terminated & any contact with CIA in the future to be by letter only." He signed the order "H."[28] Thus, with the stroke of the pen, Hoover had severed relations between the nation's two leading intelligence agencies. Years later, Helms would recount the events leading up to the split differently:

> Angleton asked if we should comply with Hoover's demand. I refused. My strong feeling was that it was up to Hoover to ferret out his own agent. I did not want to put CIA in the position of finking on the slight slip of a career FBI officer. When Hoover, who took great pride in keeping abreast of all FBI activity, no matter how marginal, learned that I had no intention of investigating the incident, he forthwith suspended all liaison between the FBI and the Agency. . . . Jim and Sam both saw the situation as a much more serious crisis than I did. My reaction was conditioned by the fact that the last thing I wanted was an all-out contretemps with the FBI on such a trivial matter. Moreover, I decided that if J. Edgar wanted to punish me or the Agency, I did not, at the moment at least, see what might be done about it. I shrugged, and suggested that this episode might not be the end of the world as we knew it. After giving Jim and Sam the benefit of my reasoning, I suggested they go home, have a stiff drink or two, and wait to see what might happen.[29]

But the situation did not improve. A couple of months later, Hoover cut off liaison with other intelligence agencies. "Criticism reached Hoover that he was discriminating against CIA. So you know what he did? One bright morning he just issued an edict to abolish the entire liaison with the Army, the Navy, the Air Force, Internal Revenue and everybody else. It was one of those unbelievable damn things. It was a nightmare," William Sullivan would tell author David Wise.[30]

Helms, however, claimed that things weren't so bad between the FBI and CIA. The two agencies continued to exchange memos and in a few weeks' time, life returned to normal. "This episode struck me as an example of Hoover's determination to show at all times he was fully in charge of every aspect of the FBI," Helms would write.[31]

Sam Papich did not take things so lightheartedly. He was disturbed over the breakdown and decided it was time to retire. He had begun to mull the possibility a year or two earlier after Hoover had become much less aggressive about pursuing Soviet espionage activities, halting many FBI programs to identify illegals. Papich had written a letter to Hoover asking him to reinstate some of the programs, but Hoover declined.

"From that point on, the relationship between Papich and Hoover chilled and any idea that Papich brought to Hoover from the CIA concerning joint counterintelligence efforts was generally rejected and accompanied by a critical remark," a congressional investigator would write.[32] In his resignation letter, Papich warned Hoover that the FBI-CIA breakdown could gravely affect national security. Then he departed, moving to New Mexico, where he became director of the governor's Organized Crime Prevention Commission.

★   ★   ★

Once former CU president Smiley admitted that his "alive and well" comments were the result of a misunderstanding, officials in the Boulder Police Department admitted that they, too, had been confused as to the facts surrounding Riha's disappearance. "I feel our information was based on a misunderstanding," Capt. Willard Spier told the *Denver Post* on February 15, 1970.[33] Spier added that there was no connection between his source and Smiley's source. "It looks like at this point there were a good many people involved in this thing, and there was a misunderstanding among a number of people." Another Boulder detective, speaking on behalf of Capt. Lowell Friesen, said Friesen had ripped up the missing-person report filed by Joyce Lebra and others after Galya told him that Riha had left Boulder and gone to the "East Coast."

The explanations were so unsatisfying that Stephen Fischer-Galati thought a grand jury should be empaneled to look into the affair. "Why did the university and Boulder police not act after Riha disappeared? And why did the Boulder police accept assurances made about Riha's safety shortly after he was known to be missing? And why did CU officials prefer to think Riha to be AWOL on personal grounds?"[34]

Mike McKevitt, who believed Riha was dead, let his investigation peter out. But the rumors persisted that Riha was a double or triple agent. One day, an FBI agent from the El Paso office went to see Joseph Smiley. Smiley told the FBI man that he "couldn't get it out of his mind that RIJA [sic] may have been a double agent for the Soviets or the Czechoslovaks." He then related the story of a Czech man who had come to Boulder in August 1968 to arrange a marriage between Riha and the man's sister. "Although the 'brother-in-law' supposedly did not speak any English, and had Riha translate every statement into Czech, it was apparent from the gestures and expressions of the 'brother-in-law' that he understood more than he let on," Smiley said.[35]

Smiley's observations raise more questions: How was it that Smiley was informed of such intimate details about a relatively unimportant faculty member? Was Riha being watched? If so, who was the informant?

Michael Todorovich, meanwhile, continued to send his long, ruminative memos to Langley, tamping down just slightly the jocular tone he used in his summaries of the "Thomas Riha Affair." One afternoon he received a phone call from a man identified in CIA records as "IDEN 1," or an "ethnic Czech contact," saying he had an urgent matter to discuss. Todorovich was leery of the caller because some years ago, the man had attempted to "exercise congressional influence in settling a claim against us."[36] Nevertheless he went ahead and met with IDEN 1. Todorovich, as usual, took pleasure in parrying the Czech's questions with his own opaque responses. IDEN 1 confided that in mid-1968 he became aware of an "espionage net" operating in the Denver area.

> The local Czech colony insists that Riha had been involved in an espionage net operated by [name deleted] as principal agent and [deletion] who functioned and perhaps continues as an espionage agent. The local Czech colony insists that Riha is not only in Czechoslovakia but is working for the Czechoslovak intelligence and has an important position. (IDEN 1 could not or would not elaborate further.) IDEN 1 further explained that Riha's relations with Mrs. Galya Tannenbaum were of a nature which placed them in continuing close contact.

The local Czechs, as our source puts it, believe Mrs. Tannenbaum may have become privy to Riha's intelligence functions and used that knowledge in an attempt to control Riha's relations with her. IDEN 1 reasons, however, that Riha became fearful of that control realizing that Mrs. Tannenbaum was a threat, and that in essence he was directed to leave via Canada for Czechoslovakia, entering Canada on a visitor's visa with a subsequent commercial flight to Prague. IDEN 1, in dwelling on Riha, reasons that the Czech professor having traveled to the USSR twice as leader of a student group must have been treated unusually well to return the second time and that in all probability has been recruited by the Russians or the Czechs for some years.[37]

Todorovich nodded his head and asked what he described as "stupid questions." Later, he found himself wondering if IDEN 1 might, in fact, know more than he was saying. The Czech informant, he would write, said "the likelihood of Dr. Riha being dead is less than one in one hundred and that Mrs. Tannenbaum would not have killed him. He concludes that if he were killed, members of any net operation in which he was involved would have done the job."

15 ★ THE HUSTON PLAN

When antiwar activists converged on Washington, DC, to protest the Vietnam War, the FBI's William Sullivan often donned old clothes and went out to talk to them. "They were obviously not hardened revolutionaries; they were seventeen- or eighteen-year-old kids who knew almost nothing about the government they were attacking," he would write in his autobiography.[1]

But Sullivan was only too willing to fight back when he felt personally threatened. During a demonstration in front of the Justice Department, the crowd began spitting, throwing stones, and yelling obscenities. The agents retreated behind a gate, but Sullivan managed to get left behind. As the crowd closed in on him, Sullivan kicked out at a demonstrator and began brandishing his black jack. Two agents rushed out and dragged Sullivan to safety.[2]

On another occasion, Sullivan and an FBI agent were touring the city by automobile. They were dressed in business suits and carrying firearms. Near Dupont Circle, the car slowed and the driver raised his camera to snap a photo of a protester. The man jeered at the two agents and began to saunter toward their vehicle. "Mr. Sullivan removed a canister of mace from his pocket, rolled the window down and sprayed mace at the man who was then about six feet from the car. I did not secure a photograph; the signal light changed and we immediately drove out of the area," the driver said.[3]

The FBI tried to track members of the Weather Underground, the Black Panthers, and Students for a Democratic Society, but they were much harder to monitor than the staid octogenarians of the Communist Party USA. What made things even tougher for FBI agents was Hoover's July 19, 1966, memorandum—the so-called "Hoover cut-off memo," which put the breaks on tactics such as burglaries, wiretapping, and buggings.

Theories abounded as to why Hoover issued the order: After Sen. Edward Long held wiretap hearings in 1965, the public had come to view the surreptitious techniques with distaste and Hoover, a master at reading public opinion, recognized the shift. Clyde Tolson had also advised Hoover to keep away from the surreptitious stuff. "If these techniques ever backfire, your image and the reputation of the Bureau will be badly damaged," he warned.[4] Finally, Hoover had reached the mandatory retirement age of seventy, which required him to get a waiver from the president each year to keep his job. "This put him into a somewhat vulnerable position," the FBI's Charles Brennan would say.[5]

The top officials at FBI headquarters sensed Hoover's vulnerability and kept a close watch on him, wondering when he would stumble and fall, when he would be forced into retirement so that they could assume the throne. Clyde Tolson was too sick to be a contender; he had suffered a series of strokes that left him so physically disabled that he took a back hallway to his office. Hoover himself often took long naps. Every morning, Hoover's automobile pulled into the courtyard of the Justice Department and "two old and sick men" would get out, Bill Sullivan would write. "Hoover would be the first to leave the car and he would walk as quickly as he could to the building. Behind him, shuffling along, was the pathetic figure of Clyde Tolson, no longer able to keep up with the other half of what we called the 'unipersonality.'"[6]

For a while, Cartha D. "Deke" DeLoach looked as if he might be the shoo-in. He was the third-highest ranking official in the FBI, behind Tolson and Hoover. DeLoach had served as liaison to LBJ's White House and had grown so close to President Johnson that he had a telephone line installed in his bedroom that connected him to the White House. He eventually came to believe that Hoover would never leave and resigned to take a job at PepsiCo.

W. Mark Felt, who would later become Watergate's "Deep Throat," also wanted Hoover's job. Felt had flunked out of law school at George Washington University three times and routinely received C's and D's on his course work, but he had managed to pull himself together and had grown into a tall, suave-looking executive.[7]

Felt directed the FBI's Inspection Division, which was akin to a police department's internal affairs unit. He was unpopular with other FBI men, but good at lying—like Bill Sullivan—who also fancied himself sitting in the director's chair one day. Felt and Sullivan became fierce rivals. Felt thought Sullivan a "mercurial little man known for his Napoleonic complex" who threw temper tantrums when he didn't get his way and engaged in backstabbing.[8]

In addition to these men, there were other high-ranking executives in the FBI who no doubt coveted the director's job, but outward expression of such ambition could bring banishment from the caffeinated offices of headquarters to a sleepy FBI outpost in the Midwest. So the palace courtiers bided their time. No one—not even Hoover—could live forever.

In May 1970, when US troops invaded Cambodia, the protests against the Vietnam War increased exponentially. Four students at Kent State University in Ohio were killed by National Guardsmen. Eleven days later, two students were killed and eleven others wounded at Jackson State in Mississippi. In Washington, DC, thousands of protesters filled the streets. President Nixon was hustled off to Camp David and the 82nd Airborne Brigade was brought in to protect the administration.

During this tumultuous period, the friendship between William Sullivan and White House lawyer Tom Charles Huston deepened. They hoped fervently that President Nixon would unshackle the intelligence community and give them back the tools they needed to defeat the homegrown terrorists. "I really was peripherally interested in the antiwar demonstrations," Huston recalled. "What I was concerned about was the 40,000 bombings that took place in one year. What I was concerned about was the thirty-nine police officers who were killed in sniping incidents."[9]

CIA officials were also unhappy with Hoover's cut-off order. "Hoover put us out of business in 1966 and 1967 when he placed sharp restrictions on intelligence collection. I was a Soviet Specialist and I wanted a better coverage of the Soviets. I felt—and still feel—that we need technical coverage on every Soviet in the country. I didn't give a damn about the Black Panthers myself, but I did about the Russians," a CIA man said.[10]

Once Hoover severed relations with the CIA and then expanded his order to include other intelligence agencies, the FBI found itself operating in a virtual vacuum. "I had never seen anything like it," Sullivan recalled. "We wouldn't share our information with anyone, and no other agency liked to give us anything because Hoover would leak it to the newspapers and use it against them if he could."[11]

Everyone in the intelligence community knew more coordination was needed, Huston said. "Particularly, as you know, at that time, the CIA and the FBI liaison had been terminated."[12]

On June 5, 1970, when the furor over Cambodia subsided, President Nixon convened a meeting of his intelligence chiefs in the Oval Office. Among them were J. Edgar Hoover, the CIA's Richard Helms, Gen. Donald Bennett of the Defense Intelligence Agency, Adm. Noel Gayler of the National Security Agency, presidential aides H. R. Haldeman and John Ehrlichman, as well as Tom Charles Huston, who had been promoted to White House adviser for internal security affairs. General Bennett, who thought he saw Nixon turning on a tape recorder as the meeting began, said "the president chewed our butts."

Nixon's talking points on the meeting were not quite so blunt, but they did portray a country on the brink of collapse. "We are now confronted with a new and grave crisis in our country—one which we know too little about. Certainly hundreds, perhaps thousands, of Americans—mostly under thirty—are determined to destroy our society," he said.[13]

Nixon asserted that foreign powers were behind the domestic upheaval and that the young extremists were developing their own "indigenous revolutionary activism," which was as dangerous as anything they could import from Cuba, China, or the Soviet Union. "Our people—perhaps as a reaction to the excesses of the McCarthy era—are unwilling to admit the possibility that 'their children' could wish to destroy their country. This is particularly true of the media and the academic community," Nixon said.

Nixon paused for a moment and looked at J. Edgar Hoover and Richard Helms. Were there any problems between the two agencies? he asked. Both men shook their heads. "Neither, apparently, wished to discuss the Riha case with other disagreements," the Church Committee would write.[14] Nixon's question was rhetorical anyway; Tom Charles Huston had already briefed him on the FBI-CIA dispute stemming from the Riha case.[15]

Nixon said he wanted the directors to review their intelligence-collection efforts and prepare a report describing what could be done to strengthen them. He asked J. Edgar Hoover to chair the committee. Hoover, in turn, appointed William Sullivan to chair a subcommittee that would actually draft the report.

The following day, the intelligence chiefs met again in Hoover's office. Hoover began the meeting saying it was his understanding that the president wanted an historical summary of the country's unrest. Tom Charles Huston, who was seated to the left of Hoover, contradicted him, saying that was not what Nixon wanted. The president wanted to know the *present-day* problems in intelligence-gathering and how to correct them, Huston said.

The room went silent. "You could hear a pin drop," remembered Sullivan.[16] The other intelligence experts then pitched in to support Huston's recollections. Hoover, red-faced, adjourned the meeting. "From that moment on, Hoover hated Huston," Sullivan would write. "He never called him by his right name, and in our conversations he never referred to him by any other name except 'that hippie,' taking his cue from Huston's two-inch sideburns."[17]

By June 23, 1970, a draft written largely by Sullivan and two aides had been completed. The draft, instead of being named after Sullivan, would become known as the Huston Plan because it was Tom Charles Huston who urged President Nixon to approve the recommendations. Under the plan, government agents would be allowed to plant electronic bugs, surreptitiously open mail, and burglarize the homes or businesses of anyone they deemed a foreign intelligence or internal security risk without getting judicial approval.

All the intelligence chiefs signed off on the draft—except Hoover. Huston and Sullivan had shown Hoover the document last, hoping that once he saw that his colleagues were in favor of the plan, he would "acquiesce."[18] Instead, Hoover exploded in anger. "For years and years and years I have approved opening mail and other similar operations, but no," Sullivan quoted Hoover as saying. "It's becoming more dangerous and we are apt to get caught."[19]

Sullivan had to proceed cautiously; Deke DeLoach had resigned and Hoover had promoted Sullivan to be assistant to the director, the Number Three post in the FBI. Sullivan didn't want to anger Hoover, yet he still hoped to salvage the Huston Plan. So he came up with a compromise. He recommended that Hoover put his objections in footnotes, which was a common procedure for interagency papers. But after Hoover added his footnotes to the report, the other intelligence chiefs balked, saying they wanted to insert their own footnotes, too. Huston tried to calm them down, saying that he would communicate their views in a separate memorandum to Nixon.[20]

At the signing ceremony, which was once again held in Hoover's office, Hoover insisted on reading the report aloud. Then he went around the room asking if anyone cared to comment. "Mr. Helms do you have anything to add?" Sullivan remembered Hoover saying.[21] "When Helms shook his head, Hoover went on to Admiral Gayler, General Bennett, and the others, and finally to 'Mr. Hutchinson' as he called Tom Huston," remembered Sullivan. "After Hoover read another page he'd go around the table again, asking each man if he had anything else to add and finally, as Hoover got to Huston, he'd ask, 'Mr. Hoffman?'"

Once the directors had signed off on the plan, Huston prepared a letter for Nixon, recommending that restrictions on bugging, wiretapping, and break-ins be lifted. He also recommended the president approve the mail-opening programs, unaware that the CIA already had a mail-opening program under way.

Huston wrote bluntly of the pros and cons. Covert mail-opening programs and break-ins were illegal, he acknowledged. Furthermore, break-ins were highly risky and could result in great embarrassment if exposed. Neverthe-less, they yielded valuable information and "can produce the type of intelli-gence which cannot be obtained in any other fashion."[22]

The implications were stunning. Tom Charles Huston, the Church Com-mittee would write, was asking "the highest political figure in the nation to sanction lawlessness within the intelligence community."[23] Despite the plan's illegalities, President Nixon approved it on July 14, 1970.

After Huston sent out a memo describing Nixon's approval, a dismayed Hoover marched into Attorney General John Mitchell's office. Mitchell, who claimed to know nothing about the Huston Plan, instructed Hoover to "sit tight" until he could confer with the president. Five days later, Nixon rescinded the Huston Plan.

Huston, "intense and agitated," trooped down to the White House Situa-tion Room and told the supervisor to contact the participating agencies and tell them to return the plan. All of the copies were returned, but Huston noticed that the staples had been removed, meaning all of the agencies had made copies.

Huston wasn't ready to admit defeat yet. In a memo to H. R. Haldeman, he wrote, "At some point Hoover has to be told who is president. He has become totally unreasonable and his conduct is detrimental to our domes-tic intelligence operations . . . if he gets his way it is going to look like he is more powerful than the president."[24]

Haldeman ignored Huston's memo, as well as his follow-up memos. Fi-nally, Huston realized that Hoover had beaten him.

On August 7, 1970, John Dean took over Huston's responsibilities for domestic intelligence. Huston remained at the White House for another ten months, spending time talking with counterintelligence officials on a special scrambler phone he kept in a safe in his office.[25] He resigned from the White House staff on June 13, 1971.

Five years later, when the Church Committee delved into the Huston Plan, they subpoenaed numerous witnesses, including Tom Charles Huston, James Jesus Angleton, and the FBI's Charles Brennan. The committee mem-bers were especially appalled at the duplicity and disingenuousness exhib-ited by the intelligence leaders while the plan was being drafted. For exam-ple, the Huston Plan requested presidential approval for overt and covert mail-opening programs, yet a covert program had already been under way for two decades. Richard Helms, J. Edgar Hoover, William Sullivan, and James Jesus Angleton knew of the program, but nothing was said when the Huston Plan was being developed.

Similarly, the FBI, at the request of Henry Kissinger, Nixon's national security adviser, had also begun wiretapping the telephones of reporters and members of Kissinger's National Security Council staff who were suspected of leaking critical information about the administration's foreign policy to the press. Seventeen wiretaps were conducted between 1969 and 1971. The FBI man who oversaw them and kept the logs and memorandum in his office was none other than William Sullivan.

Huston testified that he knew nothing about the mail-opening programs, the Kissinger wiretaps, the FBI's COINTELPRO activities, or the CIA's domestic espionage programs. When asked why the intelligence leaders went through the charade, he responded, "I wish I knew. I do not know."[26]

The committee chairman, Sen. Frank Church, pointed out that the CIA continued to open mail even after Nixon rescinded his approval of the Huston Plan. "So the Commander in Chief is not the Commander in Chief at all. He is just a problem. You do not want to inform him in the first place because he might say no. That is the truth of it. And when he did say no, you disregard it."[27]

Equally disturbing to senators was the conviction held by members of the Nixon administration that the president had the executive authority to override the US Constitution when it came to matters involving national security. Huston admitted that his thinking was wrong. "We went from this kind of sincere intention, honest intention, to develop a series of justifications and rationalizations based upon this distorted view of inherent executive power, and from that . . . you went down the road to where you ended up with these people going into the Watergate."[28]

Sen. Richard Schweiker, the liberal Republican from Pennsylvania, argued that the Huston Plan was the precursor to the May 28, 1972, break-in of the headquarters of the Democratic National Committee at the Watergate office complex. The Plumbers, a group of former FBI and CIA operatives working inside the White House, planned and executed the break-in.

"Did the Plumber's unit not do some of the same things, breaking and entry, illegal burglary that the Huston Plan proposed? Is that not a fact?" he asked the CIA's James Jesus Angleton.

"Yes," responded Angleton.

"So, in essence, they went around the back door instead of the front door. Even though the Huston Plan was dead, I believe it had nine lives," Schweiker responded.[29]

Although President Nixon revoked his approval of the Huston Plan before it could be put into action, his initial authorization nevertheless would form the core of Article II in the Impeachment Articles framed by the Judiciary Committee of the US House of Representatives.[30]

Thus, the Thomas Riha case was analogous to the proverbial flapping of a butterfly's wings, which creates an atmospheric disturbance that grows into a hurricane. The sequence went like this:

1. Riha's disappearance triggered the split between the CIA and FBI;
2. the FBI-CIA split and Hoover's subsequent decision to sever ties with other agencies created an intelligence vacuum;
3. the intelligence vacuum gave rise to the Huston Plan;
4. the failed Huston Plan led to creation of the White House Plumbers and an impeachment article against President Nixon.

Just as in a hurricane, there were other tremendous forces that led to President Nixon's resignation—among them the domestic turmoil surrounding the Vietnam War; Nixon's insatiable desire for intelligence; the death of J. Edgar Hoover in 1972; and the war between William Sullivan and W. Mark Felt over who would become the next FBI director.

Curiously, only a month after Nixon rescinded his approval, Hoover approved a vast expansion in surveillance activities. He okayed the recruitment of students on college campuses who were eighteen years of age or older; authorized a new surveillance program targeting four thousand African American students; ordered the review of seven thousand individuals on the Security Index; and approved the opening of sixty-five hundred cases on "New Left" student activists.[31] Within a year, he also had sixty-five hundred "ghetto informants" and had approved the installation of more than a dozen telephone taps, most of them on Black Panther members or their organizations.

16 ★ THIRTY-SIX DAYS

In her room at the Colorado Psychiatric Hospital, Galya shrugged off the "Colonel" persona and took up painting, transferring to the blank canvases all the images she had stored up from her life. The surging creativity had lain dormant within her, crushed beneath the depression and despair, the plotting and conniving that had carried her through her days.

Outside the brick walls of the hospital, chaos awaited her: bond hearings, preliminary court appearances, reporters, and photographers. But she had a room of her own and could paint for thirty-six days—from February 4 to March 12, 1970.

She worked until two or three o'clock in the morning, the only sounds outside her window the occasional sirens of ambulances and rattling of coal trains shuddering north through the city. In four days, she created twenty-five paintings.[1] She also wrote several autobiographical sketches, including one for the state's chief psychiatrist, Dr. John M. Macdonald, and a second and longer one for her attorney, John Kokish, and Dr. John P. Hilton, a psychiatrist hired to help defend her.

An art gallery in downtown Denver eventually agreed to put on a show of her collected works, which drew the inevitable comparison with other troubled artists. "Her work has the technique of the German expressionists while the sunny colors on some acrylics have the disturbing quality and brilliance of Van Gogh," writes the *Denver Post*.[2] The art critic singled out Galya's *Horsemen of a Dream*, which depicted two horsemen trotting down a golden hillside. She created dreamlike whorls in her canvas by dragging a comb through the thick paint. Galya also worked with pencils and watercolors. One drawing showed a young girl sitting pensively in the middle of a field, another showed a young boy slouching in a baseball uniform. The children may have represented her own children, the displaced specters in her own hallucinatory journey.

While Galya was in the psychiatric hospital, police in Denver and Boulder continued their investigations into the forgery cases. But the cyanide poisoning deaths of Gustav Ingwersen and Barbara Egbert weren't pursued with much energy once she was confined.

Psychologists and psychiatrists trooped in and out of Galya's room to administer physical and psychological exams. She was a complex person and deflected and redirected incoming questions with practiced ease. She was evasive when the state's prosecution witness, Dr. Macdonald, questioned her, but was more forthcoming with the sympathetic Dr. Hilton. For the first time, Galya began referring to herself as a "retired" colonel. She told Dr. Hilton she didn't know exactly how she became the "retired colonel," but said she inhabited the role so thoroughly it was as if she had never been anyone else.

"Being the retired Colonel I was somebody good, and I thought there was nothing that I could do that would go wrong. I was happy, flying on cloud 9, as though I had just been reincarnated. The old person didn't exist at all; all the tears that I had cried were somewhere like a dream that one doesn't remember very clearly. So complete was this new person that it seemed that I had a memory of a military past."[3]

The persona, as best she could recall, emerged in the fall of 1968 when she was trying to get financing for the two real estate developments. Or it may have emerged earlier, around the time that Leo Tanenbaum walked out of her life and Thomas Riha walked back in.

As the colonel, Galya said she felt confident and walked with a purposeful stride. She installed oversized wheels and extra-strong brakes on her car so she could make fast U-turns in the mountains. In a letter to Dr. Hilton, she writes:

> I have always liked fast powerful cars, still do. I drove the family to the mountains a lot, never feeling the least bit hesitant over the passes, and I do believe I have gone over the good ones as well as the poor surfaced ones in all of Colorado, Wyoming and New Mexico. (By contrast when I was going to Aspen riding with Leo thru the mountains I was so frightened he would put me to sleep hypnotically to drive in peace). But not after I was the Colo. Ret. I felt quite equal to the mountains, nothing frightened me about them anymore at all, they were beautiful, I felt free of all restrictions, and there was no place I could not climb, no old mine too dark, dangerous or deep to explore.[4]

When Thomas told her that he was going to marry Hana, Galya said she was so immersed in the colonel persona that she was not terribly upset.

"I was not torn with tears over the affair, in fact, I felt like a stranger to everything around me, people, places & things. There was no relationship between what I had known—what was then or what is now,"[5] she writes.

The colonel persona was shattered when her mother showed up. "At which point I was confused as all get out and down at the lowest depths. . . . I kept on going—but much happened like a TV picture flipping or rolling fast—some things I remember with Tom—my mother, Gus—the Lake Valley Project, the water & sewer district and other jobs. Everything that happened with Tom was like it happened in a dream—and I'd wake up and all would be as it was."[6]

Galya spoke affectionately of her relationship with Gus, telling Dr. Hilton how he had become part of her family. She had served him lobster when he came to dinner for the first time and he enjoyed it so much that Galya cooked him another lobster the next day for lunch. "There was nothing I wouldn't do for Gus and he in turn gave of himself freely to us."[7]

Gus had asked Galya to marry him several times, but she said she felt only friendship toward him. "I was not interested in being a bedtime playmate."[8] On Father's Day, when Gus returned from the plastics convention in New York, she hosted a large dinner party. The guests included Gus, Zdenek Cerveny, Barbara Egbert, Esther Foote, Galya's two kids, her mother, and herself.

Gus brought along his will, but Galya said she didn't pay much attention to it because she was in the kitchen cooking. She overheard Gus asking Zdenek and Esther to sign the papers. "The occasion was not a formal bit intended for any paper signing, but rather a Father's Day supper and the paper signing bit was completely incidental to the overall affair."[9]

When Galya learned that Gus had died, she said she was shocked and had urged his family to have an autopsy. "I didn't want to believe it. I suppose I acted like a slob. Cried."[10]

Leighton Whitaker, a psychologist for the state, interviewed Galya in the psychiatric hospital and administered a battery of psychological tests. She arrived for the interview clad in a sweater and slacks and spoke so quietly that he often had to ask her to speak up. He thought her movements slow and deliberate. The tests showed no psychotic thinking, no brain damage, no memory impairment. However, he noticed that she displayed a marked hostility toward men. Whitaker diagnosed her with an antisocial personality with paranoid persecutory and grandiose elements. "It may be concluded that while the patient does not demonstrate the usual signs of psychosis, her extreme need to fabricate are pathological to a severe degree, and it is doubtful whether she could sustain any more constructive behavior."[11]

Dr. Roland Brett, another expert witness for the state, also interviewed Galya. "She relates warmly and easily. In fact, she is quite a charmer, someone easy to like, and one never feels this way or relates this way to a paranoid schizophrenic. She seemed, in fact, almost naïve and extremely trusting of me."[12]

Dr. Brett thought Galya was exceptionally intelligent, with strong mathematical skills and genuine artistic talent. But he was surprised to discover her poor spelling ability. "Her spontaneous vocabulary particularly shows that she is able to function intellectually at a very high level of intelligence. However, when testing her in a formal manner or having her attempt to write out words dictated to her, she showed a very marked discrepancy between her native intelligence and her spelling ability."[13] Galya, he continued, was able to fuse fact and fiction so deftly that it was often impossible to discern the truth:

She is so bright and so facile and adept in describing events that have supposedly occurred during the past several years that one is left leaving an interview with her of feeling rather strongly that she is giving an honest picture of the situation. At these times she is *very* convincing. Later when I have compared notes with her attorney, Mr. Kokish, I find there are discrepancies, but not remarkably great discrepancy. . . . Outside of the hospital she has called herself for example a Colonel and even a General and has even had her children believing that she had a position of Colonel in the F.B.I., a somewhat ridiculous confabulation and yet she is so believable in these various roles that she plays that not only do others believe her in my opinion, but she halfway believes that she is the real Colonel or General.[14]

Galya, he said, began to fantasize she was an FBI agent after she broke up with Leo Tanenbaum, and FBI agents came to her and asked her about the photos Leo had taken in Cuba. "It is my impression that at this point Galya began to have the grandiose idea that she herself was an FBI agent simply because she helped the FBI."[15] (Dr. Brett did not know of the FBI's impersonation investigations, which dated back to the 1950s.)

Dr. Brett also conducted various psychological tests and was surprised, given Galya's creative talents, that her Rorschach Ink Blot Test was so "barren." He detected no pervasive hostility, but he did notice that she became "very aggressively angry" when talking about her mother, her brother, or various social workers.

Ultimately, he concluded Galya was sane and suffered from no mental illness. That finding, he added, "does not rule out the possibility or even the probability that she might have a sociopathic personality disorder manifested by a tendency toward pathological lying and enjoying the positive feedback she gets by conning other people into believing her stories, her special capabilities or her playing the part of a Colonel or a FBI agent, for example."

He added, "In my opinion, she is a real artist at deception, a master-innovator in taking a small amount of truth or reality in a situation and weaving an entirely believable explanation about some of the things that seem to be happening in the most bizarre fashion wherever she makes her appearance. I do not believe that this comes under the category of a mental illness. Especially with regard to the acts charged."[16]

At 9:30 P.M. on March 12, 1970, Galya's stay in the psychiatric hospital ended. So did her intense burst of creativity. She penned a suicide note and a will, then she was escorted outside, where two Boulder County sheriff's deputies awaited her. The deputies led her to a squad car and transported her to the Boulder County Jail, where her bond was initially set at $5,000.[17]

Galya couldn't scrape together the money to make bond and no one was willing to lend her money, so she sat in jail, growing more distraught with each passing day. The Boulder County facility had strict rules: Visiting hours were on Sunday afternoons, from one o'clock until three o'clock. Outsiders were not allowed to bring in cash, food, or magazines dealing with crime or sex. Inmates were allowed to write two letters a week, but the letters could contain no profanity or underlined words. Before the letters were mailed, jail officials opened them and read them to make sure they were in compliance with the rules.

Galya was poorly equipped psychologically to withstand the confinement and isolation of jail. "There is nothing to ameliorate the drag of time. Nothing is allowed to the inmate, no newspaper, pencil or paper, or reasonable reading material," she would write. "Your nerves wear raw, waiting, seemingly hopelessly waiting, to get help from a lawyer, a bondsman, or family or friend. The disease of knot [sic] knowing literally eats away at your mind and senses. There is nothing to do to help yourself. Sleep is caught in a series of catnaps between the slam of the door behind each new book-in. The breakfast marks the time of day when cereal and a bowl of coffee, minus sugar, are served in their degrading fashion. From then on there is nothing, nothing to do but lay under the glare of the light that is never turned off."[18]

A Denver businessman named Gayle Norton was one of Galya's only visitors. Norton and his wife, Jo Ann, knew John Kokish and had agreed to take Galya's two children, Jimmy and Becky, in part because the state was going to separate them. "That didn't seem right," Jo Ann Norton recalled in an interview in 2013.[19]

Galya had worked briefly for Mr. Norton in the summer of 1969, designing reports and brochures for his financial firm. On June 20, 1969—the night that Neil Armstrong walked on the moon—he had argued with her over a roll of film that he needed for a presentation in Vail. At about 10 P.M., he told Galya he was coming to her house to pick up the film. She asked him not to come, but he went anyway. When he knocked on her door, she opened it a crack and handed him a piece of paper, saying, "You will find the film here."[20] The paper contained a cryptic set of directions, which instructed him to go to an abandoned truck located in an industrial area on the west side of town. The film, she wrote, was on the floor of the truck. Norton followed the instructions and found the roll of film exactly where she said it would be. The only problem was, the film was blank. "I mean, it was there, but the thing that irritated me is that when I processed and developed it, there was not a thing on it."[21]

While Galya was in jail, Norton brought her stamps and painting supplies and small amounts of money. Although she had voluntarily agreed to give custody of her kids to the Nortons, she sometimes grew irrationally jealous and threatened Mr. Norton with physical violence. "This woman, when she became angry, was like a Jekyll and Hyde," he would say in a sworn deposition. "She was just an entirely different person. And the profanity and the vulgarity and the obscenities. It would be coming out in torrents and all of sudden there would be a cessation of that and she would become very docile, feminine, crying, imploring, pleading."[22]

In one letter to Mr. Norton, Galya writes that she had mixed emotions about taking the insanity plea. "It seems to me that if a person WANTED to declare any adult in America a nut, they could—and I hope—sincerely hope you are not caught up in the whirlpool of self excuses and rationalizations in trying to have me declared nuts. It gets so darn academic that I think the legal end forgets that it is my life and my children's lives that is at stake—real live people."[23]

She begged Mr. Norton to help her raise the bond money to get out, saying she could repay him by selling her artwork or her three rifles—two Winchesters and a .30–06. She also said that she needed time with Jimmy and Becky. She was particularly worried about Jimmy, who was building a fantasy world for himself. "There is such a desperation in his small plea to come back to me—and here I am, caged like some wild beast, and cannot even talk to him to make the change easier for him," she writes.[24] "I know the terrible hurt they felt and probably reacted to being suddenly away from me, it probably upset the apple cart something awfull [sic]—particularly Jimmy, for he needed TLC the most desperately. I certainly am not going to upset the most precious thing—the children when I'm out . . . I beg for a chance to live—Please, help for the sake of heaven itself. I won't let you down—after all I trust you most, for you have my children."[25]

The Nortons couldn't, or wouldn't, help her. Furthermore, law enforcement officials were determined to keep her jailed. She was shuttled back and forth between hearings in Boulder and Denver. As she entered and departed courtrooms, she wore her cat's-eye glasses and mink coat and tried to hide her face from photographers. Even though the trips were painful, they were preferable to sitting in jail. Often a week would go by without a visitor or a scrap of news. Waiting for someone to come during visiting hours was "absolute hell," she told Mr. Norton:

This is the most severe punishment environment any human could put upon another. The windows are so heavily frosted that all it admits is light and dark—there is no world, no sky—nothing—absolutely nothing. I am alone here—which amounts to solitary confinement, which is an absolute hell. Telling me to hang on—hang on to what, there is nothing here, no human thing to hang onto—only a miserable cage in which there is nothing to do but pace & pace & cry and cry . . . I don't know how long I can hold out—in this hell . . . I feel so abandoned, so dead—it is extremely difficult to keep myself from ending it all—There is so much of nothing here—the matrons who I see only fragmentary parts of when they shove the food through a slat. You know, when visiting hours start it is hell, watching from the time they start, hoping someone will come, and then after all is over, knowing how much more alone you are. I think that even on a death row there would be someone to talk to.[26]

In mid-April, Galya was transferred to the Denver jail, where she would remain until midsummer when her first sanity hearing was held. The Denver jail was not nearly so confining as the Boulder facility. Inmates who weren't considered dangerous were allowed out of their cells to exercise and socialize. Galya attached herself to Rebecca Haynes, the director of the women's jail. She made herself indispensable, filing and typing, scrubbing floors, vacuuming hallways. "She had to be with me almost constantly," Haynes would say. "This was a little difficult for her as well as for me because she did alienate most of the other inmates and it caused a lot of jealousy. . . . The least little thing that happened would frighten or upset her, she would immediately want to get off by herself or in my office with me."[27]

When Haynes arrived in her office each morning, Galya had a pot of coffee waiting. She was exuberant and full of laughter while she was working, but sulked and wept when she was asked to leave Haynes's office. Haynes saw how devastating incarceration was to Galya's emotional stability. "She just falls apart. She just—cannot function adequately. She becomes extremely nervous, extremely upset and just falls apart."[28]

As Galya grew accustomed to the Denver jail, the tone of her letters grew less desperate. In an April 14, 1970, letter to Mr. Norton, she reminded him of the $600 that Barbara Egbert owed her and how that the money could be used for bail. "I am not guilty of the BS I am charged with—As a woman— having been interested in a man—yes—but really is that so abnormal—Any- one's life can be twisted into something sinister if twisted enough by skilled people—that however does not necessarily make the twisted version true."[29]

17 ★ THE TRIAL

On the morning of July 8, 1970, a year and three months after Thomas Riha disappeared, Galya's sanity trial got under way in a Boulder courtroom. When she entered the courtroom, her attorney, John Kokish, was waiting for her at the defense table. With his sideburns and long, dark hair, Kokish still had the rumpled look of a reporter. But he had done his homework and was prepared for this, his first big case. At the opposing table was W. Douglas Watson, Boulder County's chief deputy district attorney. Watson was a dogged prosecutor with far more courtroom experience than Kokish and would raise objections repeatedly when the young lawyer tried to shoehorn in Galya's medical records or hearsay testimony.

Four psychiatrists—two for the prosecution and two for the defense—were sitting in the courtroom along with half a dozen lay witnesses. The psychiatrists were allowed to remain in the courtroom while the hearing was under way but the other witnesses were asked to wait in the hallway until the bailiff called their names.

The spectators arranged themselves in rows behind the bar. Many reporters were present, including Fred Gillies, whom Galya disliked and had disparagingly referred to as a "punk." The pageantry and excitement seemed out of proportion for a simple forgery case, but there was nothing simple about the case. It was the first time the public would get a prolonged look at the mysterious "colonel."

Galya wore a sleeveless dress and black flats and looked more like a businesswoman than a criminal defendant. During the hearing, she kept her eyes trained on the notepad in front of her. When a witness pointed her out, she would look up, her eyes glazed with a cocktail of sedatives and tranquilizers that she was given each night—Permitil, Tofranil, and phenobarbital.[1]

At nine o'clock Judge Barnard strode in.

"All rise," shouted the bailiff.

Barnard waved the spectators to their seats and took his seat behind the bench.

Galya had pleaded not guilty by reason of insanity to the charge that she had forged Thomas Riha's name on the $330 check to Judson Flying Service. The sanity hearing revolved around two legal questions: (1) Did Galya understand the difference between right and wrong on the day she forged the check? (2) If she understood the difference, was she capable of choosing right and refraining from doing wrong?

John Kokish and the two psychiatrists on his defense team believed that Galya suffered from manic depression, a mental illness that now is known as bipolar disorder and is characterized by alternating periods of elation and depression. The psychiatrists for the prosecution believed Galya had serious emotional problems but was nevertheless sane on the day she wrote the hot check.

Galya had waived her right to a jury trial, so it was Judge Barnard alone who would hear the evidence and render the verdict.

The judge looked at Mr. Watson and nodded. "You may proceed."

Mr. Watson called his star witness, Dr. John Macdonald, to the stand. Dr. Macdonald had received his medical training in New Zealand and served as a medical officer in the New Zealand Royal Army. After postgraduate studies in psychiatry at the University of London and the University of Edinburgh, he moved to the United States. In 1951, he joined the staff of the University of Colorado Health Sciences Center and had been there ever since. During his career, Dr. Macdonald had examined more than six hundred criminal defendants and written nearly a dozen books, including *The Murderer and His Victim*. In researching that book, he had accompanied Denver police to homicide scenes and spent long hours at the Denver morgue. One of the police officers he acknowledged in the preface was Arthur Dill, head of the homicide division and Denver's future police chief. (Dill also happened to be one of Galya's confidants; she once referred to him as an "'Ironsides' kind of a guy.")[2]

Dr. Macdonald viewed criminal defendants with an almost palpable hostility, writing that most defendants who "simulated insanity" were malingerers and imposters who hadn't the foggiest idea what a truly insane person looked like.[3]

He had a posh English accent and, as befitting a psychiatrist, seemed devoid of emotions. In truth, he had found Galya to be a frustrating subject. He had interviewed her for more than twenty-five hours in jail or the psychiatric hospital and could not break through her defense system. "Often when you would ask her a question, she would answer something that was related to the topic, but not really an answer to your question. She would start on it and then slip it aside and deal with something else and very frequently she would say, 'I don't know' or 'I don't remember' and things of this nature when you asked her questions. There was a certain inconsistency in her answers."[4]

When Dr. Macdonald tried to limit Galya's responses to "yes" or "no," she became angry with him and accused him of being a police interrogator. At other times she wept, offering up tidbits of information at the conclusion of an interview to entice him to stay longer. Dr. Macdonald testified that he was troubled by Galya's case and even after he submitted his report to court, he continued to visit her, trying to make up his mind if she was truly insane or just a very clever con artist.

During his interviews, Dr. Macdonald said he obtained Galya's general medical history, conducted a physical examination, performed several brain-wave tests, and sought corroborating information from relatives and acquaintances. He noticed that her right side seemed less sensitive than the left, but thought she might have been faking it because she jumped when he jabbed her with a pin on the right side. He said her memory was normal and her intelligence average, but conceded that she possessed far more artistic talent than the average person.

During their many hours of discussion, Galya wove dozens of falsehoods into the fabric of her life story. She was charming, likable, and generous with her time and money, as well as self-centered, narcissistic, and shallow. She was imbued with grandiose ideas and sexually promiscuous, though she had never particularly enjoyed sex.

Galya told Dr. Macdonald that she tried hard to control her temper, saying that the only person she ever physically assaulted was her first husband, Robert McPherson. "She said she had difficulty in making up her mind regarding moral standards. She said, 'They are all my own. It's anything you want to do so long as you don't hurt anybody.'"[5]

Galya gave Dr. Macdonald different names for herself and different birth dates. She said she took the name Galya from a Russian ballerina and the surname Zakharovna from Zakharov, a name that her father had used. She said she was born in Russia, then in China, then Brazil. "I should also mention that one time she said she was from another planet," the psychiatrist testified.[6] Galya also said she had once owned two lions, two black panthers, a monkey, and a baby crocodile that had to be given away because it got "rather nasty" as it got older.[7]

Galya said she liked to read and watch sports on television, but avoided movies because she said she became too engrossed in them and they frightened her. She also had adopted the European style of eating, with the fork in her left hand and the knife in her right. She said she was raised as a Roman Catholic, but had belonged to as many as fifteen different religions.

Dr. Macdonald thought Galya a prodigious liar and testified that anything she told him could have been true—or false.[8] She was able to bolster her self-esteem and get attention from others through lying.[9] He added that she had a "rather hostile" sense of humor and often laughed at other people's expense.

Although she described herself as a "clinging vine," Dr. Macdonald thought she was a controlling person who readily took command of situations. He said that when he visited Galya in the Denver jail, it seemed as if she was running the facility. When jail director Rebecca Haynes wanted to use her own office, Galya seemed to be doing her a favor by allowing her in. "Mrs. Tannenbaum was sort of accepting her apology for coming in almost as though it was her office and she was being very gracious to let the lady in. It is very difficult to describe, but I had the feeling that she was really running the women's section of the Denver County Jail; the young inmates were coming up to her and talking as though she was a sort of a source of wisdom and authority and even when she said good-bye, it was almost as though she was dismissing some flunky out the door."[10]

Galya told Dr. Macdonald that she had impersonated perhaps a dozen people in her life and inhabited the roles so completely that cities and neighborhoods where she had lived for years became unrecognizable. She claimed to have once been the wife of Henry Crown, a wealthy Chicago man who owned a hotel chain; the wife of a member of La Cosa Nostra; and the strong and capable colonel. With the exception of Thomas Riha, all of her husbands or partners were much older. While married to her second husband, Charles Russell Scimo, she said she had transported large quantities of narcotics from New York to Chicago. "I did anything. Bookmaking, I got involved in it. Anything he asked me to do, I never thought twice about it."[11] As Colonel Zakharovna, she said she used fake passports to get people out of Czechoslovakia. "Some of the persons were sent back into Czechoslovakia and they would send reports that 'a guy needed to have some dental work.' This would be a coded report meaning that this person had to be killed and later on they would get a report that the guy had his teeth filled and all was well. In fact, the man had been killed."[12]

Galya boasted that she could assemble and disassemble guns behind her back and had the grip on her .357 Magnum—which she called her "pet"—altered so it felt more balanced in her hand.[13] She also boasted that she was handy with dynamite and often worked fifteen hours a day on her car.

During the summer of 1969, Galya said her house on Logan Street was filled with people. "She was not getting much sleep at night—not because she couldn't sleep—but because of the tremendous activity going on in the home,"

Dr. Macdonald testified. The colonel persona began to fade around June 1969 when her mother arrived for a visit.

"On one occasion when I asked her if she believed in Colonel Zakharovna," he testified, "she said it was like a motion picture in which you have fade outs. You know, you have a sequence showing something and then something comes in and then goes back to what it was on originally. She would get the impression she was Mrs. Tannenbaum and then there would be a change and she would become Colonel Zakharovna and then go back to Mrs. Tannenbaum."[14]

Galya said she had been hearing voices since she was about eight years old. She said she continued to hear voices off and on throughout her life and that when she was in the psychiatric hospital, she heard a group of prominent people discussing her case. "Sometimes it is a male voice that is talking, for example, about rabbit hunting and she can actually see herself where she would be out in the country and she could see the weeds and the timber and the dog," Dr. Macdonald said.[15] At those times, Galya said she didn't see herself as a woman, but more like "a big 'He-Man' out hunting."[16]

Galya also said she had visions and claimed to have been in the Louvre Museum in Paris many times. She also mentioned the statues that had walked down from their pedestals in church to converse with her. "I was pleased as punch. I felt like I belonged to something," she told Dr. Macdonald.[17]

Galya admitted that she had tried to commit suicide more times than she could remember. She also said she had taken numerous drugs, including methamphetamines and barbiturates, and that she had been addicted to morphine in the late 1950s. She said she once fought off a man who was trying to abduct her by breaking a flashlight over his head and then running over his body with her car. She scanned the newspapers for days afterward, looking for some mention about the incident, but nothing was ever reported.

As the noon hour approached, Dr. Macdonald reached his conclusions. "Now, reviewing all this material, I think there could be no question Mrs. Tannenbaum is, indeed, a very sick woman."[18] But she was not a schizophrenic, nor did she suffer from multiple personality disorder or manic depression, he said. "I didn't see at any time from what she told me that she really has a true flight of ideas, elated moods, the constant activity that is so highly characteristic of the manic state."[19]

Instead, Dr. Macdonald diagnosed Galya with three personality disorders: hysteria, passive-aggressiveness, and sociopathy. "Let me define what I mean by hysterical personality. Hysterical personalities usually are women who are inclined to be rather self-centered, egocentric, immature people who show shallow moods," he testified.

They may be very dramatic, swinging moods from depression to feeling on top of the world and yet there is a superficial quality to these moods. You sometimes get the feeling these people really don't experience the depth of feeling, which they show. Often these people show dramatic attention-seeking behavior. . . . Finally, they tend to be very dependent, commanding people. As I look at Mrs. Tannenbaum, I think that in many ways she is very self-centered and in very many ways a very immature woman . . . she seems almost intent on attracting attention to herself.[20]

Galya's passive-aggressiveness, he testified, was evident in the way she resisted his questions. "Instead of expressing her aggression very directly, she is negative. For example, in talking to her, she would make it very difficult for you to get information. It was typical of a passive-aggressive person. Finally, you get the information, but it's only after a very great effort."[21]

Dr. Macdonald didn't go into sociopathy in detail on the witness stand, but in *The Murderer and His Victim,* he defines sociopaths as "social misfits who from an early age prove to be a problem to themselves and others."[22] Sociopaths lack the capacity for empathy and are often callous and devoid of affection. They go from job to job, unable to hold a position for long. They can't tolerate frustration and this inability can lead to many antisocial acts. "Egocentric and immature, they constitute an individualistic, rebellious group, intolerant of discipline and of the legal and social restrictions of everyday life," he writes.[23] "They show a lack of foresight which is almost beyond belief, yet may score well on intelligence tests."

The sociopathic murderer, he continues, may experience no guilt, but often "commits his crime in such a manner as to ensure his detection. . . . His conscience would appear to permit commission of the crime, yet demand punishment for the forbidden act. The apparent absence of guilt, or alternatively the inability of the individual to utilize such feelings in the control of his behavior is one of the hallmarks of sociopathy."[24]

Finally, Dr. Macdonald indicated he was done with his testimony. "Does this complete the findings of your examination?" W. Douglas Watson asked.

"I think so, yes," responded Dr. Macdonald.

"As a result of your examination, have you formed an opinion as to whether at the time of the alleged crime, that is on or about July 30th, 1969 . . . the defendant was capable of distinguishing right from wrong with respect to those acts and was capable of choosing a right and refraining from doing a wrong?"

"Yes."

"What is that opinion?"

"That she was able to choose the right and was able to distinguish right from wrong and capable of choosing right and refraining from doing the wrong."

"Thank you, Doctor," Watson responded. "I have no further questions."[25]

★   ★   ★

When the judge recessed for lunch, John Kokish reviewed his morning's notes and organized his cross-examination. Although Dr. Macdonald insisted Galya didn't fit the profile of a manic-depressive patient, Kokish intended to prove him wrong. When the judge, the attorneys, and the spectators returned to the courtroom, Dr. Macdonald again took his seat at the witness stand and John Kokish approached him.

"Now, you stated, Dr. Macdonald, that Mrs. Tannenbaum is a very sick woman. Just how sick do you think she is?"

"Well, just as the words say, very sick. I think that it is not an acute illness that she has. I think her condition fluctuates, but I think this is a sickness that involves her whole character and I think she has been sick for many, many years."

"Now, if Mrs. Tannenbaum was alleged to have killed someone, would you have found her legally insane?" asked Kokish.

"Well, I would have to know the circumstances, but if the circumstances were consistent with the kinds of psychopathology I have described, I probably would say it."

"You would say she was insane?"

"Yes."

"In other words," Kokish continued, "if a person whom she had been dependent upon and had rejected her and she had killed him, she would then be legally insane?"

"Yes. I am speculating, mind you, but I think there would be circumstances in which I would say, yes, she was insane."[26]

Over the strong objections from the prosecutor, Kokish was able to get into the record Galya's numerous hospitalizations. The records were difficult to obtain because Galya had provided different names and ages to hospital clerks.[27]

Dr. Macdonald dismissed many of Galya's stories as simply fantasies designed to draw attention to herself. "What do you think happens when you begin to break through this web?" Kokish asked.

"Two things happen," responded Dr. Macdonald. "I think that she becomes angry and impatient with you and I think that she even becomes more evasive."[28]

Kokish asked Dr. Macdonald if Galya's case had been "disturbing" him.

"Yes. I seldom spend as much time as I did examining Mrs. Tannenbaum."

"Why?" asked Kokish.

"Well it was partly a consequence of her evasiveness on certain issues; that was one factor, but another factor was that I was concerned about the decision as to whether she was legally sane or insane. It's not been one of those decisions that you can make in a relatively short period of time as you can with some persons who appear before the criminal courts."

"It was a borderline case?" asked John Kokish.

"It was a difficult case," the psychiatrist responded.[29]

John Kokish continued to question Dr. Macdonald's findings, but the psychiatrist remained unshakable. Finally, Kokish told the judge he had no more questions. Dr. Macdonald had been on the witness stand all day. The judge called a recess, saying the trial would resume at nine o'clock the following day.

The following morning, July 9, 1970, the prosecution called a third-year psychiatric resident named David L. Garver to the witness stand. Dr. Garver shared Dr. Macdonald's conclusions, testifying that he had interviewed Galya for a total of twelve hours.[30] Dr. Garver said the emotional and physical abuse that Galya had suffered during her childhood created such a sense of inadequacy and depression in her that she compensated by inventing a fantasy life. "She is fully aware at all times that she is playing a role; that this role is—that it is a fantasy which serves considerable purpose, namely of relieving this sense of inadequacy and depression."[31]

Galya, he continued, tried to escape her psychological distress by searching for men who would take care of her. She would do anything to keep them, including becoming pregnant. She also tried to bind people to her by doing favors for them. "Mrs. Tannenbaum attempts to facilitate people caring about her very much, I think, by doing everything she can to please them."[32]

Like Dr. Macdonald, Dr. Garver also found Galya to be extremely evasive when she was asked direct questions and she became angry when he tried to control the examination. But when she was allowed free rein, she related her story "happily and in a coherent and very detailed manner." Dr. Garver said he also did not believe Galya was manic-depressive, but her personality disorders—hysteria, sociopathy, and passive-aggressiveness—could have had an effect on her willpower and thus impaired her ability to choose right over wrong.

"Do you feel, Doctor, that a personality disorder can be as disabling as a psychosis?" asked Kokish.[33]

"Yes."

"Do you feel Mrs. Tannenbaum—you stated Mrs. Tannenbaum is a very sick woman?"

"That's right."

At the conclusion of Dr. Garver 's testimony, the state rested its case. During a hearing in Judge Barnard's chambers, Kokish moved for acquittal. The judge denied the motion.

After lunch, it was Kokish's turn to put on his defense. He began by calling people who knew Galya in an effort to illustrate the range and depth of her delusions.

The first was Paul Morris, a Boulder attorney who had worked with Galya from July to November 1968 on the Lake Valley Estates project. Morris testified that Galya said she knew Gov. John Rockefeller and the artist, Mark Chagall. She also confided that part of her job as a government agent had been to eliminate Communists. "Rather than bringing them to trial, she would exterminate them," he testified.[34] Morris said he didn't believe she actually killed people, but was unsure about her other claims.

"At times she tells a very convincing story. It is something you don't totally believe, but at times you don't totally disbelieve," he testified.[35]

Next up was Rebecca Haynes, who described Galya's behavior in jail. "She was a very frightened individual. The type of person who must have someone to cling to. In this particular case, she chose me."[36] Haynes testified that when she was busy with another inmate or employee, Galya would pout. "There were times when she was extremely over-wrought and she would cry and hang on to me desperately like a child will its mother."[37]

Zdenek Cerveny then took his place in the witness stand. John Kokish asked him what Thomas Riha had told him about Galya.

"I was told by him and her that she was the person who helped me to the United States."

"And did your uncle believe it?"

"Yes, he did."

"Did you believe that at that time?"

"For a time, yes."[38]

Cerveny testified that Galya told him she knew President Nixon and his daughter, Tricia, that she had millions of dollars stashed away, and that she had "eliminated" numerous people.

"Who were these people she was eliminating? Double agents?" asked Kokish.

"Mostly, yes," Cerveny responded.[39] He also testified that Galya took frequent trips to North Vietnam and Mexico.

"What was she doing in North Vietnam?" Kokish asked.

"Getting agents out of trouble," he responded.[40]

In August 1969—after Gus Ingwersen died from sodium cyanide poisoning and before Barbara Egbert was killed with potassium cyanide—Cerveny said Galya became extremely ill, experiencing cramps and fainting spells.

"Did she almost fall on Becky once?" John Kokish asked.

"Yes," he responded.[41]

(Cerveny wasn't asked on the witness stand to speculate what caused Galya's illness, but he said in an interview that he thinks Galya may have inadvertently poisoned herself with cyanide. "She called me and said, 'I'm very sick. I think I might not live.' That was after she poisoned somebody. I think she mishandled the poison she used.")[42]

Cerveny testified that Galya talked incessantly.

"How much did she talk?" asked Kokish.

"Almost all the time," responded Cerveny.

"Even when the television was on, she talked, didn't she?"

"Oh, she wasn't interested in television."[43]

John Kokish then called Eleanor Williamson, Galya's landlady, to the witness stand. Mrs. Williamson said she had rented the 248 Logan Street bungalow to Galya for about two years. One day, Galya called her and asked her to cement over an area in the basement. "She felt that there were dead bodies buried there," Mrs. Williamson testified.

"Did she explain why she thought there were dead bodies buried there?" asked Kokish.

"A doctor had owned the house before we had it," responded Williamson.

"Because a doctor was living in the house, there were dead bodies, is that what she felt?"

"Perhaps so, I don't know."[44]

Galya's ten-year-old son, Jimmy, was the next witness. After the judge admonished the boy to tell the truth, he raised his right hand and was sworn in. Jimmy was asked to identify his mother in the courtroom and pointed to Galya. Jimmy testified that his mother told him she was an army general and often took trips to Vietnam to take pictures. She also owned a special car, he testified.

"What is that car like, Jimmy?"

"It has built-in guns and bullet-proof glass."

"Built-in guns and bullet-proof glass?"

"Uh-huh and reinforced steel."[45]

When it was prosecutor W. Douglas Watson's turn to cross-examine the boy, he asked, "When your mother talked about going to Vietnam and about bullet-proof cars and things like this, is she just sort of kidding you, you think?" he asked.

"No."

"You think she is really serious? Does she really mean this or is she telling you a story?"

"I think she really means it."[46]

Watson hastily concluded his cross-examination and sat down. The judge then called a thirty-minute recess.

★ ★ ★

Upon reconvening, John Kokish called Dr. John Hilton, his primary rebuttal witness. Like Dr. Macdonald, Dr. Hilton had an impressive résumé and had interviewed hundreds of criminal defendants over the course of his career. He had privileges at all of Denver's major hospitals and had served for thirty-five years on the Denver Lunacy Commission.[47] He interviewed Galya thirty-three times and spent many hours with her.

He divided her life into three periods—when she was Gloria McPherson; when she was Galya Zakharovna; and when she was Mrs. Tannenbaum. Dr. Hilton felt Galya suffered from a "serious and deep sociopathic personality disturbance" stemming from her deprived and abused childhood.[48] Grafted onto that personality were hysteria and manic depression.

Galya's manic depression, he said, began in the late 1940s, became "florient or well-blown" in the 1950s, and progressed to hypomania on two occasions—in 1965 and in 1969. "In my opinion she was in a state of hypomania during those two periods of her life. Four years ago when Becky was born and last year."[49]

Galya's "colonel" persona was a delusion—not a fantasy—which emerged during a period of hypomania, he testified. Accompanying the delusion was a sense of enormous power and infallibility. As Galya's hypomania diminished, the delusion went away.

"She could look back and say, well, that wasn't really that?" asked Kokish.

"Yes. That is what has happened. She sometimes cannot understand how it happened but she knows it happened."[50]

Dr. Hilton also said Galya's frequent suicide attempts coincided with the depressive phase of her illness. Trying to kill herself with bichloride of mercury in 1954 was the "ultimate in poor judgment of a way out of things."

"Is it quite deadly?" asked Kokish.

"It is such a horrible death," he responded.[51] (Bichloride of mercury can shut down the kidneys and cause extensive damage to other internal organs.)

Dr. Hilton was asked how sociopathy fit into her illness.

"She is a sociopath who has a mental illness," Dr. Hilton said. "She has a sociopathic personality, a disturbance since she was a child."[52]

Dr. Hilton said Galya was in the throes of the manic phase of her illness when she chartered the flight to San Antonio and her willpower and her ability to distinguish right from wrong were greatly impaired. "Whatever she needed to do or thought she needed to do would be the right thing whether it was the wrong thing or not. She was unable to refrain from doing wrong."[53]

"Have you found evidence of paranoid thinking?"

"Yes, sir. This extends to her family. She despises them—there is something wrong with everyone in her family except her children—and it extends to people around her."

"How about Mr. Cerveny who testified yesterday?"

"He has done her wrong in spite of the many things she did to help him," he testified. "Mr. Gillies is another individual to whom she directs this paranoid thinking. He runs to the police. She says, 'The things I could have done wrong are not the things they accuse me of doing. It's part of a plot and the Boulder District Attorney is in on the plot."[54]

When Dr. Hilton finished his testimony, John Kokish called Dr. Bradford Murphey to the witness stand. Dr. Murphey also had had a long productive career, including a stint as a professor in the psychiatry department at Harvard University. He had practiced for forty years and written numerous papers, including a treatise on Munchausen syndrome, a condition named after an eighteenth-century German nobleman in which patients make up physical ailments to get attention.

Dr. Murphey spent only a few hours examining Galya and confessed that he didn't particularly enjoy assessing the mental health of criminal defendants. Unlike Dr. Macdonald, he conducted a free-form interview with Galya. She talked steadily, sometimes crying, other times becoming indignant and angry.

"Initially, in the first half hour, I felt that I was dealing with a sociopath. I was not at all certain as to whether she was trying to mislead me or not, but as her unfolding of ideas continued over that hour and a half, some of her notions were so bizarre, unusual and strange, that I felt that she was one of those individuals who is unable to think straight because of a disorder which we usually call manic-depressive insanity. I felt the story as she told it, indicated there had been periods when she was depressed to the point of irrationality, to the point of trying definitely to take her life. I felt that there were other periods where she was so expansive, so exalted in her feelings and her notions were so bizarre about having multiple personalities, that I was unable to reconcile that with my first impression of a psychopathic personality and came to the conclusion that she must have been at various times in her life incompetent by virtue of a disease we call manic-depressive insanity."[55]

Dr. Murphey said that throughout his examination he was aware that Galya might have been lying to him and he watched for evidence of deception. "I am always aware of that when I examine a patient who is charged with a crime. I came to the conclusion that although much of what she said was unrealistic and probably not true, it was not a deliberate kind of lying. It was the talk and the behavior of a sick woman. So I ended up with the diagnosis in my own mind of an individual who has been brutalized and abused as a baby and child, who had as a result developed a poorly integrated personality that made it difficult for her to make life's adjustments and that somewhere along the way she became ill with manic-depressive insanity; sometimes with depressive periods and sometimes with periods of hypomania."[56]

Dr. Murphey was of the opinion that Galya was unable to distinguish between right and wrong on July 30, 1969, the day of the charter flight to San Antonio, because of her mental illness. "I do believe that," he testified.[57]

During the cross-examination, W. Douglas Watson suggested that Dr. Murphey may have been hoodwinked.

"Is it possible, doctor, that she could just be an imposter?"

"Well, I would hate to say anything is impossible, although in this case, I am of the opinion that she is sick rather than an imposter."[58]

After Dr. Murphey's testimony was concluded, it was the prosecution's turn to call rebuttal witnesses. The first was Carol Word, the young, attractive graduate student who lunched with Thomas Riha daily. (Word loathed and feared Galya. In a 2013 interview several months before she died, she said, "I thought she was very evil, the most evil person I had ever met. I thought Thomas must be crazy hanging out with her. I thought she was going to get him in big trouble and she did.")[59]

Word testified that after Thomas disappeared, she went to Galya's home on perhaps ten to fifteen occasions. She perused Galya's library shelves, which contained law books, natural history books, art books, and almost two dozen psychology books.

"Did you have occasion to, you know, discuss the field of psychology and psychiatry with Mrs. Tannenbaum?" asked Watson.

"Yes, in a rather cursory manner as it related to Dr. Riha."

"Do you remember the substance of that discussion?"

"Well, I think that I remarked on her collection of psychology books and she said she had always been very interested because of the different employment she had had; that she had found it necessary to be able to size up people quickly and accurately and one could not do this without extensive knowledge of psychology."[60]

Finally, the prosecutor recalled Dr. Macdonald to rebut the testimony of Dr. Hilton and Dr. Murphey. Dr. Macdonald said his two colleagues had erred in their clinical diagnoses. Galya was not manic-depressive nor did she suffer from delusions. Rather, she made up outrageous stories to attract attention to herself and knew perfectly well they were false.

Dr. Macdonald said patients in the manic phase display far more excitement than Galya exhibited. If they do paint, their work is so bad that it could never be shown in an art gallery. "I think that, in fact, she is an imposter."[61]

John Kokish pounced on the word, "imposter." "When did you arrive at that imposter theory? You never mentioned that on direct examination."

"I did not use that term earlier," Dr. Macdonald responded. "I did say sociopathic personality and I think many imposters are sociopathic personalities."

Finally, the lawyers for the two sides rested their cases. The testimony had taken three days. There were still final arguments to make, but it was Friday afternoon and the judge decided to reconvene on July 15, 1970.

★ ★ ★

A week later, the two sides met again. Galya took her usual seat next to John Kokish and W. Douglas Watson sat across from them. The two lawyers then delivered their final arguments while Judge Barnard listened. After they finished, the judge said he was going to spend the next two to three hours deliberating and would reconvene the court at three o'clock that afternoon to deliver his verdict.

Before leaving the courtroom, the judge lambasted prosecutor W. Douglas Watson for claiming that the case involved the simple difference between right and wrong. "If it were all that simple then all of the words which were spoken by all of the witnesses were actually wasted because it is not a simple thing to determine the right from the wrong."[62]

When the trial reconvened that afternoon, the courtroom was crowded with spectators and reporters. The judge delivered his verdict quickly, saying he found the defendant, Galya Tannenbaum, suffering from a mental illness and that he had a reasonable doubt that she could distinguish between right or wrong on the day when she forged Thomas Riha's name to the $330 check. "It is the determination of this court on this particular case that the defendant was, on July 30, 1969, in respect to the act charged in the information, incapable of choosing the right and refraining from the wrong by reason of the destruction of her willpower as a result of her impairment of mind by disease."[63]

The judge sidestepped the question of whether Galya was a sociopath, hysteric, antisocial personality, or a manic-depressive. Instead, he noted that all four psychiatrists agreed "that the defendant was mentally ill and that this had an effect on her 'willpower.'"[64]

He pronounced Galya insane and ordered her committed indefinitely to the state mental hospital in Pueblo, a small southern Colorado city located about a hundred miles from Denver.

Law enforcement officials breathed a collective sigh of relief.

18 ★ THE SMELL OF ALMONDS

Galya leaned her head against the backseat of the sheriff's car and looked out the window. On either side of the highway were cottonwood trees, pale green prairies, and the watery shadows of tumbling, cumulous clouds. She was numb and tired, her skin sallow from being locked up in jail for six months. She had always pretended to be older than she really was and now she did resemble a woman in her mid-fifties instead of someone who was not yet forty. It was July 17, 1970, a year and four months since Thomas had disappeared.

As the automobile drew closer to the city of Pueblo, Galya gazed indifferently at the San Juans breaking on the southwestern horizon. She no doubt thought of her younger children, Jimmy and Becky. Normally, criminals ordered to the State Hospital remained for two to three years. With three more forgery cases and a burglary case pending against her, Galya realized that it was entirely possible that her children would grow up without her. The idea was painful to contemplate. Now that she was being transferred to an institution one hundred miles from Denver, she knew that her visits with Becky and Jimmy would be infrequent, if at all.

Hearing the crunch of tires winding up a driveway, she gazed at the nineteenth-century institution that would be her home indefinitely. The old buildings were surrounded by rolling green lawns and flower beds and were constructed from red brick that looked much like the brick used in construction of her grandfather's house in St. Louis.

Established in 1879, the Colorado State Hospital for many decades had served as a vast poor farm for the homeless, the elderly, and the severely mentally ill. Scattered across the five-thousand-plus acres were dairy farms, pig farms, chicken farms, vegetable gardens, classrooms, kitchens, cafeterias, dormitories, hydrotherapy pools, occupational and recreational therapy rooms, day halls, a medical and surgical unit, a nurse's home, and administrative offices.

In 1960, the average patient stay was sixteen years.[1] After such a long time, many patients no longer had family or friends in the outside world and wound up being buried in small plots on the hospital grounds, arms folded over their chests, a toothbrush or comb stuck in their pocket. By 1969, the deinstitutionalization movement was under way and the wards were being emptied out—whether the patients were ready or not.

The State Hospital had undergone much reorganization. At the time of Galya's arrival, it was organized into nine geographic divisions that represented various cities and regions of Colorado. In addition, it had wards set aside for children, the elderly, alcoholics, and a high-security ward for male defendants accused of crimes and judged to be insane. No such ward existed for female Criminal Court commitments like Galya. Instead they were mixed in with women who had entered the hospital voluntarily or had been committed in a civil proceeding.

At the same time that the hospital was releasing patients, the institution was experiencing a surge in "criminal court commitments." To accommodate the new arrivals, male patients from the high-security unit were being transferred to less secure wards. Escapes were common and the newspapers were filled with lurid stories of patients who had gone on to commit violent crimes, including rape, murder, and kidnapping.

Although the hospital had its own police force, security was lax. Patients and visitors were not thoroughly searched nor were packages and briefcases opened and inspected. Some patients—including the Criminal Court commitments—had off-ground privileges, which allowed them to work in Pueblo or go on day trips. When contraband was smuggled in, it was nearly impossible to find in the old buildings. Alcohol, drugs, and weapons were hidden in the dropped ceilings, beneath toilets and wash basins, and behind bricks and radiators.

Hospital superintendent Dr. Charles Meredith acknowledged in a deposition that parts of the hospital were quite open. "You could, if you wanted to, walk onto an open ward. You would be asked who you are and treated cordially, but you wouldn't be searched necessarily."[2]

After the sheriff's deputies had turned Galya over to the custody of the State Hospital, a physician conducted a cursory physical examination, did some psychological tests to rule out organic brain damage, and roughed out a preliminary treatment plan. She was assigned the patient number 50815 and escorted to a small female dormitory on Ward 69 of the Northeast Division. The ward was shaped like an *L*, with female dormitories at one end, male dormitories at the other, and a communal day hall in between. The female patients on Ward 69 included drug addicts, severe schizophrenics, manic-depressives, and individuals who had suffered psychotic breakdowns.

Because of the widespread publicity surrounding the Thomas Riha case, hospital administrators considered Galya one of their most "notorious" Criminal Court commitments.[3] Worried that she might escape and embarrass the institution, two staff members were assigned to watch over her. Staffers were also instructed to censor her mail, specifically looking for correspondence addressed to the local newspaper or "disturbing" letters sent to her children.

Dr. Macdonald and Dr. Hilton had advised hospital officials of Galya's previous suicide attempts, but there was really nothing the hospital staff could do except monitor her. If Galya did seem genuinely intent upon committing suicide, a green sheet would be placed in her chart and she could be checked at fifteen-minute intervals or even placed in restraints in a sequestered room until the danger passed.

A couple of days after she arrived, she was summoned to the office of Dr. David Olenik, a staff psychiatrist who was just finishing up his residency at the University of Colorado medical school. Dr. Olenik was putting in a year of service at the State Hospital in exchange for a loan that he had received to help defray his medical education. His schedule was demanding; he oversaw anywhere from fifty to seventy patients, made rounds every day, wrote up medical orders, conducted group psychotherapy sessions, taught a course on psychopathology, and was involved in patient aftercare. Dr. Olenik was far too busy to conduct one-on-one therapy sessions with patients, but he did make time to meet with Galya and her team leaders. Galya took an immediate dislike to Dr. Olenik. When he was late for an appointment, she became "infuriated, unbelievably angry," he would say.[4]

It didn't take Galya long to figure out that her mail was being censored. She circumvented the censorship by sending her letters through her defense attorney, John Kokish, which weren't opened because of attorney-client privilege. She also quickly discovered that other patients had access to more activities than she did and became resentful. "I am in fact not treated as a patient here but as a prisoner—no medication, no program, and I've seen Dr. Olenik exactly 15 min. in 2 weeks," she wrote to Dr. Hilton. "I'm certainly not a danger to anyone else to be sure—if anyone really knew me they'd know I was the biggest softie in the West."[5]

Two weeks after her arrival, she attended a formal staff meeting with a team of healthcare workers who would be responsible for her care. They included psychiatric technicians, nurses, occupational and recreational therapists, a psychologist, and a social worker. Dr. Olenik began the session by asking her what kind of emotional problems she perceived herself as having and what issues she wanted to work on during her hospital stay. "She really didn't see that she had any emotional problems," the psychiatrist recalled. "She saw that her problem was getting out. We talked a little bit about her episodes of depression and her chronic problems with men, but she really didn't see them as internal psychiatric problems that she wanted to do anything about."[6]

After interviewing Galya and reviewing her medical history, Dr. Olenik concluded that Galya was not insane but did have serious mental and emotional problems. In a deposition taken in 1973 by John Kokish, Dr. Olenik said he had decided to restrict Galya's activities so that she would have time to reflect and confront some of her deep-seated psychological problems:

You know, one would ask Galya, "What are you troubled by?" and she would say, "I'm troubled because I'm here." Well, there's nothing therapeutically to work with. As you well know, one of the hallmarks of antisocial personalities is a low frustration tolerance. And if she's not given her demands immediately, this type of person becomes anxious, angry and depressed. And I think that we worked under the theory that the anger and rage of the depression comes from an earlier time in her life. Again her childhood conflicts have been well documented by other psychiatrists as well as by myself. And the very general and oversimplified theory is that all the pain from these unresolved earlier conflicts got, so to speak, acted out in antisocial activity. And if she was in a milieu where she felt some anxiety and had to look inside and see what she was really feeling and struggling with, that she could achieve some resolution of those internal conflicts and wouldn't have to act them out in a maladaptive way getting herself in jail. So this is how we tried, if you will, to affect some kind of internal change in her so that when she was ever released from the hospital, she wouldn't have to repeat twenty years of antisocial behavior.[7]

Galya was not totally isolated nor did she have to sit in her room all day doing nothing. She could read, write letters, and paint. She considered the hospital's painting supplies inferior and pleaded with friends and family to send her better-quality paper and oil-based paints. Galya also received individual psychotherapy and attended group therapy meetings with other male and female patients who had been committed by the Criminal Courts. As the weeks passed, she was granted more privileges. She participated in a weight-reduction program, studied Spanish, and took a course on American history.[8] She also returned to the Catholic religion, going to Confession and Communion and attending Mass on Sunday mornings.[9]

The medical staff found her difficult to manage and grew concerned about the strife she created between patients. "Galya had an incredible ability to remember what she told everybody, and she would tell one thing to one person and the opposite to somebody else and soon they would be fighting with each other," Dr. Olenik recalled.[10]

She made sexual advances toward at least one man, urging him to divorce his wife. She terrified others, saying they could wind up drowned, with their heads in toilets. Dr. Olenik admitted that Galya even scared him at times. "I think it was very well put by a patient, that if you looked into her eyes, that she was a person who could possibly kill without compunction and that she had a very cold, icy, feelingless look about her."[11]

Galya took a new name for herself—Donna T—and bragged about her important contacts on the outside.[12] She made grandiose promises to some of the more vulnerable patients, telling one young girl she had Mafia contacts and could arrange a scholarship for her to study in France. During therapy sessions, she often wanted to talk about her alleged crimes, but Dr. Olenik discouraged such talk. "She initially tried to tempt us to talk about whether she did, or didn't, murder Thomas Riha. And I said, 'You know, that really wasn't my province, I wasn't the judge or a policeman and that really wasn't what she was there for.'"[13]

Two months after her arrival on Ward 69, Galya met with members of the Special Review Committee, a panel of healthcare workers who interviewed all patients who had been committed to the hospital by the Criminal Courts. A psychiatrist named Dr. Karl Waggener conducted the hearing. He questioned her aggressively, but Galya remained remarkably poised during the interrogation.

"Where do you think Thomas is—if he's not in the grave?" he asked.

"I think he is somewhere in the Soviet Union right now."

"Why this disappearing bit?"

"I don't know. I know the tension in the house was terrible."

"You've told some pretty wild yarns. Almost so ridiculous as to where the average person just wouldn't buy them. Did you think people believed all that?"

"No," she responded.

"Why did you tell them then?"

"Doctor, I really don't know."

"Tell us about how your mother mistreated you as a child. Did she beat you, tie you down to a termite-ridden post, and all that?"

"I don't know about termites, but I was put in the basement and tied to a post so I couldn't get upstairs and kick on the door."

"Why would she have treated you that way?"

"I wasn't a boy for one thing."

"She ultimately got several boys. Couldn't she have kind of let up on you a little?"

"It didn't happen."

"Why did you make the plea of not guilty by reason of insanity?"

"Everything started to fall apart so bad."

"Has it been a tendency for you to lie?"

"Yes."

"For what reason?"

"What do you mean?"

"Why do you need to lie? Why don't you just speak truthfully? Was it just to take a drab life and make it interesting?" he asked.

"Could be," she responded.[14]

By the end of the session, Dr. Waggener had developed a distaste for Galya and wrote in his clinical notes, "Mrs. Tannenbaum exudes a relatively cold feeling in the examiner."[15] He added, "A remarkable change in her affect occurred when asked the question whether she has ever murdered anyone. At that point, her eyes lit up and she smiled significantly."

Dr. Waggener and the Review Committee concluded Galya was too dangerous to be allowed off grounds and supported Dr. Olenik's decision to curtail her activities. Angered by their decision, Galya vented her frustrations to a patient named Robert George McIntyre, who had been sent to Pueblo after he was diagnosed as a schizophrenic and found criminally insane.[16]

Galya and McIntyre had discussions in the day hall that sometimes went on until three or four o'clock in the morning. She told him she was "sane as a doorbell" and took the insanity plea to keep from going to prison.[17] Despite their friendly conversations, McIntyre thought prison was exactly where she belonged. Each day he received three tablets of Mellaril, an antipsychotic drug and tranquilizer. Instead of taking the pills, he gave them to Galya. Twice, he saw her swallowing them. She had other pills in her possession, including a white pill about an inch and a half long, which she said she kept stashed behind a loose brick on the ward.

Galya told McIntyre she had poisoned two men and a woman with cyanide. One of her victims, she said, was Thomas Riha.[18] Galya said she wrapped his body in a plastic bag and placed it in a Denver sewer. Galya told another patient named David Gillard that a body could be disposed of by dissolving it in acid and then just letting it "float down the bathtub," a possible reference to a vat of chemicals found in Gus's garage.[19]

One day, when she was arguing with several other patients on the ward, a young psychiatric technician named Henry Madrid intervened. Galya looked at him appraisingly and decided to make him her confidant. Madrid was one of half a dozen psych techs assigned to the ward. He was a young married man who was in the process of getting his bachelor's degree. After going through a nine-month, in-hospital training program, he had been licensed as a psychiatric technician and had just been promoted to senior psych tech.

Although Dr. Olenik thought Madrid was cocky and overconfident, he nevertheless gave him permission to work with Galya. He warned Madrid of Galya's manipulative personality and her hostility toward men and instructed him to record his encounters with her on her medical chart. Madrid made only one extended entry.

Galya and Madrid began having marathon discussions in the day hall. Seeing them engaged in such intense conversation, other staff members thought Galya was finally opening up and confronting her problems. What they didn't know was that Galya had put Madrid in a horrifying bind that he felt he couldn't discuss with anyone.

Once or twice a month, she would come to him and tell him that she was going to kill herself. Then she would tell Madrid that it was his job to talk her out of it. "She always gave me deadlines to meet. She'd set up a date and it was usually a week or two away and she would say, 'It's up to you to work it out,'" Madrid would say in a deposition taken in 1973 by John Kokish.[20]

Madrid should have reported the suicide threats to his superiors, including Dr. Olenik, but Galya warned him that if anyone learned of her threats, she'd kill herself instantly.

"Did you believe she would do it?" Kokish asked.

"That was the chance that I had to take. And I didn't feel it was fair to gamble with her life for some mistake I would make."[21]

Galya also warned Henry that she would not tolerate being put in restraints. "If I'm restrained in any way, don't even turn your head because I'll be dead and you will have done it," Galya threatened.[22]

When Madrid asked Galya how she was going to kill herself, she said she possessed a poison that could kill her in three minutes. "I had three minutes and she said she'd never kill herself unless I was there. On my day off, or a holiday, she said, 'Don't worry. Just worry when you come on.'"[23]

Galya showed Henry various pills and a capsule containing a white powdery substance. Madrid managed to persuade her to flush most of the stuff down the toilet, but he didn't report the drugs to his supervisors because Galya said she would kill Madrid and his entire family, as well as Dr. Olenik and several other psych techs.

"She threatened you?" asked John Kokish.

"That's correct. Anybody that kind of crossed her the wrong way, she said they could be eliminated just like that."

"Do you believe she could do that?"

"I wasn't about to test it out."[24]

"Did she indicate the drugs were dangerous?"

"She did."

"What did she say they were?"

"She said, 'This stuff will kill you in no seconds flat.'"[25]

Madrid worked hard to keep Galya's trust while simultaneously trying to encourage her to dispose of the drugs. "So I was working kind of two ways. I didn't want to depress her so bad that I might cause her to commit suicide."[26]

"What justified your actions in your mind for not reporting the incidents of drugs?" Kokish asked.

"She says anybody gets in her way, that's it. She says she's a pro at it. She says she has enough experience to not be able to point the finger at herself, that she can point it at anybody she wants."[27]

Madrid also came to believe that Galya was capable of murder and had, in fact, murdered people. He grew afraid of her, but tried to suppress the fear because he knew she could pick up on it.

"Did she indicate that she had killed people in the past?" asked John Kokish.

"Numerous people."[28]

Madrid said that Galya alluded to killing several women with a poison-laced drink. She added that she hadn't really murdered them—"I just poured the stuff."[29] She made a similar statement about a man she killed. "When she killed that one dude with the gun, she said, 'Well I didn't tell him to step in front of the gun. I was just aiming it and he stepped in front and I pulled the trigger.' She said, 'My finger slipped.'"[30]

"Did you believe her?"

"What proof did I have to disbelieve her? What proof did I have to believe her?"

"Did Mrs. Tannenbaum strike you as a truthful person in your experiences with her?"

"In that respect, yes, because this is how she threatened me. She put that word you are talking about—that fear—in me because she says, 'Let any of these things go out and that's it for you, baby.'"[31]

Galya hinted to Madrid that she had buried Thomas Riha's body in a wooded area near the town of Aspen, Colorado. "She drew this painting that was out in the woods and it's got a little red bird on it and she was always saying, 'Here lies my secret.'"[32]

★ ★ ★

On October 29, 1970, Galya was taken back to Denver for another sanity hearing in connection with the charge that she forged documents related to the sale of Thomas Riha's Volkswagen. This time it was a jury—not a judge—that would render the verdict. Back in the noisy confines of the Denver County Jail, Galya felt bleak and depressed. The blankets, she would write, were passed "from body to body, with no cleaning, sterilization or de-bugging in between."[33] The lights were left on all night long and the constant slamming of the steel doors kept her awake. She wept and cried, telling several of the matrons she didn't want to go on living. She told one guard that she had cyanide stashed at the State Hospital beneath a piece of furniture. She told another she hid cyanide behind a hospital filing cabinet. To a third, she said she had cyanide taped to a desk.

During a search of her Denver jail cell, a cone-shaped packet of pills was found in her clothing bag.[34] Galya denied knowledge of the pills, saying another inmate must have put them in the bag. Later that evening, when her cell was searched again, an envelope of pills, including ten Mellaril tablets, was found beneath her pillow.[35] Galya shrugged when confronted with the stash, saying pills were easy to come by in the State Hospital.

When jury selection began the next day, Galya took her seat in the courtroom next to John Kokish. She seemed only half awake as attorneys for the two sides began questioning potential jurors. Suddenly, she bent over and vomited into a trash can. The judge immediately halted the trial and the contents of the trash can were seized and submitted to a lab for analysis.

That analysis showed Galya had ingested a mixture of barbiturates, tranquilizers, and Dilantin.[36] A jail official thought Galya obtained the pills from an epileptic female prisoner who rode to court with her that morning on a Denver County Sheriff's Department bus.[37] The judge postponed the trial for a month and Galya was sent back to the State Hospital.

In early December 1970, Galya was returned to Denver, only this time she was incarcerated in the Arapahoe County Jail because the judge thought drugs too easy to come by in the Denver facility. Many of the same expert and lay witnesses took the stand, including Galya's son, Jimmy. After the child testified, the judge called a twenty-minute recess so mother and son could talk privately in his chambers.

Several new witnesses testified, including Eleanor Gale, who worked in public relations at Loretto Heights College. Gale said she went to Galya's home for dinner in the summer of 1969. Galya was wearing heavy gloves and goggles. "She said she was cooking on a laser stove she invented."[38] Eleanor offered to help with the cooking, but Galya refused, saying it was too "dangerous."

Robert Stroessner, the curator at the Denver Art Museum, said Galya attended a fundraising gala in June or July 1969. She was "handsomely dressed" in a pink gown and offered to help the museum raise $1 million for a Rembrandt painting.[39]

The case went to the jury about three o'clock on a Saturday afternoon. During their deliberations, the panel—five men and seven women—argued heatedly. Several wept. By noon on Monday, December 22, 1970, they had reached a unanimous verdict.

Galya, who had her hair pulled back in a severe bun, sat impassively as the judge read the verdict. This time, the jury concluded that Galya was sane on the day she forged documents relating to the sale of Riha's car. But they also strongly believed she was mentally ill and would benefit from hospitalization and treatment.

Galya was returned to the State Hospital. Christmas was only a few days away and the ward had a celebratory feel as packages and cards arrived for patients. The medical staff thought Galya was adjusting to the ward nicely and that the time had come to give her more opportunities to socialize.[40]

In reality, Galya's mental health was deteriorating badly. She continued to boast to her fellow patients that she had killed people and she threatened to kill people in the hospital, including Dr. Olenik.

In late December 1970 or early January 1971, Galya met with Henry Madrid and gave him a package wrapped in two paper towels. She didn't say what was in the package, but told him she kept the material taped beneath a washbasin and could get more if she needed it. Madrid thought it was strychnine or cyanide. "She said, 'Get rid of it.' 'Even smelling this stuff will kill you.' 'There's nothing to get it out of you.'"[41]

Madrid took the package home, rewrapped it, and hid it on the top shelf of his garage behind some boxes. He told no one about it, not even his wife. When Galya asked him about it, he told her that he had disposed of the package. She seemed satisfied with his answer.

As Madrid was returning from dinner one evening, Galya waylaid him and drew him into a small office. She said she had been having dreams they were having sex together and tried to seduce him. Madrid gently pushed her away, reminding her that he was a hospital employee. "And she started crying a little bit, but I must have been standing there a little while talking and I said, 'I can't, Galya, this would blow up everything I'm trying to help you with.'"[42] Galya accepted the explanation, but continued to tease him, urging him to run away with her. She said money was no obstacle for her and they could go to Spain together or perhaps she would buy him a Jaguar.

With Madrid's encouragement, Galya became the unofficial "secretary" for Ward 69 and began typing academic papers for psych techs like Henry Madrid who were attending college. When Dr. Olenik and one of the nursing supervisors learned what she was doing, they thought it gave her too much power over the staff and ordered it stopped. "She was exerting some degree of control over the people who were responsible for taking care of her," Dr. Olenik recalled. "It was a lever that she would have used to extract favors."[43]

On the morning of March 4, 1971, Galya was informed of the decision. She grew angry, telling one staff member she felt like that little girl who had been tied up in the basement so many decades ago. She wrote several letters that day, including one to her daughter and another to John Kokish.

The letter to her daughter is filled with genuine regret. She told her that her only happiness in life came from being with her children, but that financial strain had often ruined their time together. "There were a lot of things I would do differently today in trying to raise you—but when you were very, very small—I had only my personal life experience to rely upon—and it had been *brutal*," she writes. "I deeply *regret* spanking you so much—that it happened was my inability to know of better methods to teach some measure of morality."[44]

Galya's letter to John Kokish contained none of that remorse. Instead she railed out against Dr. Olenik. "Dr. Olenik acts capriciously—he has systematically taken away *everything* that made me feel good about myself. There has NEVER been a valid reason for any of it." She went on to say that she had never killed anyone. "I didn't do Tom—or Gus or Barb in—I went nuts with hurt over losing them." She added, "I suppose this is all academic now anyhow—because I will be free of it all before too many hours elapse— Thanks for your interest—Everyone has what they wanted now—Galya."[45]

The following day, Friday, March 5, Galya seemed uncharacteristically ebullient. Her good spirits continued the following day. She gave a philodendron to a staffer named Eleanor Vierra, asking her to return the vase after Vierra had repotted the plant. Around five o'clock in the afternoon, on her way to dinner, she spotted Henry Madrid. Two new psych techs had taken over Galya's case and she hadn't seen much of him lately. She was late for the evening meal and as she hurried past him, she whispered, "Today's the day. Do you want to talk about it later?"

"Okay," he responded.[46]

About 7:30 P.M., a tech named Dorothy Bell Bailey stopped by Galya's room and asked her if she wanted to attend her square dance lesson that evening. Galya shook her head, saying that she had other things to do. At 9:30 P.M., she met Henry in a conference room on the female side of the ward. She was wearing a sheath dress and green suede shoes with black soles. As she began talking about her kids, she grew morose and sad. To cheer her up, Madrid retrieved a philosophy book they both enjoyed reading and they went over some passages together.

Her mood lightened, then darkened as her thoughts returned to her children. At about 10 P.M., Madrid left the room for fifteen minutes. A psych tech popped her head in and asked Galya what she was doing. "Waiting for Henry," she responded. When Madrid returned, she was still reading the philosophy book. She had purchased a Coca-Cola from a vending machine and asked Henry if he wanted some. He declined.

Galya asked Henry for a cigarette and smoked it leisurely. Then she stood up and went to the bathroom. He heard the toilet flush and water running in the sink. She exited the bathroom, zipping up the front of her dress. She returned to her chair, put one foot up on the coffee table, and they continued to talk. Then she asked for his hand.

"I took it," she muttered. A few moments later, her head dropped back and she began mumbling.

"Oh God, dammit, you took the son of a gun!" Henry yelled. He raced from the room to get help.[47]

Moments later, he returned, accompanied by the nursing supervisor and two female psych techs. All three noticed a sweetish smell, like almonds, in the air.

Galya's head and neck were arched back and a brown substance was foaming from her mouth. Her body was shaking all over and the nurse realized she was convulsing. She loosened Galya's clothing. One aide ran to get oxygen. Another looked around to find out what Galya had swallowed. She saw the empty Coca-Cola can in the trash, shook it, and then dropped it back in the wastebasket.

Henry began preparing a charcoal mixture that would bind with whatever was in Galya's stomach. But the nurse told him not to administer the charcoal until they knew exactly what Galya had ingested.[48] Galya was loaded onto a stretcher and taken to the hospital's medical unit. Her stomach was pumped and she was given fluids, oxygen, and Ritalin. But the resuscitation efforts failed. She slipped into a deep coma and was pronounced dead at 12:40 A.M. on Sunday, March 7, 1971.

★ ★ ★

The letters Galya had written to her daughter and John Kokish reached his office on Saturday and sat unopened until Monday morning. Had Galya mailed the letter to her daughter through normal channels, the medical staff might have opened it and been alerted to her plans to commit suicide. But Galya was determined to kill herself this time. Even Dr. Olenik would describe the incident as a genuine suicide attempt and not a "gesture," which he defined as more of a cry for help than a genuine attempt to end one's life.

Authorities found three notes in Galya's room. Two contained instructions for disposing of her personal effects, including directions that her body be donated to the University of Colorado medical school. The third was a suicide note. In the note, which is dated March 6, 1971, Galya blames Dr. Olenik for her death:

> I hold him singularly responsible. I do show feelings—but I admit they are not exaggerated feelings—and would require a concerned and skilled eye to see. Anyhow I'm free now and beyond being put down again. The many put downs and negative situations here have made it crystal clear that my value as a person is less than nothing, and with the emotional contact with my children prohibited by Dr. Olenik and no one left—there is little point in hurting without an end in sight—or even help in sight. After all, I've been here 8 months now and have nothing but a long line of put downs done out of sheer caprice by the dictator of the ward.[49]

Galya once again proclaimed her innocence in the disappearance of Thomas Riha and the deaths of Gustav Ingwersen and Barbara Egbert. She added that it was her money that was used for the down payment on Riha's house. "After eight months of incarceration, with only myself to rely on for any sort of activity mental or otherwise, and after the sum total of put downs, I cannot go anymore."

On March 7, an autopsy was conducted at a Pueblo hospital. One thousand micrograms of sodium cyanide were found in the gastric contents of her stomach and one hundred micrograms in her blood. Officials later concluded she had ingested close to a gram of sodium cyanide.[50]

Henry Madrid turned over to hospital police the packet Galya had given him. When a technician in the hospital laboratory analyzed the contents, he concluded that it contained eleven grams of potassium cyanide—enough to kill a dozen people. Galya had stashed the package under a refrigerator in the employee lounge.[51]

On March 10, Colorado's lieutenant governor, John Vanderhoof, ordered the Colorado Bureau of Investigation (CBI) to investigate Galya's death. Investigators began their inquiry that day and over the next week interviewed numerous people, including the medical staff on duty the night Galya committed suicide, as well as the hospital's top administrators, the Pueblo County coroner, and other officials. While the CBI officials were in the hospital, a stabbing occurred in the maximum-security unit for male patients and another man escaped after being transferred to a less secure ward.

CBI investigators quickly learned that Henry Madrid had been present at Galya's death. At 7:20 P.M. on the evening of March 10, CBI director John MacIvor and two investigators went to his Pueblo home and conducted a tape-recorded interview. Madrid spoke honestly of his relationship with Galya, telling them of her frequent threats of suicide and why he didn't inform his supervisors. He told them about the package that Galya had given him and said she had also shown him several gelatin capsules containing a white substance that she claimed was cyanide. Madrid admitted that he had violated hospital rules, but he defended his actions, saying he was trying to protect Galya and other members of the medical staff. He was subsequently asked to take a lie detector test—and passed. Galya, he said, made three statements at the time of her death: "I took it." "Give me your hand," and "I didn't kill Riha."[52]

The next day, CBI investigators proceeded to the morgue to view Galya's body. The back of her shoulders and arms, both sides of her neck, and her mouth had a pinkish color. A physician on duty said the color was typical of cyanide poisoning. CBI officials took photographs and hair samples and fingerprinted Galya's right hand. That evening, they did an extensive interview with Dr. Olenik, who explained his reasons for limiting Galya's activities. He conceded that it was entirely possible that Galya had committed suicide because her typing privileges had been rescinded. "She used heavy activity as a method of acting out her frustrations, thus never personally experiencing her true feelings," he said.[53]

The CBI investigators learned at least eight members of the medical staff, including Dr. Olenik, had heard rumors that Galya possessed cyanide. Dr. Olenik discounted the rumors, saying Galya was a "pathological liar." Nevertheless, several searches of the ward had been conducted. In Galya's room, hospital aides found thirty-two aspirin, a sharpened knitting needle, and rubber tubing.[54]

One important question remained unanswered: How did Galya get the cyanide into the hospital? There were several theories. No body cavity search was conducted when she was first admitted to the hospital in July 1970, leading the Pueblo County coroner to believe she had stashed the cyanide in her vagina, which he said was "loose" from a medical condition that she developed while giving birth.[55]

Galya could also have stolen the poison from the hospital laboratory, which stocked both sodium cyanide and potassium cyanide. A CBI investigator had walked unnoticed through the open door of the hospital's laboratory and remained for ten minutes. No one asked for his identification. While he was in the lab, he saw a glass container of potassium cyanide in the back of the room. Later he learned cleaning personnel had keys to the lab and no security was maintained. "Obviously, unknown persons would be able to gain access to this area," he wrote.[56]

Ultimately, CBI investigators were unable to definitely answer the question of where Galya got the cyanide, but they favored the coroner's "loose vagina" theory. "Had the hospital established a strict procedure for searches of all incoming patients, upon admission, that would include body cavity searches, the possibility of patients smuggling contraband into the hospital would be severely hampered."[57] To bolster the theory—and perhaps to protect the State Hospital from a lawsuit—the CBI noted that both forms of cyanide had been discovered in Galya's house at 248 Logan Street.

But Galya had been in custody since February 4, 1970, and it would have been extremely difficult for her to keep such dangerous substances hidden while she was being shuttled between the psychiatric hospital, the Boulder jail, the Denver jail, and various court hearings.

It was also rumored that Galya kept cyanide in a pendant she wore around her neck, but neither hospital officials nor criminal investigators found any such pendant during their searches.

While the CBI officials were conducting their investigation, Dr. David Olenik was doing his own "psychological autopsy." The psychiatrist, aware of the axiom that behind every suicidal wish is a homicidal impulse, knew that Galya's rage at him was no doubt a factor in her decision to kill herself. "It was very, very probable," he would later admit.[58]

When Dr. Olenik talked to Henry Madrid, he was surprised to learn of Galya's frequent suicide threats, her possession of drugs, and the packet she had given him. But Madrid defended his actions, telling Dr. Olenik that he didn't inform him of Galya's threats because he couldn't take a chance that Galya might kill herself or Dr. Olenik. "My disclosing it and you would have been dead because of negligence on my part," Madrid told the psychiatrist. "Maybe you could live with it, but I couldn't."[59]

In retrospect, Dr. Olenik realized that Henry Madrid was not equipped to deal with Galya. "Mr. Madrid was a very strong-headed guy who had difficulty in listening to what I had to say and what other staff had to say about his relationship with Galya. I think that he perceived himself because of his mental health worker status as being a little bit above the average psych tech. And I personally was not impressed with his competence. I feel that he was very overconfident and perhaps in all good faith took a bite of [sic] more than he could chew," he admitted in the deposition taken by John Kokish.[60]

"What did you tell him about Mrs. Tannenbaum that he didn't seem to appreciate?" asked Kokish.

"Well, in general, I think I pointed out that she had chronic problems with men and to beware of her manipulations; that a constant theme throughout all of her life had been that she wanted to control men, and that she had had a traumatic childhood in terms of her father leaving, abandoning the family when she was about four years old, and at some level she was always searching for a father or a man to be close to. There was a great deal of hostility also in terms of her relationships with men, symbolically again directed at a father who left her. I think we warned Henry not to get too deeply involved."[61]

"I notice you thought it was an anger thing that she killed herself in front of Mr. Madrid," Kokish asked.

"Oh, yes, I believe this epitomizes one of the diabolical features of Galya's character, under the guise of peace and love and friendship, having this man with her at the last moment of her death. If we really look at it we see that this is the psychiatric technician who devoted an incredible amount of time trying to help her with her problems in the best way that he knew how and her final parting act was to apparently ingest some cyanide and grab him by the hand and essentially ruin his career as a psychiatric technician. I see this as an incredibly hostile act."

"So she got you and him at the same time?"

"She really got all of us," Dr. Olenik said, including John Kokish in his statement. "It's so ironic that males who tried to be close to her and tried to be helpful to her—her psych technician, or doctor, or lawyer—there was always a very angry element that we could never do enough for her."[62]

After Galya died, Dr. Olenik talked to Galya's mother, Margaret Forest. Galya blamed her mother for everything that had gone wrong in her life, including her stint in the Illinois prison and her breakup with Leo Tanenbaum.

Mrs. Forest was saddened by Galya's death, but she knew her daughter's shortcomings well. "Her mother described her as having a problem with lying all of her life and always creating turmoil wherever she went," Dr. Olenik recalled. "And as I piece together the history, it sounds like this was so even in terms of her death; Galya still lives on in people who are presently fighting and arguing about her. And if I may be casual, she may still be laughing at us from the grave."[63]

PART IV ★

"WHAT WOULD THE RUSSIANS THINK?"

19 ★ TORPEDOES AND SUBMARINES

Bill Sullivan managed to hang onto his job at the FBI, blaming the genesis of the Huston Plan on other members of the intelligence community. But Hoover knew better. For decades he had had his own spies inside the Bureau keeping tabs on his agents. "We called those guys 'submarines,' because they worked in secret below the surface, always trying to ingratiate themselves with the director," Sullivan would write in his autobiography.[1]

W. Mark Felt was not only Hoover's top enforcer in the Inspections Bureau, but also an experienced submariner. After the Huston Plan debacle, he began to watch Sullivan, noticing how he tried to ingratiate himself with Henry Kissinger, Nixon's national security adviser; Kissinger's deputy, Alexander Haig; and Robert Mardian, an assistant attorney general in the Justice Department's Internal Security Division.

Felt believed that Sullivan was making a play to unseat Hoover by deliberately playing on the "paranoia and political obsessions" of the Nixon White House. "In my opinion, Sullivan was responsible for the excesses in the domestic intelligence gathering in the Nixon White House," he would allege in his autobiography years later.[2]

On October 12, 1970, tensions between Hoover and Sullivan worsened after Sullivan made a few off-the-cuff remarks at a newspaper editors' conference about Hoover's longtime nemesis, the Communist Party USA. Sullivan told the group it was "nonsense" to link antiwar radicals to a Communist plot.[3] In fact, he said, the CPUSA's membership totaled only about three thousand people and no longer posed a threat at all.[4] By the time Sullivan returned to the office, Hoover had read a wire story about his remarks and was livid, worried that Congress might reduce his budget.

Hoover decided it was time for Sullivan to go and tried to ease him out in bureaucratic fashion by realigning the chain of command. He created a new position of deputy associate director and gave the slot to Mark Felt.

Felt had been gunning for Sullivan's job. Just a few months earlier, he had sent Hoover a note thanking the director for sending him an autographed color photo of himself. "This is a prized possession and I am having it suitably framed to occupy the place of honor in my office," he gushed.[5] When Hoover called Felt in to tell him he was being promoted, he instructed him to keep tabs on Sullivan.

"Felt," Hoover said, "I need someone who can control Sullivan. I think you know he has been getting out of hand."

"Yes sir," responded Felt.

"Watch everything that comes out of the Domestic Intelligence Division very closely. They are going too far," Hoover added.

"Mr. Hoover, I'll do my best," Felt responded.[6]

Sullivan was angry—and hurt. His bond with J. Edgar went deeper than a mere professional relationship. Sullivan had always been there for Hoover, bucking him up when the "press jackals" were after him or complimenting him on a particularly excellent presentation before the House Appropriations Committee. Hoover, too, had always treated Sullivan like a son, consistently giving him excellent marks on his yearly evaluations. Now the treacherous W. Mark Felt had come between them.

After much soul-searching and consultations with two dozen colleagues, Sullivan penned an anguished letter to Hoover. He recapped his long career in the FBI, describing how he had often put the Bureau ahead of his family. Sullivan assured the director that he was still loyal to the Bureau, warning him about surrounding himself with flatterers. "You claim you do not want 'yes men' but you become furious at any employee who says 'no' to you," he wrote. "If you are going to equate loyalty with 'yes men,' 'rubber stamps,' 'apple polishers,' flatterers, self-promoters and timid, cringing, frightened sycophants, you are not only departing from the meaning of loyalty you are in addition harming yourself and the organization."[7]

Sullivan said he wanted to see Hoover retire in a blaze of glory, but hoped that Hoover's successor would not enjoy the same power. "We humans are not saintly enough to possess and handle it properly in every instance."

Sullivan mailed the letter and waited for a response. It arrived three days later. Hoover demanded that Sullivan take his accrued leave and retire. But Sullivan had no intention of quietly slipping off into retirement.

The veteran of numerous COINTELPRO operations, Sullivan was an old fox himself. Two weeks before the showdown, he had gathered up all the letters and transcripts associated with the seventeen Kissinger wiretaps and stuffed them into his battered, olive-green briefcase. He gave the briefcase, which had his initials embossed on it, to the FBI's Charles Brennan and told him to take it to Robert Mardian. "Mr. Mardian accepted it—without commenting about the contents of the briefcase and it appeared as if he had expected it," Brennan later reported. Sullivan rationalized his decision, saying he feared Hoover might "blackmail Nixon and Kissinger and hang onto his job forever."[8]

Hoover soon learned the wiretap documents were missing and directed a team of agents—led by W. Mark Felt—to recover them. Felt relished the opportunity to ingratiate further himself with the director and to damage Sullivan in his effort to recover what he called the "purloined special files."[9]

An FBI reconstruction of events written on May 12, 1973—just as the US Senate was about to begin televised hearings into Watergate and fifteen months before Nixon resigned—fills in some of the details of what happened next. Mardian contacted his boss, Attorney General John Mitchell, who said that he would contact the White House. Mardian was then instructed to fly to San Clemente to meet with President Nixon. Nixon gave Mardian two orders: (1) Take the Sullivan material to the White House; and (2) make sure Sullivan's documents matched White House summaries.

Shortly thereafter Mardian delivered the satchel to Dr. Henry Kissinger and General Alexander Haig at the White House. In Kissinger's and Haig's presence, White House correspondence checked against chronological check list which listed all material sent to White House to date. The White House summaries in possession of Kissinger were checked, found intact. As best Mardian recalls he then gave the list to Mr. H. R. Haldeman who checked the summaries in his possession against the check list. Two summaries found missing. After check was made Mardian said he took the satchel, which he believes contained summaries, the check list and telephone surveillance logs, and delivered them to the Oval Room in the White House.[10]

Mardian declined to identify the recipient, but presidential aide John Ehrlichman writes that he stored the material in a safe in his outer office.

While Sullivan was on leave, he began drafting another lengthy letter to Hoover. He listed twenty-five mistakes that Hoover and the FBI had made, ranging from the director's feeding of information to Communist witch-hunter Sen. Joe McCarthy; to the Bureau's failure to hire African American and Jewish applicants; to the FBI's abysmal record on organized crime. He also devoted several paragraphs to Sam Papich, one of the casualties in the Riha affair:

"You falsely accused me of writing the two fine letters which Sam J. Papich, former liaison with CIA, had written trying to prevent you from further damaging the Bureau. I never wrote the letters but I would have been proud to have done so and had you listened to Mr. Papich, one of the finest and most able men this Bureau ever had, we would not be in the horrible condition we are in today and there would have been no need of my writing this letter to you. Like myself, Mr. Papich was most fond of the Bureau but he saw it was deteriorating and tried to prevent it. After the reception his two fine letters received he knew the cause was hopeless and retired. Perhaps I should have done the same thing at the time but I still clung to the hope that changes could be brought about orderly and quietly and once more the Bureau would be moving ahead and doing what the people thought it had been doing all along."[11]

In a strange reversal of roles, Sullivan closed by saying perhaps it was Hoover who should retire. No FBI employee had ever dared to talk to Hoover like that. On September 30, 1971, he relieved Sullivan of his duties for "insolence and insubordination."[12] He appointed a Felt ally, Alex Rosen, to replace Sullivan and put another Felt ally, Charles W. Bates, in charge of the General Investigative Division.

A week later, when Sullivan returned to the Bureau to fill out paperwork, he was met by W. Mark Felt, who questioned him about the purloined wiretap files. Sullivan refused to answer, saying that it was a matter for Hoover and John Mitchell to settle. "I pointed out to Sullivan that he was still on the Bureau's rolls and that I was his superior and that I was ordering him to disclose the person or persons who had instructed him to refuse to answer." But Sullivan stood his ground.[13]

Unable to restrain himself, Felt called Sullivan a "Judas."

Sullivan challenged him to a fistfight.

Felt declined. "He was like a little banty rooster and I think he really would have fought me had I accepted his challenge, although I am half again his size," Felt recalled.[14]

Sullivan turned in his keys, his blackjack, his revolver and holster. He wanted to keep his FBI badge, a courtesy normally allowed high-ranking officials, who had them mounted on plaques, but Hoover refused. So Sullivan departed, leaving behind his own autographed photo of J. Edgar Hoover.

★ ★ ★

Hoover knew his days were numbered, figuring Nixon would come for him after the 1972 general election. But it was death who reached him first. In the early morning hours of May 2, 1972, Hoover was found dead of a heart attack in his home.

Afterward his body lay in state at the Capitol Rotunda. Politicians and rank-and-file FBI men paid their last respects, including Bill Sullivan, who felt more regret than sorrow. Had he known the "egomaniacal old rogue" was going to die so soon, he writes, he would have kept his mouth shut.[15]

In retirement, Sullivan was as busy as ever. He penned his memoirs and was frequently recalled to Washington to testify before various House and Senate committees investigating excesses of the FBI during the Hoover years.

In the fall of 1977, just before he was scheduled to testify before a congressional committee investigating the assassinations of John F. Kennedy, Martin Luther King, and Malcolm X, he was accidentally shot and killed in a hunting accident near his New Hampshire home.

The twenty-one-year-old shooter, Robert Daniels Jr., said he had mistaken Sullivan for a white-tailed deer. The son of a New Hampshire state trooper, Daniels was fined $500 and his hunting license was suspended for ten years.

William Kunstler, a prominent attorney, urged then US Attorney Griffin Bell to investigate Sullivan's death. "I am not suggesting that murder took place in New Hampshire on Nov. 9, 1977, but simply that there is sufficient smoke to indicate that it might have," he said in an April 21, 1978, letter.[16] The Justice Department declined, saying it saw no basis for initiating an investigation.

20 ★ THE FINK

On September 24, 1975, the CIA's newly retired counterintelligence chief, James Jesus Angleton, appeared before a US Senate panel investigating the nation's intelligence agencies. Looking malnourished, as if the secrets that he had guarded for three decades had been feeding on his own body, Angleton lowered himself into a chair in the hearing room. When he spoke, his voice was a reedy baritone and the senators had to lean in to hear him.

Angleton was the CIA's counterespionage chieftain who chain-smoked Virginia Slims, lunched with notorious double agent Kim Philby, and was known by a plethora of nicknames, including Mother, the Gray Ghost, and the Black Knight. When Philby decamped to the Soviet Union, Angleton had been deeply shaken and his mind had grown warped as he hunted for a phantasmagoric mole who had somehow burrowed into the Agency.

"Angleton had a compulsive approach to anything he took on—whether hunting spies, raising orchids, or catching trout—and surrounded himself and his staff with an aura of mystery, hinting at dark secrets and intrigues too sensitive to share," David Robarge writes.[1] "What makes Angleton such a conundrum for the historian and biographer is that he was losing his sense of proportion and his ability to live with uncertainty right around the time, 1959–63, when it became startlingly evident—agents compromised, operations blown, spies uncovered—that something was seriously amiss with Western intelligence and more aggressive CI and security were needed."

For years, Angleton had run an agency within the Agency that was answerable to no one. But just a few months earlier, he had been fired from his job after the *New York Times* published a story alleging Angleton was the mastermind behind a huge and illegal domestic spying operation.

Still reeling from his dismissal, Angleton had been called before the Church Committee to explain his activities. He was ready to spill some secrets of his own, including several seemingly casual remarks that would only deepen the mystery surrounding the disappearance of Thomas Riha.

The Church Committee, formally known as the Senate Select Committee to Study Governmental Operations with Respect to Intelligence Activities, had its origins in the Watergate hearings when it was learned that several US presidents had directed the nation's intelligence agencies to spy on antiwar demonstrators.[2] Journalist Seymour Hersh, in an article published on December 22, 1974, reported that the CIA had amassed files on ten thousand unwitting Americans.[3] James Jesus Angleton, he writes, directed the collection efforts. "Mr. Angleton was permitted to continue his alleged domestic operations because of the great power he wields inside the agency as director of counterintelligence," Hersh writes. But Angleton, who knew that the CIA was forbidden by its charter from engaging in domestic espionage, told Hersh that CIA's counterintelligence operatives didn't spy on Americans. "We know our jurisdiction," he insisted.[4]

Over the next sixteen months, the Church Committee would hold nearly 170 meetings,[5] interview 800 witnesses in public and closed sessions, and publish 14 reports, many of which ran into hundreds of pages.[6] Its chairman, Frank Church, was an Idaho Democrat and thirty-two years old in 1956 when he was first elected to the Senate. His fellow Democrats on the committee included Walter Mondale, who would run against Ronald Reagan in 1984, losing disastrously; and Colorado's Gary Hart, whose presidential campaign in 1988 would end in humiliation after the *Miami Herald* reported that he was having an affair with Donna Rice.

The Republican members of the Church Committee were among the lions of the Senate—Arizona's Barry Goldwater, who ran for president against LBJ in 1964; John Tower of Texas, a member of the Armed Services Committee, who would push through Reagan's military agenda; and Tennessee lawmaker Howard Baker, future Majority leader and Reagan's White House chief of staff, who asked the famous question during the Watergate hearings: "What did the president know and when did he know it?"[7]

Denver Post reporter Fred Gillies hoped that Senator Hart could pry loose information on the Riha case. Hart, who was looking down the road toward his presidential campaign, needed the goodwill of the *Denver Post,* the state's largest newspaper, and promised to do what he could.

(A spokesman for Gary Hart said in a 2014 email that Hart "recalls nothing about that case and it did not come up in the Church committee hearings that he recalls."[8] But Fred Gillies's voluminous files and the official transcripts of the Church Committee make clear that Hart's recollection is in error. Those documents show that Hart was in frequent communication with Fred Gillies, often dropping him a note or asking one of his staffers to give Gillies an update on the Senate investigation.)

Gillies prepared a list of questions to be posed to the various US intelligence agencies and sent them to Senator Hart. Hart, in turn, passed the lists to committee staffers, assuring Gillies "the *Denver Post* will be the first to know anything about the Riha matter."[9]

By then, Gillies was the foremost expert in the country on the case. Yet his questions reveal how much was still unknown about Thomas Riha and Galya Tannenbaum.[10] Galya's death had not ended speculation about the whereabouts of Thomas Riha. In fact, many people thought Galya had been done in by the same sinister forces that spirited off Professor Riha.

Robert Byrnes, the former CIA operative and history professor at the University of Indiana, helped fuel that speculation. In 1973, four years after Riha had disappeared, Byrnes told Riha's friend, Donald Fanger, that Riha was apparently "alive and well" and living in Bratislava, Slovakia, a city that straddles the Danube River and is located between Austria and Hungary.

Byrnes was secretive about how he learned of Riha's whereabouts, telling Fanger that he had received the information from an American historian of Slovak descent whom he had known for fifteen years. The historian, in turn, had gotten his information from a Czech-born woman who was now a Canadian citizen. Byrnes did not identify the American historian nor the woman who actually had seen Riha. The woman, he said, didn't want to be identified because she hoped to return to Bratislava in the future with her husband, a Canadian scientist. In a November 5, 1973, letter to Donald Fanger, he writes:

> Briefly, this Canadian woman went to school in Bratislava with Tom in the 1940s and knew him very well. While she was in Bratislava with her husband in the last academic year on an exchange program, she met Tom accidentally. She and her husband had dinner several times with Tom and his wife in the Carlton Hotel in Bratislava, and she is absolutely certain that this is the Tom Riha we knew and who she knew 30 years ago. She believes that Tom's wife is the Czechoslovak scholar whom he met and married in the United States and who she thought separated from Tom or perhaps even was divorced from him just before Tom's disappearance. However, she is not convinced of this because all four acted as though nothing had happened between 1947 and 1972. The Canadian woman had read about Tom's disappearance several years ago and was naturally deeply interested and puzzled by it all, but this was never mentioned by anyone.[11]

Donald Fanger was mystified by details in the letter and shared Byrnes's correspondence with Peter Kress, Thomas's uncle in Oakland. In a subsequent letter to Byrnes, Fanger writes, "He [Kress] verifies my own understanding that in the late summer of 1946, when Tom's mother came to California, Tom was a student at a business college, living in Prague with his father. He had not gone to high school because of the Nazi Occupation and this business school was the next best thing."[12] Fanger went on to say that Riha had never mentioned Bratislava, nor did his mother. "I certainly never heard anything from him indicating that he had spent any time in Slovakia. I wonder, then, about the Canadian woman's statement that she went to school there with Tom 'in the 1940s.'"[13]

Fanger also found other things in the Canadian woman's account puzzling, including her description of Tom's wife as a Czech scholar whom he married in the United States. "The Czech girl Tom married was no scholar at all, and, after taking a beautician's course in Boulder, went back to New York, where she is now, so far as I know, working in a bank."[14]

Hoping to confirm the sighting, Fanger asked Byrnes to forward to the Canadian woman a picture of Thomas Riha to make sure that this was indeed the man she had dined with. "Riha is not so uncommon a name, and I suspect that there may be some confusion in the mind of your informant."

Byrnes passed along the photo to the woman, who confirmed that the man in the photo was indeed the man she had met in Bratislava. Curiously, though, Byrnes waited two years to relay the news to Donald Fanger, saying that he had "just forgotten it."[15] Byrnes added that the woman who had seen Riha in Bratislava believed he was "an intelligence agent" and that anyone who got involved in the case was in danger. For that reason, she wanted to remain anonymous.

This thirdhand sighting of Riha would become a critical part of the Church Committee's findings. Senator Hart asked Angleton if he was familiar with Thomas Riha. "I am, indeed," responded Angleton:

SENATOR HART: Do you have any information for this committee as to what happened to Prof. Thomas Riha?

MR. ANGLETON: What has happened to the subject?

SENATOR HART: He has disappeared.

MR. ANGLETON: I haven't heard anything. I have not actually inquired, but I have no knowledge. I think I heard speculation at one time, but it was back, more or less, in the *res gestae* of this trouble, that he was in Czechoslovakia, but I do not know.

SENATOR HART: In your previous deposition, you stated that counterintelligence information was only as good as relations between the FBI and CIA. That is a paraphrase of what you said. And since there was a termination of relationship between Mr. Hoover, the FBI and the CIA in the spring of 1970 over the Riha case, I think the committee might look into this termination with some degree of intensity.

MR. ANGLETON: I would like to suggest, Senator, that it was much deeper than that. It was a cutting off of all liaison with the intelligence community with the exception of the White House.

SENATOR HART: Over this one case?

MR. ANGLETON: Over this one case. Once having established the principle with us, then it was simply a matter of a short period of time when the liaison office itself was done away within the Bureau.[16]

Senator Hart appeared to be taken aback by Angleton's response. But he had the FBI's Charles D. Brennan lined up to testify on the Riha matter and decided to save his follow-up questions for him. After Brennan was sworn in, Hart asked him why the Riha case had led to the breakdown between the CIA and FBI. Brennan responded that J. Edgar Hoover had no "close regard" for the CIA and it was a way for Hoover to demonstrate his power.

SENATOR HART: But, to your knowledge, it had nothing to do with whether Professor Riha was an agent, double-agent, or was working for any agency of our Government or any other Government?

MR. BRENNAN: No, and to my recollection, this is the sad part of it. It just—I mean Mr. Riha just apparently happened to pop into a set of circumstances where the real vital question here was the fact that an FBI agent disclosed something to a CIA agent which disturbed Mr. Hoover.

SENATOR HART: Without going to great lengths—it is fairly crucial in the case because the purported FBI agent who spoke to the CIA agent said, "Calm this thing down. Get out to the press that Riha is alive and well." Riha, as you know, disappeared and has never been found. If an unnamed FBI agent knew something about Professor Riha that he was not telling anyone else, I think that is fairly important. You do not have any information on what happened to Professor Riha?

MR. BRENNAN: My recollection is that he left this country, voluntarily, and that there was no indication or evidence to indicate that, as many alleged from that section of the country, that he had been spirited off by Communist agents. As I recollect, he was possibly of Czechoslovakian background. He was in this country, teaching here, and he suddenly disappeared. The information which the FBI had available to it at that time indicated that he had voluntarily left, and there was no substantiation of any involvement in any intelligence activity or any spying. There was just no basis for the flap that arose, as I recall the incident, and this is why I say it would seem then to me to be a relatively ridiculous situation which blows up to the point where it leads to a cutoff in relations between the two agencies.[17]

Senator Hart accepted what James Angleton and Charles D. Brennan said about Riha's whereabouts, even going along with the notion that Riha had left his home, his career, his friends, his books, and his artwork for "personal reasons," that is, the divorce with Hana.

In a statement to the press, the senator wrote, "Thomas Riha, is, most probably, living somewhere today in Eastern Europe, possibly in Czeckoslovakia [sic]. He was sighted there in 1973. Why he left the United States remains unclear: personal reasons were probably the basis for his decision to leave."[18]

When Zdenek Cerveny saw Hart's statement, he tried to reach the senator by telephone to ask him about the purported sighting. Hart refused to take his phone calls. "My hope ended when that underhanded guy—Gart Hart—tried to get some publicity for himself by pretending he was interested in what happened to my uncle," he said in an interview in 2014. "He just wanted to get into the newspapers. He was a fink, to put it kindly."[19]

Cerveny, who had been appointed conservator for Riha's estate, had a legitimate interest in finding out if his uncle was alive. Eventually he hired Denver attorney Martin Buckley to help him. Buckley contacted Robert Byrnes by letter. In a lengthy, three-page response, Byrnes rambled on about Riha's selection as an exchange student in 1958 and the alleged Bratislava sighting. This time, Byrnes described the Czech-born woman who had seen Riha in Bratislava as "X" and introduced another witness whom he called "Y."

He writes, "X asserted that a friend, Y, who was present, was also convinced it was Riha. Moreover, Y told X that Y and Riha had often lunched together and that both Riha and Y were employed at the Slovak Academy of Sciences and at the university in Bratislava. Both claim that they had known Riha well in the 1940s when they had all gone to school together, I believe in Bratislava, where Riha had concentrated on the study of Russian and English."[20]

Byrnes went on to say that on a subsequent visit to Bratislava, the spouse of X tried to get in touch with Y to confirm the sighting, but was unsuccessful. "Y had moved from the apartment, was no longer at the previous position, and simply could not be found," he writes. "In short, there are very serious questions about this alleged sighting in Bratislava. I do not know X, and I am not competent to reach any conclusions concerning X's vision, memory or judgment."[21]

Cerveny's attorney eventually filed a federal Freedom of Information Act lawsuit with the CIA in an attempt to uncover the identities of the people who had purportedly seen Riha in Bratislava. The CIA steadfastly refused to release names, arguing that the lives of the informants could be endangered and that they could become the objects of harassment and embarrassment if their relationship with the CIA were to become known.

Stansfield Turner, the new CIA director, even weighed in on the case, writing in an affidavit that the CIA did not know the identity of the Czech woman and had taken no steps to verify the information.[22]

Cerveny remained skeptical of the CIA's motives, alleging in his lawsuit that the Agency had thwarted local police from investigating Riha's disappearance and now wanted to cover up what it had done.[23] He asked US District Court Judge Richard P. Matsch, who was presiding over the FOIA case, to look at the CIA's documents himself.

But Matsch—a blunt-talking Federal Court judge who was appointed to the bench by President Richard Nixon and was known for the strict order that he kept in his courtroom—refused. In a memorandum, he writes that the CIA had made a good-faith effort to meet the requirements of the Freedom of Information Act. "A moment's reflection upon recent political history and the excesses of the internal security investigations in the 1950s should be sufficient to signal caution in dealing with unverified derogatory material within the files of an intelligence-gathering agency of government."[24]

During the course of the lawsuit, the CIA acknowledged that it had in its possession eleven letters written by Thomas Riha or sent to him from the Soviet Union between 1958 and 1963. The letters were captured as part of the CIA's huge mail-opening program, Operation HTLINGUAL. The Agency refused to release the letters.

Among the most mysterious documents pried loose through Cerveny's lawsuit were several heavily redacted messages or letters that originated with the US Army's Intelligence and Security Command. Although the author and recipient of the letters are whited out, some details can be gleaned. The letters were written in the spring of 1971 by a former or current military intelligence official based in Miami, Florida, to an intelligence operative in Colorado. The letter-writer boasts of having penetrated a group of Cuban exiles in Florida who had hatched a new plot to overthrow Fidel Castro, whom he refers to as that "whiskered creep."[25]

Almost as an aside, the writer said that he verified that Thomas Riha had been seen in Canada a month following his disappearance. "He showed up at a bookstore in Montreal (a drop for the other side) and spent about two hours there, buying several books which he ordered sent to Boulder. Evidentally [sic] he intended to return. I'm also pretty sure he was dealing with KGB or some sister group (possibly the Russian-controlled Czech intel people) and not our people. Anyway, he is probably now drinking vodka with Kim Philby and Donald McLean or maybe, as my Canadian contact suggests, he is in Algeria. Anybody's guess?????"[26]

(The bookstore was likely a reference to the antiquarian shop in Montreal owned by former Polish fighter Philip Lozinski. An invoice in the Boulder police department records shows Riha owed the bookstore $26.70 for two books. But the invoice shows the books were purchased in August 1968—not in April 1969—a month after his disappearance.)[27]

The letter-writer also mentioned Lawrence Havelock, the Czech-born man who in the fall of 1968 set off an explosion in a bathroom of a plane that was preparing to land in Denver. Havelock was reportedly the sole survivor of an air force cargo plane that crashed in the Philippines carrying the stolen loot of Madame Nhu, the beautiful sister-in-law of South Vietnam's president, Ngo Dinh Diem. "I haven't heard a word from Colorado but you might be interested in knowing that I've verified Havelock's presence about the Diem plane. I'm not at liberty to impart to you where I got the info but suffice it to say it came from the area of Langley, Virginia."[28] In a second letter, he adds, "What's the situation now on Havelock? I'm still interested in that Diem thing but think he is the key. Do you figure him to walk out of that prison or is there a possibility that he will suffer an 'accident?'"[29]

The author's musings about a possible "accident" are prophetic. On July 3, 1973, Havelock was in the prison's computer room when he began to feel ill. His instructor told him to lie down on the floor where he began making strange noises. By the time he was taken to the prison hospital, his pulse had slowed and he showed no sign of life. He was pronounced dead of a massive heart attack at 2:15 P.M.[30] He was two months shy of his fifty-second birthday.

His wife, Oleta, believed her husband had been murdered and sought help from Fred Gillies in unraveling the case. Gillies worked diligently on the case, including filing Freedom of Information Act requests with the Bureau of Prisons. But he apparently was never able to gather enough information to write a story about it.

21 ★ MISSPELLINGS AND MURDER

Within Galya, creativity and destruction slumbered side by side. But it was her destructive side that was stronger and rose from the communal bed to walk through the world. From the time she was a little girl, she writes that she felt like a "a reject from the family assembly line."[1] Fearing humiliation from her classmates and relatives, she retreated into a private world roiling with a toxic mixture of fantasy, self-pity, depression, and resentment.

By the time she reached adulthood, she had begun compensating for her feelings of inadequacy by lying and inventing new personas for herself. She also began forging checks, skipping out on rent, and embezzling funds from her employers. In 1968–69, a period of severe financial distress, she crossed the line into murder. Despite her oft-repeated claims of innocence, the evidence shows that she did kill Thomas Riha, Gustav Ingwersen, and Barbara Egbert, and that she may have gone on to kill again if she hadn't been taken into custody.

Before her sanity hearing on the forgery charge, a number of psychologists and psychiatrists diagnosed her as a sociopath. Had she been facing murder charges, she may well have been diagnosed as a psychopath, Dr. Macdonald acknowledged in his court testimony.

Psychiatrist Ursula Wilder describes psychopaths as predators. They approach "life with remorselessness, manipulation, pursuit of risk and excitement, and sharp, short-term tactical abilities alongside poor long-term and strategic planning."[2]

Psychopaths can be men or women, highly functioning CEOs, or rank-and-file workers. They are sometimes violent, but not always. They are also deceptive, manipulative, shallow, irresponsible, devoid of guilt, and tend to look at people as either predators or prey. "Psychopaths are glib and charming and they use these attributes to manipulate others into trusting and believing in them. This may lead to people giving them money, voting them into office, or, possibly being murdered by them," the FBI writes in its *Law Enforcement Bulletin.*[3]

Galya's extreme evasion under questioning, which so frustrated Dr. Macdonald, was likely an attempt to keep her stories straight so that she would not inadvertently incriminate herself. By the time she reached the State Hospital, she could no longer repress her secrets and began boasting to other patients and staffers about the people she killed.

Two days before Galya committed suicide, she wrote a letter to attorney John Kokish blaming her troubles on Dr. Olenik and insisting that she didn't kill anyone. Galya undoubtedly knew the attorney would relay her last words to the world and may have slipped into death gratified by the idea that she might yet be perceived as an innocent who had been wrongly accused. At the very least, her death would be payback to the despised Dr. Olenik, who took away her typing privileges and psychologically thrust her back down into that dark cellar where her fantasies first bloomed.

Galya also knew her suicide would generate chaos inside and outside the hospital. She felt at home with chaos. It mirrored her own insides. Even her mother, Margaret Forest, admitted after her daughter's death that Galya created chaos wherever she went.

Galya kept on her bookshelf a copy of Fydor Dostoyevsky's *Crime and Punishment,* a gripping psychological novel about a penniless law student in St. Petersburg named Rodion Romanovich Raskolnikov, who murders an elderly pawnbroker and her developmentally disabled half sister with an ax. Raskolnikov is a haughty young man who argues in an article published before the murders that extraordinary people have the right to commit crimes, including murder, in pursuit of endeavors that will benefit humanity.

Afterward, though, Raskolnikov's conscience troubles him and he is plunged into a feverish world of guilt and fear. He begins to behave irrationally, heedlessly drawing attention to himself as the possible murderer. Against his better judgment, he spars with Porfiry Petrovich, the St. Petersburg policeman investigating the murders, subjecting himself unnecessarily to the policeman's clever traps.

On one occasion, the inspector exclaims, "Why you're just like a child that wants to play with the matches! And why are you so worried? Why are you thrusting yourself on us like this? For what reason? Eh?"[4]

Similarly, Galya considered herself a woman of superior intellect. "She called herself a doer and these active people are the ones who control society," Carol Word testified.[5]

Like Raskolnikov, Galya called attention to herself, brazenly carting off Riha's possessions and making innumerable extravagant claims about herself, not the least of which was that she was a colonel in military intelligence.

She also sparred with detectives, confident in her ability to avoid traps. When she was questioned by the Denver police, the Boulder police, and the FBI, she didn't even request a lawyer to be present. What's more, Galya often contacted the police herself. After Denver homicide cops went to Boulder to compare notes with their counterparts, Galya made "numerous phone calls"[6] to Denver police. When Det. Charles McCormick finally called her back, she talked at length about Thomas, assuring the investigator that Riha was alive and living in Montreal.

Dr. Macdonald, in *The Murderer and His Victim,* writes that sociopaths often commit their crimes in a way that ensures their detection. As an example, he cites a bank robber who forgets that the gas tank of his getaway car is empty. "His conscience would appear to permit commission of the crime, yet demand punishment for the forbidden act."[7] A surprising number of criminals, including murderers, he writes, sooner or later feel an overwhelming compulsion to confess their crimes. "Even though the murderer may not volunteer a confession, his total behavior may be such as to draw attention to himself as the guilty person."[8]

Galya littered her trail with clues both large and small that linked her to the three deaths. She poisoned Gus and Barbara with cyanide and it's likely she also used cyanide to kill Thomas Riha, although his body has never been recovered and it's impossible to say with certainty what he died from.

Dr. Macdonald writes that women tend to kill their victims with poison, which is exactly how Zdenek Cerveny believes his uncle died. "She poisoned Thomas just like she poisoned Gustav Ingwersen and Barbara Egbert," he said.[9] "I don't think she could have shot anybody. She was too cowardly."[10]

Boulder lawyer Dennis Blewitt theorized to Boulder police that when Thomas and Galya embarked upon a strategy to keep Hana from getting any of Riha's assets, Galya decided to double-cross Thomas and take everything for herself. The evidence supports his theory.

Records show that on March 1, 1969—two weeks before Riha's disappearance—Galya wrote a letter to Robert Stroessner, a curator for the Denver Art Museum, saying she wanted to donate some artwork to the museum. One of the pieces was a Pietà appraised at $8,000, which Galya wanted to be a sale-gift combination, with the museum paying her $1,200 and issuing a tax credit letter for the remaining $6,800 to her daughter.[11]

On March 10—five days before Riha disappeared—Stroessner drove to Boulder to look over the artwork. Thomas was at the university and Galya let him in with her key. The pieces were still on display throughout his house. Galya told Stroessner that the paintings and statues had been obtained during World War II and had been in her possession ever since. "Tannenbaum told me her husband had died and she was disposing of the house," Stroessner told Fred Gillies. "I was amazed at the quality of the material. It was very, very nice."[12]

Galya's spelling errors strongly link her to the death of Thomas, Gus, and Barbara. Just as fingerprints offer clues to a killer's identity, a consistent pattern of misspellings in letters, notes, and legal documents can do the same. Galya's misspellings showed up in documents that were passed off as having been written by Thomas, Gus, Barbara, and Hana. On the basis of these characteristic misspellings, a powerful argument can be made that the first three were killed by one person and that one person was Galya. The spelling errors became more frequent when Galya was under stress or when she typed her letters.

Galya consistently misspelled "consider" as "concider" and "extremely" as "extreemly" in letters written *before* and *after* the murders.[13] Hana's lawyer, Gerald Caplan, was the first to notice the mistakes. Barbara's friends and family members also noticed the errors. So did members of Gustav Ingwersen's family.

Other misspellings that show up in her writings include "littarly," "polution," "integraty," "reversable," "aquainted," "beginer," "porole," "galant," "scandle," "eligable," "recomendation," "maintanance," "appartment," "withdrawl," "asprin," "refering," "releiving," "endevor," "scheem," and "protine."[14]

After Thomas Riha disappeared, Galya forged numerous letters in Riha's name, which contain her signature misspellings. One of the earliest is the March 20, 1969, letter purportedly written by Thomas to a Boulder real estate firm asking the firm to sell his house and to make sure that Galya was repaid the $7,000 that she had allegedly loaned him to buy the home. The letter begins, "I, Thomas Riha, after having given *conciderable* thought and *concideration* to my situation do hereby declare that it is my desire and intention to sell the house at 1055 5th Street, Boulder, Colorado." (He actually lived on 6th Street.) Other misspellings include "settleing" and "judgement." Additional correspondence containing her spelling mistakes include:

- An April 20, 1969, letter allegedly written by Thomas Riha and sent to Wheeler Realty, reminding the firm to compute the interest on Galya's $7,000 note. "I would like to *emphasise* that my concern is satisfaction of the two notes," the letter states. "While I do not wish to go into details as to my situation, I will state that it is very serious, and my wife is an *extreemly* dangerous person."

- An April 28, 1969, letter to First National Bank in which Thomas continues to talk about his wife's treachery. "I do not want to go into detail of all the problem that has come about except to state that my wife Hana is an *extreemly* dangerous person." [15]

- A May 1, 1969, letter purportedly written by Thomas to the Boulder county clerk explaining why he fired his attorney, Richard Hopkins. "Since a *conciderable* fee has been paid to Mr. Hopkins, I do not expect additional charges, but rather a possible refund."

- A May 15, 1969, letter allegedly written by Riha to Montgomery Ward's in which he complains about the company's rude collection efforts and refers to his marital "*hassel.*"

- A June 16, 1969, letter to University of Chicago Press, which begins by thanking the publisher for sending Riha a copy of his just-published book, *Readings in Russian Civilization.* "The gesture of sending the book was a pleasant break in my tragic e*xistance,*" the letter states.[16]

The letters containing Riha's signature were submitted to handwriting expert Ben Garcia, who concluded they were all forgeries. Garcia also concluded that Riha's signature on the $7,000 IOU to Galya was a forgery. The forgeries had been done "not by various persons, but written by one person and only one person."[17] Although Garcia could not say definitely it was Galya who had forged Riha's signature, he did conclude that many of the typed documents were prepared on a typewriter that she owned.

Galya also had a financial motive in killing Riha. She received roughly $70,000 in today's dollars from Riha's estate by using his credit cards, siphoning off his savings, cashing his royalty checks, and from monies obtained through the sale of his home, his car, and his artwork.[18]

Gus's will was also riddled with Galya's odd grammatical phrases and spelling mistakes. As mentioned, the preamble to his will states, "I wish to state that I have given long deliberate thought to the relationship that has existed between myself and my sons and their *famlies,* and because they have displayed no *visable* care or concern for me in my *lonliness* and age, I have come to these decisions." Additional misspellings in the will include "grandaughters" and "specimins."[19]

Other evidence also link Galya to Gus's death. Galya told Denver police that she had loaned Gus $10,000 for a business venture, a statement that was similar to her claim of loaning Thomas $7,000 for the house. In fact, by the time Galya met Gus, she was dead broke, with no visible means of support except for a couple of hundred dollars she had received from forged checks written on Gus's bank account and the money dribbling in through the sale of Riha's assets. Handwriting expert Ben Garcia, who was also an old friend of Gus's, found Gus's signature on the will to be a forgery, as well as his signature on the purported loan documents.

There was also the ten-year-old boy who dashed into Probate Court the day after Gus died and dropped the will on the counter, as well as the unidentified woman who called afterward to make sure the will had been delivered. "It is suspected that the courier that delivered the will was one of Mrs. Tannenbaum's sons and that the caller was Mrs. Tannenbaum herself," Denver homicide detective Charles McCormick writes in a February 1, 1971, memo.[20]

The nut bread found on Gus's table was the subject of debate inside the Denver Police Department. A lab analysis showed the nut bread to be uncontaminated with cyanide, leading one detective to theorize that Gus had accidently ingested a portion of the cake that *did* contain cyanide. That seems unlikely because a few of the almost invisible cyanide crystals surely would have adhered to the portion of the nut bread that underwent laboratory analysis.

A more likely scenario is that Galya gave Gus a piece of the nut bread containing cyanide. He ate it and died. Then she placed an uncontaminated piece of nut bread on the table. She freely admitted to police that she had baked the nut bread for Gus and when that piece was shown to be cyanide free, it would have reinforced the idea that she was innocent.

Galya is also the chief suspect in the cyanide poisoning death of Barbara Egbert. The suicide note and will purportedly written by Barbara contain Galya's signature misspellings: "Always I have been *concidered* [sic] but in the end not good enough. . . . I have taken jobs which made me *misserable* for short times. . . . I cannot stand anymore, and so I choose to leave this *existance.*"[21]

Barbara's suicide note and will were later found to be forgeries. The typewriter used to type the letters also matched a typewriter that was later seized from Galya's house. Financial gain doesn't appear to be the primary motive in Barbara's death, although Galya purportedly pawned the $125 gold Omega watch that Barbara had received from her parents.[22]

"Galya was a cheap crook," McCormick reflected in an interview. "The material wealth she inherited from these deaths was nothing."[23]

Barbara's parents believed that Galya killed their daughter because she had information that would implicate Galya in Gus's death. Furthermore, none of Barbara's family members or close friends believed Barbara was despondent enough to kill herself.

Only Galya believed that.

The night before Barbara's body was found, Galya had called Barbara's ex-husband urging him to check up on Barbara. It was the same MO she had used when Gus died. "Mrs. Tannenbaum had made a similar phone call forecasting death when she called Mr. Ingwersen's daughter in Boulder the night before Gus Ingwersen was found dead. Also Mrs. Tannenbaum stated that her reason for notifying the relatives of both Mr. Ingwersen and Mrs. Egbert of her concern for them was the fact that both had failed to appear for dinner with Mrs. Tannenbaum the night before they were found dead," Detective McCormick writes in his February 1, 1971, memo.[24]

Galya inadvertently tipped her hand when Barbara's sister came to see her after Barbara died. Thinking Barbara had died from an overdose of pills, the sister asked Galya where the pills had come from. Galya blurted out, "No, it wasn't pills," and then grew silent. At that moment, only Galya knew how Barbara died.

Galya grew emboldened with each successive murder. Denver and Boulder police records suggest that she may have been plotting to defraud—and possibly murder—a fourth victim named Lee Hedenberg before she was finally jailed. Mrs. Hedenberg was a widow, her son was in Vietnam, and she wanted help obtaining a passport and preparing a will. She had given Galya a vast amount of financial data about herself and her deceased husband, including two deeds of trust. When she learned Galya was a murder suspect, she became frightened and contacted her attorney, who advised her to call the Denver police. "He feels his client was next on the list (to die)," a detective would write.[25]

Galya staged the deaths of Gus and Barbara to make them look like suicides. Gus was lying peacefully on the couch, clad in a white shirt, tie, and dress shoes, despite the stifling heat and the extraordinary death throes he must have gone through. Similarly, Barbara was peacefully lying in the middle of her small garden apartment, her body artfully arranged and lying among color-coordinated pillows and rose petals. Although Thomas's body has never been recovered, witnesses said his table was set for breakfast, despite the fact he rarely ate breakfast.

The stagings reflect Galya's artistic sensibilities and her need for order. "Crime scene staging is the physical manifestation of a person's imagination for how things should appear when trying to turn a murder scene into a legitimate death scene," says scholar and cold crime investigator Laura G. Pettler.[26]

Detective McCormick said he has "no doubt" that Galya staged the deaths of Barbara Egbert and Gustav Ingwersen.[27] But in his memo summarizing the two cases, he wrote that police nevertheless still had "insufficient evidence" to file charges against Galya:

The inconsistencies and contradictions found in the evidence surrounding these two deaths when coupled with the strange and unique personality of Galya Tannenbaum gives much impetus to suspicion of foul play. This is particularly true when considered along with the unexplained disappearance, and probable death of Professor Thomas Rhea [sic] of Boulder. Mrs. Tannenbaum's claims of being a general in Army Intelligence and an agent for the C.I.A. are obviously absurd. However her boasts of being a trained killer and indeed of having "poisoned people by the droves" may be worthy of note.[28]

22 ★ THE INFORMANT AND THE "USEFUL IDIOT"

If a serial killer is someone who commits three or more murders over a period of time, then Galya fit that definition. She was also something else—she was an FBI informant.

Her relationship with the Bureau began in the early 1950s, when she was working as a bookkeeper for the city of Wellston, Missouri, and reportedly witnessed the mayor, Leo Hayes, altering ballots after the polls closed. An FBI memo dated June 23, 1954, states that Galya had "been contacted by agents of the St. Louis Office and has furnished information with respect to the political setup in the city of Wellston."[1]

FBI records don't say whether Galya continued to provide information when she moved to Chicago, but it's very likely that she did. The Communist Party USA, which was founded in Chicago, was J. Edgar Hoover's nemesis. Together with William Sullivan, Hoover spent decades trying to destroy it. At the time of Riha's disappearance, the FBI had about three hundred paid informants monitoring the Communist Party USA.[2]

An index card in Galya's FBI dossier shows she worked as a security informant, or "SI." Security informants were individuals specifically tasked to gain information on CPUSA. While living in Chicago, Galya made contacts with several Communists and alleged Communist front groups. The contacts are obscure and not ones she would have likely stumbled into on her own, which suggests she was being directed by an FBI handler. The contacts include the following:

- Vladimir V. Denisov, deputy chief editor of Moscow's Novosti Press Agency, who was in Chicago for the Soviet Technical Book Exhibit at the Museum of Science and Industry;
- The Chicago Council of American-Soviet Friendship, whose parent organization was alleged to be a front for the CPUSA;

- Leonard Karlin, a member of the National Lawyers Guild. The Lawyers Guild was also alleged to be a Communist front and intensively monitored for three and a half decades by the FBI.
- The Institute for Cybercultural Research. In May 1965, Galya drove from Chicago to New York City by herself to attend a conference sponsored by the Institute, an organization focused on a future when workers would be replaced by machines and millions of jobs would be shed.[3] The conference drew eight hundred visitors from the Soviet Union and Warsaw Pact countries and the place was crawling with informants. Galya happened to sit next to another FBI informant during dinner. She introduced herself as Galya Zakharovna, told him she spoke fluent Russian, and that her father was a major general in Russia. When the man mentioned that he wanted to purchase a Russian-made Western Electric telephone, she gave him the name of a Russian government minister and added that she could arrange a tour of the USSR for him.[4]

There is also Galya's relationship with Leo Tanenbaum. Tanenbaum was a card-carrying Communist and in 1960 took a trip to Cuba to observe Fidel Castro's revolution. The FBI had been watching Leo for years and even had an informant working in his design firm.

After Galya broke up with Leo, she became involved with Thomas Riha. His academic friends are doubtful they met in Chicago, but Galya's daughter said she saw Riha's name on her mother's mailbox. Riha appeared to be the primary reason why Galya decided to move a thousand miles west to Colorado, where she had no friends or family. (Boulder lawyer Dennis Blewitt, who was active in the antiwar movement and an associate of Leonard Karlin, speculated that Galya was sent to Boulder to keep tabs on him)[5]

It's not known whether Galya was directed to make contact with Thomas or if she just happened to run into him while he was finishing up his book for the University of Chicago Press. But the FBI's Chicago office would have undoubtedly been aware of his presence, just like they were of Leo Tanenbaum. In addition to vetting him as a double agent, the FBI had been capturing Riha's mail since the mid-1950s as part of Operation HTLINGUAL.

Thomas and Galya seemed a mismatched couple. He was a bachelor. She had had four lovers or husbands. He was a cosmopolitan European. She was a Midwesterner who had never left the United States. He held a doctorate, she possessed a high school diploma. He prized orderliness. She produced chaos. What brought them together? What kept them together? Was it love? Sex? Espionage? Or greed?

There could have been a little sex and a little espionage in their relationship, but greed appears to have been the glue that bound them together. Thomas needed Galya to help him find a way to keep his assets from Hana. And Galya needed Thomas's assets to keep her family from starving.

Hana, who has had more than fifty years to ponder her brief marriage, is convinced that both Galya *and* Thomas planned to murder her the night of the ether incident. In other words, Thomas was not a bystander, but a full participant in the plan, she said. "They had a gun, they had ether. They were ready to do what they had to do. Fortunately, I tricked them. I opened the window and called for help."[6]

Hana believes that once she had been rendered unconscious by ether, Galya and Thomas planned to kill her with cyanide and make it look like she committed suicide. "If I disappeared without a trace, people would look for me. That wasn't the plan. They had to start nice and slow."[7] The motive, she said, was "financial." Galya and Thomas hoped to cash in on the life insurance policy that Thomas insisted Hana sign on the night of their wedding.[8]

When the plan failed, Hana speculated that Galya killed Thomas because he knew too much. "She had to get rid of him. She knew there was no other way. Maybe she thought he would spill the beans."[9]

Thomas's friends and relatives are incredulous that Thomas intended to murder Hana. Scare her, maybe. But murder her? No way.

Still, there are unexplained aspects to the case, not least of which was Thomas's strange relationship with Galya. "She had access to the house more than I did. She was everywhere. She had him under her finger. He was like a puppet. Whatever she says, goes," Hana recalled.[10]

Carol Word, the young graduate student who lunched with Riha nearly every day, described Riha's relationship to Galya in similar terms. Testifying at Galya's sanity trial, Word said, "Mrs. Tannenbaum burst into Riha's office and forcefully propelled him out of the office and slammed the door."[11]

Much is known about Galya's life from her autobiographical writings, court transcripts, depositions, and police records. But Thomas Riha remains an enigmatic figure. His early life offers clues to the forces that shaped him and why he may not have been the genial professor and social butterfly that his academic colleagues remembered.

When he landed in the United States in 1947, he was eighteen years old and had spent the last eight years living with the family of his half sister and hiding from the Nazis. His grandparents suddenly vanished from his life in 1939 and his mother disappeared a year later. Friends and relatives said he had an uneasy relationship with his mother, a beautiful, dominating woman who reappeared in Prague after the war only to divorce his father and later marry a former American military officer.

His relationship with his mother could have colored his relationship with other women, which is important to understanding his relationship with Galya. Similarly, knowledge of his sexual orientation would not only help illuminate his connection to Galya, but also help resolve the question of whether he was, in fact, an intelligence agent for the United States, a foreign government, or both.

Riha's niece and nephew and many of his friends describe him as a heterosexual male with a normal sexual appetite. But other acquaintances saw a different side. Robert Schwind, who knew Riha in the army, described him as a man with an insatiable sex drive. Yet Hana saw no evidence of that behavior. "His sexual appetite was not for women," she said.[12]

If Thomas was homosexual, he could have boasted of his sexual exploits to keep his army buddies from finding out.[13] In the 1950s and 1960s, gay men and women were socially ostracized and often fired from their jobs if their sexual orientation were to become known. Homosexuality was also associated with communism and thousands lost their jobs when President Eisenhower in the 1950s signed an executive order purging individuals with "sexual perversions" from the federal government's payroll.[14]

If Galya were threatening to inform university officials of Thomas's sexual orientation, marrying Hana would have "immunized" him from her allegations and protected his reputation and quite possibly his job. It would also explain his rush to get married, his decision to divorce Hana four months later, and the strange hold that Galya seemed to have over him.

Knowing Thomas's sexual orientation could also help definitely answer the question of whether he was an intelligence agent. Proficient in five languages and knowledgeable about the customs and habits of Czechoslovakia and the Soviet Union, he was a natural candidate to become an agent or a double agent. He also possessed the controlling, yet risk-taking personality of many spies, which was evident in his interactions with both Czech and Soviet intelligence agents during his 1958 trip abroad.

He also was a facile liar, a necessary trait for anyone leading a double life. He lied about his family's origins, lied to the FBI about the recruitment package offered by the Czechs, lied to Hana, and lied to his friends.

But did all that add up to him being a spy? When he first went missing, FBI and CIA officials denied that they had any connection to him. Military intelligence officials also denied any connection to Thomas. Their denials were to be expected. Further, if Thomas did work for them, the two agencies would have never have revealed that information because it's classified.

That said, no records have surfaced contradicting their denials. The CIA did admit to the Church Committee that it had considered using Riha as an "intelligence source" during his stay in the Soviet Union, but added that "CIA's interest in Riha was canceled and he was never contacted."[15]

The CIA never explained why it had "canceled" its interest in Thomas. Similarly, the FBI never explained why Riha had no "double agent potential" after vetting him in 1960.[16]

If the two intelligence agencies had uncovered evidence that Riha was homosexual during their background investigations, they could have rejected him on that basis. At that time, both agencies were leery of hiring homosexuals because they thought they could be blackmailed. "I don't think the CIA or the FBI would have wanted to employ anyone who was homosexual. J. Edgar Hoover, who may have been homosexual himself, was particularly fierce in persecuting homosexuals," recalled Francis Randall, a retired Russian history professor whose friendship with Thomas Riha dates back to their graduate student days at Columbia University.[17]

Riha appears to have had no access to scientific or military information. Furthermore, no documents have surfaced suggesting he was acting as a courier or recruiter for a foreign government. Had he been any kind of "agent" at all, he would mostly likely have been an informational agent, that is, someone who supplied the United States, and possibly the Czechs and the Soviets, with publicly available information that could be found in daily newspapers and journals.

Francis Randall said that the CIA occasionally did seek "estimates" from him on various subjects and speculated that the CIA could have sought the same sort of information from Riha. "He was a decent American liberal democrat, as am I, and would not have had the qualms that one would have later about working with the CIA."[18]

And yet, the idea that Riha was a double agent of some sort can't be completely ruled out. "IDEN 1," in his conversation with the CIA's Michael Todorovich, raised the possibility that Galya had learned that Riha was working for the Czech StB and used that knowledge to control him. If he were indeed an espionage agent for the KGB or StB, it would explain why Riha gladly would have preferred to be seen as Galya's puppet rather than risk arrest.

Riha went to the Soviet Union frequently and he had a business relationship with a travel agency based in Montreal. Travel agencies often served as fronts for the CIA during the Cold War and many spies had their base of operations in Canada. There's also a March 10, 1971, letter from the Boulder police to the Soviet Embassy in Washington, DC, inquiring about an employee named Galina Utiekhina (or Utickhina), whose name appeared among Riha's possessions.[19] Perhaps this was his contact person in the event he had to escape the United States quickly. Other documents belonging to Riha, including his passport, are also missing from Boulder Police Department files even though they were recovered during searches of Galya's home.

Riha's StB dossier could throw more light on the "agent" question, but most of it has been destroyed. During his 1958 visit to Czechoslovakia, the Czechs did give Riha permission to work in an archive that was off limits to foreigners. The Communist government could have demanded a favor in return. They also had a "hammer" to hold over Riha's head—members of the Cerveny family and one of his uncles were still living in Czechoslovakia.

Riha's nephew, Zdenek Cerveny, thinks that Thomas was naive and may have seen himself as a peacemaker between the two world powers. "He was almost a useful idiot. He thought there could be peace with the Russians. He liked Russian culture and his Russian friends. He could not imagine how repressive the Russians could be."[20]

EPILOGUE

With such an abundance of evidence, the question becomes: Why didn't the local police arrest Galya and charge her with murder? The answer is because Galya managed to con everyone—the police, university administrators, the FBI, and the CIA. No one, especially the FBI and CIA, wanted to admit that a convicted con artist had hoodwinked them, especially when the woman was the killer herself. "What would the Russians think," mused Howard Dougherty, one of Riha's Boulder colleagues, "if they knew Galya Tannenbaum had used the CIA as a conduit for information?"[1]

That said, a fog of espionage lay over the case. Much of the fog, or misinformation, was the handiwork of the FBI's William Sullivan and his minions, who were masters of thousands of COINTELPRO operations. The fog only thickened as multiple jurisdictions tried to wrestle with the high-profile investigation.

On Saturday evening, March 15, 1969, just eighteen hours or so after Riha left Jan Sorensen's birthday party, Galya asked Zdenek Cerveny to come to her house. When he arrived, she told him that Riha had left Boulder to get away from Hana. It's the first mention of Riha's vanishing—and the reason for it.

The story made its way to the Boulder police and the Denver police, the FBI and CIA, Immigration and Naturalization Service and the Defense Intelligence Agency. The story was circulated and recirculated to law enforcement officials within these organizations and to outside organizations. It became a self-reinforcing loop.

But it made no sense.

The idea that Thomas would leave Boulder to get away from his wife was preposterous. He was a man who had survived the privations of war, worked his way through the country's finest universities, and had a home, friends, and a career in Boulder. Law enforcement officials, the federal intelligence agencies, and university administrators believed the story because they wanted to believe it. Only Thomas's friends remained unconvinced.

It's also possible that in the early weeks following his disappearance, officials really did believe Thomas had left Boulder to get away from his wife and that the matter would resolve itself. It also gave the FBI and CIA time to do their own sleuthing without having the local cops involved.

Joseph Smiley, the university president who was told by the CIA that Riha was "alive and well," thought that relaying that message to the public would calm speculation. But it only increased the suspicion that something more was afoot. And there was: Galya was on the loose, audaciously selling off Thomas's belongings and plotting her next murders. Having gotten away with killing Thomas, she felt more emboldened to do away with Gus and Barbara.

By the fall of 1969, six months after Thomas had vanished and Gus and Barbara were dead of cyanide poisoning, police in Denver and Boulder, as well as agents in the FBI and CIA, must have realized, with a sinking feeling, that they had inadvertently allowed a killer to run free and that the killer was Galya.

Having made such a terrible blunder, which would lead to great embarrassment, the federal agencies didn't come clean but continued to circulate the "alive and well" rumor. The FBI's actions rose to obstruction of justice when Boulder detective Ralph Ruzicka contacted Merrill Smith, an FBI agent stationed in Boulder, in late October 1969.

"I asked Agent Smith if I should bother looking for a body of Professor Riha and Agent Smith said no, it would be a waste of time," Ruzicka recounted. "This led me to possibly believe that the FBI had some knowledge of Mr. Riha's activities and whereabouts."[2]

When Ruzicka pressed Agent Smith for more information, the FBI man said he would make some additional inquiries. "He called back and said, 'Files indicate that another government agency advised Riha left Boulder to get away from his wife, and that he has not left the country. This is strictly off the record do not quote me.'"

The "government agency" that Smith most likely was referring to was the CIA because the language of the message is similar to the language CIA counterintelligence official Jane Roman used in an April 1969 memo in which she wrote, "Riha has been having difficulties with his wife, and he recently 'ran away from her.'"

Thomas's friends throughout the world were warned to keep away from the case. The CIA had the global reach to issue such warnings. Thomas's friends naturally assumed the warnings were related to espionage—not that the intelligence agency was trying to cover up its bungling.

Ted Curran, Thomas's friend from Columbia University, was working for the State Department in Mexico City when he learned that Thomas had disappeared. In an interview, he said he went to the CIA station in Mexico City and asked about it. "They checked and this was really something: The local station guy came back to me and said, 'You don't want to know.' And he said, 'I suggest you drop it.' Well, I'm afraid I did."[3]

Riha's friend, Libor Brom, was told "not to be interested" in the case. Scholars in Chicago and Boulder received similar, passively worded messages.[4]

Given what was at stake, officials in the CIA and FBI were alarmed in the spring of 1970, when Denver district attorney Mike McKevitt threatened to drag university president Joseph Smiley before a grand jury. The whole sordid mess could come out.

Both agencies had a lot to lose, but the FBI had the most at stake. It had vetted Thomas as a double agent. It had used Galya as an informant. And the FBI had been extremely duplicitous in saying it wasn't investigating Thomas when, in fact, it had accumulated so much evidence on him through its impersonation investigation of Galya.

Hoover, who was then in his twilight years and trying to hang on to his job, did not want that information to come out—ever. He described the case as one of "extreme importance" in his letter to Special Agent in Charge Scott Werner in which he commended Werner for his heated response to the CIA's Michael Todorovich.[5]

The role of the intelligence agencies in the Riha affair moved from obstruction to cover-up in 1973, when former CIA operative Robert Byrnes put out the report that a friend of a friend—a woman he referred to as X— had run into Thomas in Bratislava, Czechoslovakia.

It was important for the CIA and FBI to show that Thomas was still alive; the Church Committee was about to embark upon a historic investigation into illegal activities of the nation's intelligence agencies. If Thomas were presumed to be alive, the committee would pass over the case without much interest. But if he was dead, they might start digging in earnest, and eventually uncover how both the CIA and the FBI obstructed justice, lied to congressmen, and allowed a murderer to kill two more people. "The man who said Riha is in Czechoslovakia had a purpose—to act as a launderer," charged Slavic scholar Stephen Fischer-Galati.

Riha never resurfaced in the United States or any other country. Local police did only a halfhearted search for him and his remains have never been found. After killing Thomas, Galya disposed of his body, possibly in one of the hundreds of abandoned mines in the Rocky Mountains. Others have suggested a more grisly ending—that Riha's body was dissolved in the coffin-sized vat of acid in Gustav Ingwersen's garage.

After Galya committed suicide, the homicide investigations in Denver and Boulder withered and died. Like the FBI and CIA, law enforcement officials didn't want anyone probing too deeply for fear their missteps and omissions would be exposed.

Galya—the con artist who couldn't spell—had duped them all.

NOTES

PROLOGUE

1. The events described in this chapter are primarily taken from eight depositions conducted by Boulder attorney Gerald Caplan in the days following the ether incident. The depositions are part of the Boulder Police Department's Thomas Riha case (P69–7940) and were obtained by the author on Jan. 11, 2014, in response to a Colorado Open Records Act (CORA) request. Hereafter, the Boulder Police Department documents received under CORA are identified as BPD files.
2. Carol Word, interview by Fred Gillies, n.d., Fred Gillies Collection. Fred Gillies was a *Denver Post* reporter who reported on the Thomas Riha case for a decade. After he died, his nephew loaned me a box of documents that Fred kept on the case. Hereafter documents and interviews obtained from Gillies identified as Gillies Collection.
3. Thomas Riha, songbook, BPD files.
4. Carol Word, interview by Fred Gillies, n.d., Gillies Collection.
5. Galya Tannenbaum, "The Galya Tannenbaum Story," ca. 1970, Galya Tannenbaum Collection, Mss. 02647, History Colorado, Stephen H. Hart Research Center, Denver, CO, Box 1, FF 1, 12; hereafter identified as Tannenbaum Collection.
6. Galya Tannenbaum, interview by John Olson, Jan. 20, 1970, BPD files.
7. Tannenbaum, "The Galya Tannenbaum Story," 1.
8. Sandia National Laboratory: FBI interview, Galya Tannenbaum, Jan. 28, 1970, https://www.archives.gov/files/research/jfk/releases/docid-32989553.pdf. Feb. 13, 2020.
9. Galya Tannenbaum, address book, BPD files.
10. Howard A. Dougherty, interview by Fred Gillies, Oct. 8, 1975, Gillies Collection.
11. Donald Fanger, interview by author, Sept. 30, 2013.
12. Jarmila Zakova, interview by author, May 24, 2016.
13. Deposition, Rose Grossman, Mar. 17, 1969, BPD files.
14. Zdenek Cerveny, interview by author, Oct. 9, 2014.
15. Civil Action No. 19211, Complaint in Annulment or, in the Alternative, Divorce, Feb. 10, 1969, Colorado State Archives. Divorce proceeding was later transferred to Boulder County and renumbered Civil Action 24241.
16. Deposition, Veva P. Nye, Mar. 10, 1969, BPD files, 21.
17. Deposition, Hana Riha, Mar. 10, 1969, BPD files, 5.
18. Deposition, Rose Grossman, Mar. 17, 1969, BPD files, 2–9.
19. Deposition, Veva P. Nye, Mar. 10, 1969, 30.
20. Deposition, Veva P. Nye, Mar. 10, 1969, 32.

21. Deposition, Veva P. Nye, Mar. 10, 1969, 33.
22. Affidavit, David Regosin, Mar. 18, 1969, BPD files.
23. Deposition, Hana Riha, Mar. 10, 1969, 9.
24. Deposition, Hana Riha, Mar. 10, 1969, 11.
25. Deposition, Hana Riha, Mar. 10, 1969, 12.
26. Deposition, Hana Riha, Mar. 10, 1969, 16–17.
27. Deposition, Hana Riha, Mar. 10, 1969, 17.
28. Deposition, Hana Riha, Mar. 10, 1969, 24.
29. Deposition, Hana Riha, Mar. 10, 1969, 26.
30. Deposition, Hana Riha, Mar. 10, 1969, 26.
31. Deposition, Hana Riha, Mar. 10, 1969, 36–37.
32. Deposition, Hana Riha, Mar. 10, 1969, 38–39.
33. Deposition, Hana Riha, Mar. 10, 1969, 39.
34. Deposition, Hana Riha, Mar. 10, 1969, 41–42.
35. Deposition, Hana Riha, Mar. 10, 1969, 41.
36. Deposition, Hana Riha, Mar. 10, 1969, 41.
37. Deposition, Hana Riha, Mar. 10, 1969, 42.
38. Deposition, Hana Riha, Mar. 10, 1969, 44.
39. Deposition, Richard Wilson, Mar. 14, 1969, BPD files, 5.
40. Deposition, Richard Wilson, Mar. 14, 1969, 5.
41. Deposition, Douglas J. Dorsey, Mar. 13, 1969, BPD files, 2.
42. Deposition, Dale Stange, Mar. 15, 1969, BPD files, 4.
43. Deposition, Dale Stange, Mar. 15, 1969, 4–5.
44. Deposition, Douglas J. Dorsey, Mar. 13, 1969, 10.
45. Deposition, Douglas J. Dorsey, Mar. 13, 1969, 10–11.
46. Deposition, Douglas J. Dorsey, Mar. 13, 1969, 12.
47. Willard Spier, interview by Fred Gillies, Dec. 10, 1969, Gillies Collection.
48. Deposition, Margaret Hanson, Mar. 17, 1969, BPD files, 11.
49. Hana Riha, interview by author, Aug. 30, 2020.
50. Gerald Caplan, interview by author, Dec. 23, 2014.
51. Gerald Caplan, "A Twentieth Century Mystery," *Boulder County Bar Newsletter,* Sept. 2011.
52. Memorandum, Gerald Caplan, n.d., BPD files.
53. Gerald Caplan, interview by author, Dec. 23, 2014.
54. Gerald Caplan, interview by Denver police, Sept. 24, 1969; Hana Marie Hruska Riha to Immigration Service, Mar. 8, 1969; Hana Marie Hruska Riha to Immigration Service, Mar. 9, 1969, BPD files.
55. Denver police notes, Sept. 24, 1969, BPD files.
56. Hana Riha, interview by author, Jan. 12, 2015.
57. Joyce Lebra, "Tom Riha's Disappearance," June 11, 1970, Gillies Collection.
58. Carol Word, interview by Fred Gillies, Jan. 2, 1970, Gillies Collection.
59. Zdenek Cerveny, interview by author, Oct. 9, 2014.
60. Carol Word, interview by Fred Gillies, n.d., Gillies Collection.

1. CRAZY BILLY

1. Max Holland, *Leak: Why Mark Felt Became Deep Throat* (Lawrence: Univ. Press of Kansas, 2012), 145.

2. Sir Walter Scott, *Marmion,* ed. Henry Morley (London: Cassell & Co., 1888), https://www.gutenberg.org/files/4010/4010-h/4010-h.htm.
3. W. M. Felt to Mr. Tolson, "Inspection—Domestic Intelligence Division," May 26, 1969, https://archive.org/details/WilliamC.Sullivan/Sullivan%2C%20William%20C.%20-7/page/n9/mode/2up?q=Felt.
4. FBI, "Galya Tannenbaum Impersonation," Dec. 24, 1969, FBI-FOIA response to author.
5. Felt to Tolson, "Inspection—Domestic Intelligence Division," May 26, 1969.
6. Felt to Tolson, "Inspection—Domestic Intelligence Division," May 26, 1969.
7. Felt to Tolson, "Inspection—Domestic Intelligence Division," May 26, 1969.
8. Felt to Tolson, "Inspection—Domestic Intelligence Division," May 26, 1969.
9. J. Edgar Hoover to William C. Sullivan, Dec. 12, 1962, https://archive.org/details/WilliamC.Sullivan/Sullivan%2C%20William%20C.%20-5/page/n161/mode/2up.
10. William C. Sullivan and Bill Brown, *The Bureau: My Thirty Years in Hoover's FBI* (New York: W. W. Norton & Company, 1970), 171–72.
11. Beverly Gage, "What an Uncensored Letter to M. L. K. Reveals," *NYT Magazine,* Nov. 16, 2014.
12. Holland, *Leak,* 16.
13. D. A. Bryce to Director, Federal Bureau of Investigation, Mar. 3, 1942, https://archive.org/details/WilliamC.Sullivan/Sullivan%2C%20William%20C.%20-1/page/n129/mode/2up?q=March+3%2C+1942.
14. Sullivan, *The Bureau,* 80.
15. Report, Federal Bureau of Investigation, May 6, 1941, https://archive.org/details/WilliamC.Sullivan/Sullivan%2C%20William%20C.%20-1/page/n9/mode/2up.
16. Sullivan and Brown, *The Bureau,* 33.
17. William C. Sullivan to J. Edgar Hoover, Aug. 11, 1951, https://archive.org/details/WilliamC.Sullivan/Sullivan%2C%20William%20C.%20-3/page/n13/mode/2up.
18. H. L. Edwards to Mr. Mohr, Jan. 25, 1955, https://archive.org/details/WilliamC.Sullivan/Sullivan%2C%20William%20C.%20-3/page/n219/mode/2up?q=1955.
19. J. Edgar Hoover to G. B. Norris, Sept. 24, 1953, https://archive.org/details/WilliamC.Sullivan/Sullivan%2C%20William%20C.%20-3/page/n115/mode/2up?q=1955.
20. J. Edgar Hoover to William C. Sullivan, May 26, 1969, https://archive.org/details/WilliamC.Sullivan/Sullivan%2C%20William%20C.%20-7/page/n15/mode/2up?q=Felt.
21. *New York Times,* Aug. 27, 2009.
22. J. Edgar Hoover to William Sullivan, Apr. 24, 1970, https://archive.org/details/WilliamC.Sullivan/Sullivan%2C%20William%20C.%20-7/page/n49/mode/2up?q=Felt.
23. US Senate, 94th Congress, 2nd Session, Select Committee to Study Governmental Operations with Respect to Intelligence Activities, Book III, Final Report, Supplementary Detailed Staff Reports on Intelligence Activities and the Rights of Americans, Apr. 23, 1976, courtesy Mary Ferrell Foundation, 930–31.
24. Timothy Naftali, "An Oral History Interview with Tom Charles Huston," June 27, 2008, Richard Nixon Oral History Project, Richard Nixon Presidential Li-

brary and Museum, National Archives and Records Administration, https://
www.nixonlibrary.gov/sites/default/files/forresearchers/find/histories/Tom_
Charles_Huston_II.pdf.
25. Naftali, "An Oral History Interview . . . Huston," 19.
26. Naftali, "An Oral History Interview . . . Huston," 17
27. Stanley I. Kutler, *Abuse of Power* (New York: Simon & Schuster, 1997), 5.
28. Kutler, *Abuse of Power,* 14.
29. Sullivan and Brown, *The Bureau,* 206.
30. US Senate, 94th Congress, 1st Session, Select Committee to Study Governmental Operations with Respect to Intelligence Activities, vol. 2, Huston Plan, Sept.
23, 24, and 25, 1975, courtesy Mary Ferrell Foundation, 17.
31. FBI report, "Thomas Riha aka Thomas Andrew Charles Riha—Soviet Intelligence Services—Recruitment of Students," Aug. 31, 1960, FBI-FOIA response
to author.
32. Director, FBI, to SAC, Denver, Apr. 18, 1969, FBI-FOIA response to author.

2. GALYA

1. The description of Galya's childhood is taken from several untitled autobiographical sketches that Galya wrote in 1970 while she was in jail or hospitalized for psychiatric treatment. They can be found in the Galya Tannenbaum Collection, Mss.
02647, History Colorado, Stephen H. Hart Research Center, Denver, CO.
2. Galya Tannenbaum, "Personal History, 1931–58," Tannenbaum Collection, Box
1, FF2, 2.
3. Galya Tannenbaum, "Personal History," 5.
4. Galya Tannenbaum, "Personal History," 8.
5. Galya Tannenbaum, "Personal History," 10.
6. Galya Tannenbaum, "Personal History," 11.
7. Galya Tannenbaum, "Personal History," 22.
8. Galya Tannenbaum, "Personal History," 15.
9. Galya Tannenbaum, "Personal History," 31.
10. Galya Tannenbaum, "Personal History," 28–29.
11. Galya Tannenbaum, "Personal History," 36.
12. Galya Tannenbaum, interview by John R. Olson, Jan. 20, 1970, BPD files, 1.
13. Tannenbaum interview, Jan. 20, 1970, 4–6.
14. Galya Tannenbaum, "Personal History," 39.
15. Galya Tannenbaum, "Personal History," 39, 40.
16. Bolling Air Force Base Hospital, medical records, Sept. 16–29, 1948, Tannenbaum Collection, Box 1, FF7.
17. Margaret Ann McPherson, birth certificate, Tannenbaum Collection, Box 1, FF6.
18. Galya Tannenbaum, "Personal History," 44.
19. Galya Tannenbaum, "Personal History," 46.
20. Keith McGechie, probation report, Feb. 27, 1970, Tannenbaum Collection, Box
1, FF22.
21. FBI, Impersonation Report, June 12, 1951, FBI-FOIA response to author.
22. FBI, Impersonation Report, June 12, 1951.
23. FBI, Impersonation Report, June 12, 1951, 2.
24. Affidavit, Gloria Ann McPherson, July 24, 1951, FBI-FOIA response to author.

25. J. P. Hilton, "Review of Hospital Records of Galya Tannenbaum," Tannenbaum Collection, Box 2, FF 31.
26. *St. Louis Globe Democrat,* Nov. 19, 1954, FBI-FOIA response to author.
27. Galya Tannenbaum, "Personal History," 55.
28. Jewish Hospital of St. Louis, medical notes, Tannenbaum Collection, Box 1, FF 7.

3. THOMAS

1. Police notes, Jan. 29, 1970, BPD files.
2. Trial Transcript, *State of Colorado v. Tannenbaum,* Criminal Action 4971, Twentieth Judicial District, July 8–10 and July 15, 1970, Colorado State Archives, 310–11.
3. Cadastral office, Prague, land registers, records for House No. 28 in the street Nové Zámecké Schody.
4. Police registration form, 1850–1914, Prague, Czech Republic.
5. Donald Fanger, "Thomas Riha (1929–1969?)," *Slavic Review* 30, no. 4 (Dec. 1971): 945–46, Gillies Collection.
6. Fanger, "Thomas Riha (1929–1969?)," 945–46.
7. News clipping, n.d., courtesy Vonnie Perkins.
8. Robert Gerwath, *Hitler's Hangman: The Life of Heydrich* (New Haven, CT: Yale Univ. Press, 2011), 251.
9. Vojtech Blodig, Ludmila Chiadkova, and Miroslava Langhamerova, *Places of Suffering and Braveness, the Facilities of Nazi Repression in Terezin and Litomerice* (Prague, Czech Republic: Jitka Kejrova, V RAJI Publishing, 2003), 24.
10. Jarmila Zakova, interview by author, May 24, 2016.
11. Karel Kress file, National Archives, Czech Republic.
12. Zdenek Cerveny, interview by author, Oct. 9, 2014.
13. Police registration form, Prague, Czech Republic.
14. Police registration form, Prague, Czech Republic.
15. Gerwath, *Hitler's Hangman,* 282.
16. Milan Pelant, interview by author, May 20, 2016.
17. Police registration form, Prague, Czech Republic.
18. Zdenek Cerveny, interview by author, May 24, 2016.
19. Jarmila Zakova, interview by author, May 24, 2016.
20. Zakova interview, May 24, 2016.
21. Cerveny interview, Oct. 9, 2014.
22. Ruth Kressova Rihova, National Parliament Headquarters, Prague, 1945, National Archives, Czech Republic.
23. New York passenger lists, 1820–1957, courtesy Vonnie Perkins.
24. Stephen Foehr, "The Jig-saw Man," *Colorado Quarterly* 28, no. 4 (Winter 1980): 67.
25. Donald Fanger to James McKevitt, Feb. 2, 1970, BPD files.
26. Donald Fanger, interview by author, Apr. 23, 2014.
27. James N. Roethe, "Summary of Interviews with Sam J. Papich," Mar. 5, 1975, Rockefeller Commission, courtesy Mary Ferrell Foundation.
28. Roethe, "Summary of Interviews."
29. Certificate of naturalization, Dec. 19, 1952, Exhibit to Criminal Action No. 5003, District Court for County of Boulder, Colorado State Archives.
30. Bruce Parrott to Fred Gillies, Sept. 7, 1971, Gillies Collection.

31. Richard Helms with William Hood, *A Look over My Shoulder: A Life in the Central Intelligence Agency* (New York: Random House Publishing Group, 2003), 124.
32. Duane R. Clarridge, *A Spy for All Seasons* (New York: Scribner, 1997), 37.
33. Thomas K. Latimer to Sen. Frank Church, Nov. 19, 1975, Gillies Collection.
34. Oren Jarinkes, interview by author, Mar. 17, 2020.
35. Robert L. Schwind, interview by author, Nov. 28, 2014.
36. Schwind, interview, Nov. 18, 2014.
37. Ted Curran, interview by author, Sept. 17, 2013.
38. Peter Bridges, interview by author, Aug. 29, 2014.
39. Donald Fanger, interview by author, Sept. 30, 2013.
40. "UC Executive Kills Himself, Cook Leaps off Golden Gate Bridge," *San Bernardino Sun,* Aug. 11, 1958, California Digital Newspaper Collection.
41. "Back Home," *San Bernardino Sun,* May 31, 1946, California Digital Newspaper Collection.
42. "Kerr's Assistant Jumps off Bridge," *Madera Tribune,* Aug. 11, 1958, California Digital Newspaper Collection.
43. "UC Executive Kills Himself, Cook Leaps off Golden Gate Bridge," *San Bernardino Sun,* Aug 11, 1958, California Digital Newspaper Collection.
44. "Kerr's Assistant Jumps off Bridge."
45. Cerveny interview, Oct. 9, 2014.
46. Cerveny interview, Oct. 9, 2014.
47. Thomas Riha, "Russian Émigrés in Czechoslovakia between the Wars" (MA thesis, Univ. of California, Berkeley, 1951).
48. Loren Graham, interview by author, Apr. 13, 2012.
49. Richard Pipes, interview by author, Sept. 2, 2014.

4. BEHIND THE IRON CURTAIN

1. Indiana Univ., Robert F. Byrnes papers, 1875–1997, bulk 1960–89, Collection No. C 388.3, IUC and CIA, "GSEAs in Intel Work at Time of Application."
2. Richard Wortman, interview by author, Sept. 18, 2013.
3. Richard Helms with William Hood, *A Look over My Shoulder: A Life in the Central Intelligence Agency* (New York: Presidio Press, 2003), 220.
4. Robert Francis Byrnes obituary, *New York Times,* July 3, 1997.
5. Donald Fanger, interview by author, Sept. 30, 2013.
6. Anne Fisher, interview by author, May 21, 2014.
7. Robert Byrnes to Martin Buckley, June 18, 1976, Gillies Collection.
8. SAC, Boston, to Director, FBI, June 30, 1960, FBI-FOIA response to author.
9. "Punishment information," Thomas Riha file, Institute for the Study of Totalitarian Regimes, Jan. 1, 1951, Czech Republic.
10. Thomas Carba, Alexandr Korab, and David Borek, *Legacy* (Prague, Czech Republic: Museum of Communism, 2003), 36.
11. Jan H. Vitvar, Pavel Zacek, Anna Pavilikova, Miroslav Urbanek, Vladimir Bosak et al., *Prague Through the Lens of the Secret Police* (Prague, Czech Republic: Institute for the Study of Totalitarian Regimes, 2008), 7.
12. Jan H. Vitvar et al., *Prague,* 8.
13. Jarmila Zakova, interview by author, May 24, 2016.
14. SAC, Boston, to Director, FBI, Aug. 31, 1960, Gillies Collection.

15. Zdenek Cerveny, interview by author, May 24, 2016.
16. Cerveny interview, May 24, 2016.
17. Cerveny interview, May 24, 2016.
18. Wortman interview, Sept. 18, 2013.
19. Wortman interview, Sept. 18, 2013.
20. SAC, Boston, to Director, FBI, Aug. 31, 1960, Gillies Collection.
21. Thomas Riha, "The Soviet Education of a Young Historian of Russia," Robert F. Byrnes papers, Indiana Univ., C 388.6, Soviet Education Experience, 1958–69, 5.
22. Riha, "The Soviet Education of a Young Historian," 9–10.
23. Riha, "The Soviet Education of a Young Historian," 1–2.
24. Riha, "The Soviet Education of a Young Historian," 29.
25. FBI report, Aug. 31, 1960, FBI-FOIA response to author. The "double agent" reference appears three times in documents I received under the Freedom of Information Act, but was deleted in documents that Fred Gillies received in his FOIA request filed in the 1970s. In addition, two of the "double agent" comments are deleted from the Riha file recently placed on the Internet. A handwritten note, which states, "No dissemination since this was attempt to develop possible double agent," is also illegible on the Internet file.
26. SAC, Boston, to Director, FBI, May 25, 1960, FBI-FOIA response to author.
27. SAC, Boston, to Director, FBI, May 25, 1960, FBI-FOIA response to author.
28. FBI Report, Boston, to [Name deleted], Aug. 31, 1960, FBI-FOIA response to Fred Gillies, Gillies Collection.
29. FBI Report, Boston, to [Name deleted], Aug. 31, 1960, FBI-FOIA response to Fred Gillies, Gillies Collection.
30. Loren R. Graham, *Moscow Stories* (Bloomington: Indiana Univ. Press, 2006), 170.
31. FBI Report, Boston, to [Name deleted], Aug. 31, 1960, FBI-FOIA response to Fred Gillies, Gillies Collection.

5. CHICAGO

1. "Chicago Associates of Prof. Riha Disavow Claims by Mrs. Tannenbaum," *Rocky Mountain News,* Jan. 29, 1970.
2. "Chicago Associates of Prof. Riha Disavow Claims by Mrs. Tannenbaum."
3. Zdenek Cerveny, interview by author, Oct. 9, 2014.
4. Ernest Tross, "Appraisal for Insurance Purposes," Feb. 22, 1969, Gillies Collection.
5. Richard Wortman, interview by author, Sept. 18, 2013.
6. Jarmila Zakova, interview by author, May 24, 2016.
7. Zakova interview, May 24, 2016.
8. Zakova interview, May 24, 2016.
9. Tom Mangold, *Cold Warrior: The CIA's Master Spy Hunter* (New York: Simon and Schuster, 1991), 68.
10. Robert Byrnes to Martin Buckley, June 18, 1976, Gillies Collection.
11. Margie S., interview by author, July 20, 2012.
12. Colorado Bureau of Investigation, report, Apr. 8, 1971, courtesy John Kokish.
13. Galya Tannenbaum, "Personal History 1958–1961," Tannenbaum Collection, Box 1, FF4, 2.
14. Tannenbaum, "Personal History," 3.

15. Tannenbaum, "Personal History," 14.
16. Tannenbaum, "Personal History," 14.
17. Tannenbaum, "Personal History," 14.
18. Tannenbaum, "Personal History," 15.
19. Tannenbaum, "Personal History," 34.
20. Tannenbaum, "Personal History," 30.
21. Keith McGechie, probation report, Feb. 27, 1970, Tannenbaum Collection, Box 1, FF 22.
22. Tannenbaum, "Personal History," 46.
23. Tannenbaum, "Personal History," 17.
24. Trial transcript, *State of Colorado v Galya Tannenbaum,* Criminal Action 4971, July 8–10 and July 15, 1970, Colorado State Archives, 86.
25. Trial transcript, 233.
26. SAC, Chicago, to Director, FBI, Sept. 9, 1965, FBI-FOIA response to author.
27. US Senate, 94th Congress, 2nd Session, Select Committee to Study Governmental Operations with Respect to Intelligence Activities, Book III, Final Report, Supplementary Detailed Staff Reports on Intelligence Activities and the Rights of Americans, Apr. 23, 1976, courtesy Mary Ferrell Foundation, 416.
28. US Senate, Select Committee to Study Governmental Operations, Book III, Final Report, 511.
29. SAC, Chicago, to Director, FBI, Sept. 9, 1965, FBI-FOIA response to author.
30. Galya Tannenbaum, description of relationship with Leo Tanenbaum, Jan. 30, 1967, courtesy Becky Perkins.
31. Rebecca Eva Tanenbaum, birth certificate, courtesy Becky Perkins.
32. Margie S., interview by author, Aug. 30, 2016.
33. Tannenbaum, description of relationship with Leo Tanenbaum.
34. Tannenbaum, description of relationship with Leo Tanenbaum.
35. A. Rosen to Mr. DeLoach, Jan. 27, 1970, FBI-FOIA response to author.
36. Rosen to DeLoach, Jan. 27, 1970, 8–9.
37. Galya Tannenbaum, interview by John R. Olson, Jan. 20, 1970, BPD files, 2.
38. Wortman interview, Sept. 18, 2013.
39. *Gloria Tanenbaum v Leo Tanenbaum,* Paternity Suit Settlement Agreement and Order, No. 67-M1–160013, The Municipal Court of Chicago, First Municipal District of the Circuit Court of Cook County, IL, Apr. 18, 1968, courtesy Becky Perkins.

6. BOULDER

1. "The '60s: A Boulder Flashback," *Denver Post,* Apr. 18, 1982.
2. Gretchen King, interview by author, Sept. 11, 2014.
3. Jim Jankowski, interview by author, Oct. 10, 2014.
4. Boyd Hill, interview by author, Dec. 31, 2014.
5. Joyce Lebra, interview by author, May 27, 2014.
6. Lebra interview, May 27, 2014.
7. Libor Brom, "Commitment or Holocaust," Aug. 30, 1980, https://www.marian land.com/libor001.html.
8. Brom, "Commitment or Holocaust."
9. Libor Brom, "Where Is Your America?" Aug. 1982, https://www.marianland .com/liborbr.html.

10. Galya Tannenbaum, interview by John R. Olson, Jan. 20, 1970, BPD files, 10.
11. G. T. Rees to Sgt. Det. R. C. Diezi, Feb. 3, 1970, BPD files.
12. Thomas Riha's promissory note to Galya Tannenbaum, Sept. 1967, BPD files.
13. Tannenbaum interview, Jan. 20, 1970, 10.
14. Tannenbaum interview, Jan. 20, 1970, 11.
15. Thomas Riha, faculty vita, Apr. 20, 1967, Exhibit to Criminal Action No. 5003, Boulder District Court, Colorado State Archives.
16. Elizabeth Israels Perry, interview by author, May 30, 2014.
17. Thomas Riha, annual faculty report, Exhibit to Criminal Action No. 5003, Boulder District Court, Colorado State Archives.
18. Franziska Stein, interview by author, Nov. 1, 2013.
19. Franziska Stein, "Before the Traces Disappear," manuscript excerpt provided to author.
20. Franziska Stein, interview by author, Nov. 1, 2013.
21. Franziska Stein, interview by author, Feb. 5, 2014.
22. Dennis Blewitt, interview by author, Sept. 3, 2013.
23. "FBI Spying on the National Lawyers Guild," June 27, 2007, www.counterpunch .org.
24. Blewitt interview, Sept. 3, 2013.
25. Galya Tannenbaum to Dennis Blewitt, Mar. 18, 1968, BPD files.
26. Dennis Blewitt to Galya Tannenbaum, n.d., BPD files.
27. Blewitt interview, Sept. 3, 2013.
28. Dennis Blewitt, interview by author, Apr. 25, 2012.
29. Blewitt interview, Sept. 3, 2013.
30. Galya Tannenbaum, interview by FBI, Feb. 3, 1970, FBI-FOIA response to author.
31. Articles of incorporation, Aug. 30, 1968, BPD files.
32. Articles of incorporation, Aug. 2, 1968, BPD files.
33. Galya Tannenbaum to Sister Kostka, Jan. 2, 1969, BPD files.
34. Trial transcript, *State of Colorado v Galya Tannenbaum,* Criminal Action 4971, July 8–10 and July 15, 1970, Colorado State Archives, 179.
35. A. Rosen to Mr. DeLoach, Jan. 27, 1970, FBI-FOIA response to author.
36. Galya Tannenbaum to David Zimberoff, Jan. 31, 1969, BPD files.
37. Galya Tanenbaum to Chicago Bar Association, Dec. 4, 1968, BPD files.
38. Max J. Putzel to Fred Gillies, June 9, 1971, Gillies Collection.
39. Franziska Stein, interview by author, Nov. 1, 2013.
40. Putzel to Gillies, June 9, 1971.
41. Bohdan Philip Jan Lozinski obituary, *South Coast Today,* Nov. 13, 2002.
42. Philip Lozinski's invoice to Thomas Riha, Dec. 15, 1969, BPD files.
43. YouTube interview, Milos Foreman.
44. Jarmila Zakova, interview by author, May 24, 2016.
45. Zakova interview, May 24, 2016.
46. Zakova interview, May 24, 2016.
47. Zdenek Cerveny, interview by author, Oct. 9, 2014.
48. Deposition, Rose Grossman, Mar. 17, 1969, BPD files, 7.
49. Deposition, Rose Grossman, Mar. 17, 1969, 7.
50. Hana Riha, interview by author, Jan. 12, 2015.
51. H. Riha interview, Jan. 12, 2015.
52. Jankowski interview, Oct. 10, 2014.

53. Anne Fisher, interview by author, May 21, 2014.
54. Invitation, "Wedding Supper of Hanicka Hruska and Tomas Riha," Oct. 13, 1968, Gillies Collection.
55. Stein interview, Nov. 1, 2013.
56. Anne Fisher, interview by author, May 21, 2014.
57. Tannenbaum interview, Jan. 20, 1970, 14.
58. Fred Gillies, Calendar notation, Oct. 28, 1968, Gillies Collection.
59. H. Riha interview, Jan. 12, 2015.
60. H. Riha interview, Jan. 12, 2015.
61. H. Riha interview, Jan. 12, 2015.
62. H. Riha interview, Jan. 12, 2015.
63. H. Riha interview, Jan. 12, 2015. Hana said she doesn't remember how much the life insurance policy was worth.
64. H. Riha interview, Jan. 12, 2015.
65. H. Riha interview, Jan. 12, 2015.
66. H. Riha interview, Jan. 12, 2015.
67. H. Riha interview, Jan. 12, 2015.
68. H. Riha interview, Jan. 12, 2015.
69. Tannenbaum interview, Jan. 20, 1970, 20.
70. H. Riha interview, Jan. 12, 2015.
71. Galya Tannenbaum, interview by Ralph Ruzicka, Jan. 23, 1970, BPD files, 6.
72. Zdenek Cerveny, interview by author, Oct. 9, 2014.
73. Cerveny interview, Oct. 9, 2014.
74. Fred Gillies, Calendar notation, Mar. 24–26, 1969, Gillies Collection; Dunham obituary, *New York Times*, Apr. 9, 2001.
75. Complaint in Annulment or, in the alternative, Divorce, *Thomas Riha v Hana Riha*, Civil Action No. 19211 (divorce proceeding later transferred to Boulder County and renumbered Civil Action 24241), Feb. 10, 1969, Colorado State Archives.
76. Ernest Tross to Thomas Riha, "Appraisal for Insurance Purpose of a Collection of Objects of Art," Feb. 22, 1969, Gillies Collection.
77. Tannenbaum interview, Jan. 20, 1970, 19.
78. Carol Word, interview by Fred Gillies, n.d., Gillies Collection.
79. Copy of check, Mar. 4, 1969, BPD files.
80. Fred Gillies, calendar notation, Mar. 4, 1969, Gillies Collection.
81. Joyce Lebra, "Tom Riha's Disappearance," June 11, 1970, Gillies Collection.
82. Tannenbaum interview, Jan. 20, 1970, 20.

7. NEIGHBORHOOD WATCH

1. Fred Gillies, calendar notation, Mar. 14, 1969, Gillies Collection.
2. Carol Word, interview by Fred Gillies, n.d., Gillies Collection.
3. Thomas Riha to Donald Fanger, Mar. 15, 1969, BPD files.
4. Obituary, *Boulder Daily Camera*, May 25, 2013.
5. Patricia P. Faulkner, activity log, June 4, 1970, Gillies Collection.
6. Memorandum, "Galya Tannenbaum Impersonation," Dec. 24, 1970, FBI-FOIA response to author.
7. Thomas Riha to Wheeler Realty, Mar. 20, 1969, BPD files.
8. Joyce Lebra, "Tom Riha's Disappearance," June 11, 1970, Gillies Collection.

9. "Riha Had Questions: Is University Padding Gov't Fund Requests," *Gadfly,* Feb. 13, 1970, Gillies Collection.
10. Fred Gillies, notes, n.d., Gillies Collection.
11. Gillies, notes, n.d.
12. Ruth Ann Cook to Libor Brom, Apr. 25, 1969, Gillies Collection.
13. Libor Brom to Ruth Ann Cook, May 1, 1969, Gillies Collection.
14. Ruth Ann Cook to Libor Brom, May 6, 1969, Gillies Collection.
15. Stephen Fischer-Galati, interview by Fred Gillies, Dec. 17, 1969, Gillies Collection.
16. Anne Fisher, interview by author, Apr. 28, 2015.
17. Lebra, "Tom Riha's Disappearance."
18. Officer Alps to Capt. Spier, n.d., BPD files.
19. Lebra, "Tom Riha's Disappearance."
20. "Organizers Remember '71 Chicano Protest at UTEP," *Prospector,* Sept. 9, 2014.
21. Lebra, "Tom Riha's Disappearance."
22. Boyd Hill, interview by author, Dec. 31, 2014.

8. COUNTRY COUSINS AND SOCIALITES

1. "The More Things Change . . . ," *Boulder Planet,* Dec. 23, 1998, courtesy Carnegie Branch Library for Local History, Boulder, CO.
2. "The '60s: A Boulder Flashback," *Denver Post,* Apr. 18, 1982, courtesy Carnegie Library for Local History, Boulder, CO.
3. Todorovich's background is taken from a memoir written by Michael M. Todorovich, entitled *Michael M. Todorovich, His Autobiography, 1912–2004,* private printing, courtesy Don Bolich.
4. Todorovich, *Michael M. Todorovich,* 236.
5. Todorovich, *Michael M. Todorovich,* 208.
6. Todorovich, *Michael M. Todorovich,* 309.
7. US Senate, 94th Congress, 2nd Session, Select Committee to Study Governmental Operations with Respect to Intelligence Activities, Book III, Final Report, Supplementary Detailed Staff Reports on Intelligence Activities and the Rights of Americans, Apr. 23, 1976, courtesy Mary Ferrell Foundation, 712.
8. G. Gordon Liddy, *Will* (New York: St. Martin's Press, 1980), 119.
9. Turner Publishing, ed., *Society of Former Special Agents of the FBI* (Nashville, TN: Turner Publishing Co., 1998), 245.
10. Liddy, *Will,* 191.
11. "Havelock, 52, Dies in Prison; Less Than Month Till Parole," *Denver Post,* July 7, 1973, Gillies Collection.
12. "Fire-Charred Rest Room of Continental Jet, Air Force Vet Held in Airliner Sabotage," *Arizona Republic,* Nov. 21, 1968; death certificate of Lawrence B. Havelock, Gillies Collection.
13. "Spies, Terrorists Attracted to Treasure Hunters' Circles," *Manila Times,* May 31, 2002.
14. "Fire-Charred Rest Room of Continental Jet, Air Force Vet Held in Airliner Sabotage," *Arizona Republic,* Nov. 21, 1968.
15. Stephen Fischer-Galati to [Name deleted], Apr. 5, 1969, CIA-FOIA response to author.
16. Chief, Denver Office, to Director, Domestic Contact Service, Apr. 7, 1969, CIA-FOIA response to author.

17. Michael M. Todorovich, memorandum, Apr. 8, 1969, CIA-FOIA response to author.
18. Todorovich, memorandum, Apr. 8, 1969.
19. Todorovich, memorandum, Apr. 8, 1969.
20. Mike Todorovich to Director, Domestic Contact Service, Apr. 10, 1969, CIA-FOIA response to author.
21. "Riha's Absence Mysterious," *Colorado Daily,* Apr. 14, 1969, FBI-FOIA response to author.
22. "Riha's Absence Mysterious."
23. Stephen Fischer-Galati to Nathan B. Lenvin, Apr. 7, 1969, FBI-FOIA response to author.,
24. James N. Roethe, "Summary of Interviews with Sam J. Papich," Mar. 5, 1975, Rockefeller Commission, courtesy Mary Ferrell Foundation.
25. S. J. Papich to D. J. Brennan, Apr. 16, 1969, FBI- FOIA response to Fred Gillies, Gillies Collection.
26. FBI, memorandum, Dec. 24, 1969, FBI-FOIA response to author.
27. FBI, memorandum, Dec. 24, 1969.
28. FBI, memorandum, Jan. 22, 1970, FBI-FOIA response to author.

9. GUS

1. Galya Tannenbaum, interview by John R. Olson, Jan. 20, 1970, BPD files, 3.
2. "Doctor Upholds Galya's Sanity," *Denver Post,* Dec. 11, 1970.
3. "Galya's Attorney Asks for a Mistrial," *Rocky Mountain News,* Dec. 15, 1970.
4. "Riha's Book Collection Was Meant to Be Read," *Rocky Mountain News,* Feb. 27, 1970, Gillies Collection.
5. Thomas Riha to Wheeler Realty, Apr. 20, 1969, BPD files.
6. Ralph Ruzicka, interview by Fred Gillies, Aug. 18, 1970, Gillies Collection.
7. Thomas Riha to Boulder County Clerk, May 1, 1969, Civil Action 24241 (divorce), Colorado State Archives.
8. Classified advertising statement, Mar. 28, 1969, Gillies Collection.
9. "Witness Testifies Galya Used Mrs. Riha Name," *Denver Post,* Mar. 30, 1970.
10. "Curator Heard in Galya Case," *Denver Post,* Dec. 12, 1970, Gillies Collection.
11. Thomas Riha to Morris Philipson, June 16, 1969; copy of checks for $2,100 and $126.34, Gillies Collection.
12. William Briggs, interview by Fred Gillies, n.d., Gillies Collection.
13. W. E. Briggs to Thomas Riha, Apr. 10, 1969, BPD files.
14. Dan Smith, interview by Fred Gillies, Dec. 8, 1969, Gillies Collection.
15. Otis Sword, interview by Boulder police, Jan. 19, 1970, BPD files.
16. "Doctor Upholds Galya's Sanity," *Denver Post,* Dec. 11, 1970, Gillies Collection.
17. Zdenek Cerveny, interview by author, Oct. 9, 2014.
18. "Galya Called 'Very Bright,'" *Denver Post,* Dec. 15, 1970, Gillies Collection.
19. Cerveny interview, Oct. 9, 2014.
20. Dr. George Ogura, autopsy report of Gustav Ingwersen, June 18, 1969, courtesy Denver Medical Examiner's Office.
21. Obituary, *Rocky Mountain News,* June 26, 1969.
22. Pete Ingwersen, interview by author, June 22, 2020.
23. P. Ingwersen interview.
24. T. L. Lohr, supplementary DPD report, Feb. 27, 1970, courtesy Charlie McCormick.
25. Lohr, supplementary report, Feb. 27, 1970.

26. Tom Lohr, interview by author, Sept. 16, 2020.
27. Galya Tannenbaum to Dr. Hilton, n.d., Tannenbaum Collection, Box 2, FF 31.
28. Obituary, *Rocky Mountain News,* June 26, 1969.
29. Galya Tannenbaum to Dr. Hilton, n.d., Tannenbaum Collection, Box 2, FF 31.
30. Tannenbaum to Dr. Hilton, n.d.
31. Mildred Probert, interview by Denver police, July 30, 1969, Denver Police Department, Colorado Open Records Act response to author; hereafter known as DPD records.
32. Irene Theis, interview by Denver police, July 31, 1969, DPD records.
33. Galya Tannenbaum, interview by Denver police, July 8, 1969, DPD records.
34. Gertrude H. Bromley, interview by Denver police, June 22, 1969, DPD records.
35. C. B. McCormick to Sgt. M. J. Mullins, report, Feb. 1, 1971, DPD records.
36. Barney Gross, interview by Denver police, July 7, 1969, DPD records.
37. Denver police offense report, June 18, 1969, DPD records.
38. Pete Ingwersen, interview by author, June 22, 2020.
39. The family was told Gus had a handkerchief in his hand or near him, but the police report doesn't mention a handkerchief.
40. Denver police offense report, June 18, 1969, DPD records.
41. Donald Ingwersen, interview by Denver police, June 20, 1969, DPD records.
42. Martin J. Finnerty, interview by Denver police, July 8, 1969, DPD records.
43. Finnerty interview, July 8, 1969.
44. Gustav Ingwersen, last will and testament, DPD records.
45. McCormick to Mullins, report, Feb. 1, 1971.
46. Phillip Villalovos, interview by author, Oct. 11, 2020.
47. Denver police notes, June 20, 1969, DPD records.
48. DPD records show Galya wrote a $115.50 check on May 19, 1969; a $135 check on May 28, 1969; a $45.75 check on June 2, 1969; a $45 check on June 5, 1969, and another $45 check on June 5, 1969.
49. George Ogura, interview by author, Sept. 23, 2008.
50. Ogura interview, May 25, 2012.
51. Ogura interview, May 25, 2012.
52. Ogura, autopsy report of Gustav Ingwersen, June 20, 1969.
53. McCormick to Mullins, report, Feb. 1, 1971.
54. Denver police notes, June 21, 1969, DPD records.
55. Robert Ingwersen to Det. Phillip Villalovos, Dec. 28, 1969, DPD records.
56. Dale Crippen, interview by Denver police, July 31, 1969, DPD records.
57. Phillip Villalovos, interview by author, Oct. 11, 2020.
58. Villalovos interview, Oct. 11, 2020.
59. Tannenbaum interview, July 8, 1969.
60. McCormick to Mullins, report, Feb. 1, 1971.
61. Tannenbaum interview, July 8, 1969.
62. Tannenbaum interview, July 8, 1969.
63. Galya Tannenbaum to Dennis Blewitt, n.d., BPD files.
64. Tannenbaum to Blewitt, n.d.
65. Tannenbaum to Blewitt, n.d.
66. Galya Tannenbaum to Dennis Blewitt, Aug. 5, 1969, BPD files.
67. "Riha's Nephew Fears Missing Scholar Is Dead," *Rocky Mountain News,* Jan. 27, 1970.

68. Copy of check, Sept. 9, 1969, BPD files.
69. Neil King, interview by author, Sept. 11, 2014.
70. Lohr, supplementary report, Feb. 27, 1970, courtesy Charlie McCormick.
71. Lohr, supplementary report, Feb. 27, 1970.

10. BARBARA

1. Dr. George Ogura, autopsy report of Barbara Egbert, Sept. 15, 1969, courtesy Denver Medical Examiner's Office.
2. Maryann Hendee to Denver police, ca. Sept. 1969, DPD records.
3. Barbara Egbert, undated and unsigned typescript found during police search of her apartment, DPD records.
4. B. Egbert, undated and unsigned typescript.
5. Barbara Egbert to Marianna, Christmas 1967, DPD records.
6. Sonia Choquette, *Diary of a Psychic: Shattering the Myths* (Carlsbad, CA: Hay House Publishing, 2003), 161–62.
7. "Maurice Doreal and His Brotherhood of the White Temple Awaited the Apocalypse in Colorado," *Westword,* Oct. 28, 2015.
8. "Maurice Doreal and His Brotherhood of the White Temple," *Westword,* Oct. 28, 2015.
9. Mary Ann Hendee to Denver police, Oct. 6, 1969, DPD files.
10. Maryann Hendee, statement to Denver police, Oct. 6, 1969, DPD records.
11. Barbara Egbert to Mother and Dad, Sept. 10, 1969, DPD records.
12. Hendee, statement to Denver police, Oct. 6, 1969.
13. John Egbert, statement to Denver police, Sept. 17, 1969, DPD records.
14. Egbert, statement to Denver police, Sept. 17, 1969.
15. Supplemental police report, Barbara Egbert, Sept. 13, 1969, DPD records.
16. Barbara Egbert, suicide note, n.d., DPD files.
17. Egbert, suicide note.
18. Barbara Egbert, last will and testament, n.d., DPD files.
19. Dr. George Ogura, autopsy report of Barbara Egbert, Sept. 13, 1969, courtesy Denver Medical Examiner's Office.
20. Ogura, autopsy report of Barbara Egbert, Sept. 13, 1969.
21. Galya Tannenbaum to boys, Sept. 15, 1969, DPD records.
22. Eugene and Constance Hall, interview by Denver police, Sept. 15, 1969, DPD records.
23. Clinton D. Smith to Det. Phillip Villalovos, n.d., DPD records.
24. Smith to Villalovos, n.d.
25. Maryann Hendee to Mr. Smith, Jan. 14, 1970, DPD records.
26. Charles McCormick, interview by author, Sept. 14, 2020.
27. "Barbara Egbert" notes, Tannenbaum Collection, Box 4, FF 65. It's unclear if these notes were written by Galya Tannenbaum for John Kokish or if they were notes written by the Denver police during an interview of Galya Tannenbaum and later furnished to John Kokish.
28. Galya Tannenbaum, interview by Denver police, Sept. 18, 1969, DPD records.
29. Ben Garcia to Donald Ingwersen, Aug. 6, 1969, DPD records.
30. C. B. McCormick to M. J. Mullins, summary report, Feb. 1, 1971, DPD records.
31. McCormick to Mullins, summary report, Feb. 1, 1971.

32. Charles McCormick, interview by author, Sept. 14, 2020.

33. McCormick interview, Sept. 14, 2020.

34. Tom Lohr, interview by author, Sept. 16, 2020.

11. "BAG OF SNAKES"

1. Willard Spier, interview by Denver police, Sept. 22, 1969, BPD files.

2. Ray Mathias, interview by Denver police, Sept. 22, 1969, BPD files.

3. FBI, "Galya Tannenbaum Impersonation," Dec. 24, 1969, FBI-FOIA response to author.

4. FBI, "Galya Tannenbaum Impersonation," Dec. 24, 1969.

5. Divorce decree, Complaint in Annulment or, in the alternative, Divorce, *Thomas Riha v Hana Riha,* Civil Action No. 24241, Sept. 30, 1969, Colorado State Archives.

6. Hana Riha and Rose Grossman, interviews by Denver police, Sept. 24, 1969, BPD files.

7. Denver police, supplemental report, Sept. 24, 1969, BPD files.

8. Galya Tannenbaum, telephone interview by Denver police, Sept. 24, 1969, BPD files.

9. Tannenbaum telephone interview, Sept. 24, 1969.

10. Esther Rose Foote, affidavit, Oct. 8, 1969, DPD records.

11. Foote, affidavit, Oct. 8, 1969.

12. Esther Foote, telephone interview by Denver police, Sept. 23, 1969, BPD files.

13. Esther Foote, interview by Denver police, Sept. 25, 1969, DPD records.

14. Foote interview, Sept. 25, 1969.

15. Interview report, W. G. Nelson to R. R. Lundquist, Feb. 20, 1970, BPD files.

16. Zdenek Cerveny, interview by author, Oct. 9, 2014.

17. Galya Tannenbaum, description of Denver Jail, Tannenbaum Collection, Box 1, FF 16,17.

18. Richard Scherwitz's affidavit for search warrant, Oct. 28, 1969, DPD records.

19. "Daniel Hoffman, Denver Trial Lawyer for Decades, Dies," *Denver Business Journal,* Sept. 1, 2009.

20. John Kokish, interview by author, Mar. 22, 2012.

21. Zdenek Cerveny, interview by Boulder police, Oct 28, 1969, BPD files.

22. US Senate, 94th Congress, 2nd Session, Select Committee to Study Governmental Operations with Respect to Intelligence Activities, Book III, Final Report, Supplementary Detailed Staff Reports on Intelligence Activities and the Rights of Americans, Apr. 23, 1976, 8.

23. US Senate, 94th Congress, 1st Session, Select Committee to Study Governmental Operations with Respect to Intelligence Activities, vol. 2, Huston Plan, Sept. 23, 24, and 25, 1975, courtesy Mary Ferrell Foundation, 129.

24. US Senate, Select Committee to Study Governmental Operations, , 2:129–31.

25. Margie S., interview by author, July 20, 2012.

26. BPD notes, n.d., BPD files.

27. R. R. Ruzicka and Robert Diezi to District Attorney Stanley Johnson, Feb. 25, 1970, BPD files.

12. MAKING MUD

1. Zdenek Cerveny, interview by author, Oct. 9, 2014.
2. Fred Gillies, interview by author, Sept. 3, 2013.
3. Willard Spier, interview by Fred Gillies, Dec. 3, 1969, Gillies Collection.
4. Willard Spier, interview by Fred Gillies, Dec. 4, 1969, Gillies Collection.
5. Ralph Ruzicka, interview by Fred Gillies, Dec. 17, 1969, Gillies Collection.
6. Glen Reichert, interview by Fred Gillies, Dec. 15, 1969, Gillies Collection.
7. George Seaton, interview by Fred Gillies, Feb. 22, 1970, Gillies Collection.
8. Michael M. Todorovich to Director, Domestic Contact Service, Dec. 29, 1969, CIA-FOIA response to author.
9. Todorovich to Director, Domestic Contact Service, Dec. 29, 1969.
10. Michael M. Todorovich to Director, Domestic Contact Service, Dec. 30, 1969, CIA-FOIA response.
11. "Nearly a Year after Son's Disappearance, Riha's Mother Dead," *Denver Post,* Mar. 1, 1970.
12. Scott Werner to Ruth Ann Cook, Dec. 29, 1969, FBI-FOIA response to author.
13. Ruth Cook to Scott Werner, Dec. 5, 1969, FBI-FOIA response.
14. Ruth Ann Cook to Scott Werner, Jan. 11, 1970, FBI-FOIA response to author.
15. Libor Brom, interview by Fred Gillies, n.d., Gillies Collection.
16. "Nearly a Year after Son's Disappearance, Riha's Mother Dead."
17. Donald Brotzman to John Mitchell, Jan. 8, 1970, FBI-FOIA response to author.
18. Brotzman to Mitchell, Jan. 8, 1970.
19. J. Edgar Hoover to Donald G. Brotzman, Jan. 15, 1970, FBI-FOIA response to author.
20. FBI, "Galya Tannenbaum Impersonation," Dec. 24, 1969, FBI-FOIA response to author.
21. FBI, "Galya Tannenbaum Impersonation," Dec. 24, 1969.
22. George Bodley, interview by Fred Gillies, Feb. 17, 1970, Gillies Collection.
23. "Mystery Surrounds Riha '69 Tax Return," *Denver Post,* Feb. 8, 1970.
24. "Forgotten Envelope Sheds Light on Riha," *Denver Post,* Jan. 15, 1978.

13. SIGHTINGS

1. Earl Morrelli, statement, Feb. 19, 1970, BPD files.
2. Detective notes, Feb. 13, 1970, BPD files.
3. Richard Hopkins, interview by BPD, Jan. 12, 1970, BPD files.
4. Dennis Blewitt, interview by BPD, Jan. 12, 1970, BPD files.
5. Blewitt interview, Jan. 12, 1970.
6. Blewitt interview, Jan. 12, 1970.
7. BPD notes, Jan. 18, 1970, BPD files.
8. BPD notes, Jan. 18, 1970.
9. BPD notes, Jan. 28, 1970, BPD files.
10. Sgt. G. D. "Shorty" Walker to Lt. Ruzicka, Jan. 25, 1970, BPD files.
11. [Name illegible] to Ralph Ruzicka, n.d., BPD files.
12. BPD notes, n.d., BPD files.
13. Donald L. Hansen to Ralph Ruzicka, June 23, 1970, BPD files.

14. Sgt. Andrews, follow-up report, June 24, 1970, BPD files.
15. BPD notes, Apr. 23, 1971, BPD files.
16. Report, Robert Diezi to Willard Spier and Ralph Ruzicka, Jan. 19, 1970, BPD files.
17. BPD notes, Jan. 29, 1970, BPD files.
18. BPD notes, Jan. 26, 1970, BPD files.
19. Joyce Lebra to Mr. Paddock, Jan. 25, 1970, BPD files.
20. BPD notes, Feb. 19, 1970, BPD files.
21. BPD notes, Feb. 20, 1970, BPD files.
22. BPD notes, Feb. 20, 1970.
23. BPD notes, Feb. 20, 1970.
24. Otto Stockmar to BPD, Nov. 15, 1970, BPD files.
25. Stockmar to BPD, Nov. 15, 1970.
26. Galya Tannenbaum, interview by John R. Olson, Jan. 20, 1970, BPD files, 6.
27. Tannenbaum interview, Jan. 20, 1970, 7.
28. Tannenbaum interview, Jan. 20, 1970, 25.
29. Report, R. R. Ruzicka and Robert Diezi to District Attorney's Office, "Mrs. Galya Tannenbaum Forgery," Feb. 25, 1970, BPD files.
30. "Drug and Narcotic Evidence Examination Worksheet and Report," Jan. 30, 1970, BPD files.
31. "Mrs. Galya Tannenbaum Forgery," BPD files.
32. Galya Tannenbaum, interview by BPD, Jan. 23, 1970, BPD files.
33. Galya Tannenbaum, interview by FBI, Feb. 3, 1970, FBI-FOIA response to author.
34. Tannenbaum interview, Feb. 3, 1970.
35. Tannenbaum interview, Feb. 3, 1970.
36. "Mrs. Tannenbaum out on Bail," *Denver Post,* Jan. 30, 1970.
37. "Pleas of Innocent Entered," *Denver Post,* Feb. 5, 1970.
38. "In News Game, It's Digging That Counts," *Rocky Mountain News,* Feb. 3, 1970.
39. BPD notes, Feb. 12, 1970, BPD files.
40. "In News Game, It's Digging That Counts."

14. "H" BOMB

1. "MxKevitt Is Swamped with Riha Case Leads," *Rocky Mountain News,* Feb. 15, 1970.
2. David Wise, *American Police State* (New York: Random House, 1976), 263.
3. Robert L. Schwind to James B. McKevitt, Feb. 6, 1970, BPD files.
4. Robert L. Schwind, interview by author, Nov. 28, 2014.
5. Wise, *American Police State,* 264.
6. Transcript, Donald Fanger and Mike McKevitt, n.d., BPD files.
7. Walt Nelson, note, n.d., BPD files.
8. Michael M. Todorovich, memorandum, Feb. 3, 1970, CIA-FOIA response to author.
9. Denver Field Chief to Domestic Contact Service, Feb. 4, 1970, CIA-FOIA response to author.
10. Michael Todorovich, memorandum, Feb. 12, 1970, CIA-FOIA response to author.
11. Todorovich, memorandum, Feb. 12, 1970.
12. SAC, Denver, to Director, FBI, Feb. [day illegible], 1970, FBI-FOIA response to Fred Gillies, Gillies Collection.

13. Deputy Director for Intelligence to Director of Intelligence, Feb. 24, 1970, CIA-FOIA response to author.
14. SAC, Denver, to Director, FBI, Feb. [day illegible], 1970, FBI-FOIA response to Fred Gillies, Gillies Collection.
15. J. Edgar Hoover to Scott Werner, Feb. 13, 1970, FBI- FOIA response to author.
16. Wise, *The American Police State,* 264.
17. "MxKevitt Is Swamped with Riha Case Leads."
18. Chief, Denver Office to Director, Domestic Contact Service, Feb. 16, 1970, CIA-FOIA response to author.
19. Chief, Denver Office to Director, Domestic Contact Service, Feb. 16, 1970.
20. Richard Helms with William Hood, *A Look over My Shoulder: A Life in the Central Intelligence Agency* (New York: Random House Publishing Group, 2003), 269–70.
21. [Name deleted] to W. C. Sullivan, Feb. 20, 1970, FBI- FOIA response to author.
22. Helms with Hood, *A Look over My Shoulder,* 24.
23. Helms with Hood, *A Look over My Shoulder,* 273.
24. [Name deleted] to W. C. Sullivan, Feb. 18, 1970, FBI-FOIA response to author.
25. Richard Helms to J. Edgar Hoover, Feb. 26, 1970, Univ. of Colorado Boulder Libraries, Special Collections and Archives, Gary Hart Papers.
26. Helms to Hoover, Feb. 26, 1970.
27. Helms to Hoover, Feb. 26, 1970.
28. Helms to Hoover, Feb. 26, 1970.
29. Helms with Hood, *A Look over My Shoulder,* 271.
30. Wise, *American Police State,* 266.
31. Helms with Hood, *A Look over My Shoulder,* 270.
32. James N. Roethe, "Summary of interviews with Sam J. Papich," Mar. 5, 1975, courtesy Mary Ferrell Foundation. In one of these interviews, Papich states that the "alive and well information" was passed along to the FBI from the Denver police. That might have been true as Galya appeared to have a relationship with Art Dill, a Denver detective who would later become police chief.
33. "Reports of Riha's Safety Discounted," *Denver Post,* Feb. 15, 1970.
34. "Riha Grand Jury Probe Urged by CU Professor," *Denver Post,* Feb. 16, 1970.
35. SAC, El Paso, to Director, FBI, May 8, 1970, FBI-FOIA response to author.
36. Chief, Denver Office, to Director, Domestic Contact Service, June 4, 1970, CIA-FOIA response to Fred Gillies, Gillies Collection.
37. Chief, Denver Office, to Director, Domestic Contact Service, June 4, 1970.

15. THE HUSTON PLAN

1. William C. Sullivan with Bill Brown, *The Bureau: My Thirty Years in Hoover's FBI* (New York: W. W. Norton and Co., 1979), 156.
2. [Name deleted], affidavit, Oct. 4, 1971, https://archive.org/details/WilliamC.Sullivan/Sullivan%2C%20William%20C.%20-8/page/n17/mode/2up.
3. [Name deleted], affidavit, Oct. 5, 1971, https://archive.org/details/WilliamC.Sullivan/Sullivan%2C%20William%20C.%20-8/page/n19/mode/2up.
4. US Senate, 94th Congress, 2nd Session, Select Committee to Study Governmental Operations with Respect to Intelligence Activities, Book III, Final Report,

Supplementary Detailed Staff Reports on Intelligence Activities and the Rights of Americans, Apr. 23, 1976, courtesy Mary Ferrell Foundation, 932.

5. US Senate, 94th Congress, 1st Session, Select Committee to Study Governmental Operations with Respect to Intelligence Activities, vol. 2, Huston Plan, Sept. 23, 24, and 25, 1975, courtesy Mary Ferrell Foundation, 97.

6. Sullivan with Brown, *The Bureau,* 222.

7. FBI, Applicant-Special Agent report, Jan. 12, 1942, https://archive.org/details/ MarkFelt/1124498-000%20---%2067E-HQ-276576%20---%20Section%201/page /n15/mode/2up.

8. Mark Felt and John O'Connor, *A G-Man's Life* (New York: Public Affairs, 2006), 97.

9. Church Committee, Huston Plan, 13.

10. Church Committee, Final Report, 972.

11. Sullivan with Brown, *The Bureau,* 208.

12. Church Committee, Huston Plan, 9.

13. Church Committee, Huston Plan, 396.

14. Church Committee, Final Report, 943.

15. Church Committee, Huston Plan, 9.

16. Sullivan with Brown, *The Bureau,* 210.

17. Sullivan with Brown, *The Bureau,* 209.

18. Sullivan with Brown, *The Bureau,* 5.

19. Church Committee, Final Report, 942.

20. Church Committee, Huston Plan, 7.

21. Sullivan with Brown, *The Bureau,* 214.

22. Church Committee, Final Report, 954.

23. Church Committee, Final Report, 954.

24. Church Committee, Final Report, 960.

25. Church Committee, Final Report, 961.

26. Church Committee, Huston Plan, 33.

27. Church Committee, Huston Plan, 59.

28. Church Committee, Huston Plan, 45.

29. Church Committee, Huston Plan, 71.

30. Church Committee, Final Report, 926.

31. Church Committee, Huston Plan, 116.

16. THIRTY-SIX DAYS

1. Trial transcript, *State of Colorado v Galya Tannenbaum,* Criminal Action 4971, July 8–10 and July 15, 1970, Colorado State Archives, 100.

2. "Galya Tannenbaum's Art Exhibit," *Denver Post,* Mar. 22, 1970.

3. Galya Tannenbaum to Dr. Hilton, n.d., Galya Tannenbaum Collection, Box 2, FF 31.

4. Tannenbaum to Dr. Hilton, n.d.

5. Galya Tannenbaum, sketch, Tannenbaum Collection, Box 1, FF 5.

6. Tannenbaum, sketch.

7. Galya Tannenbaum to Dr. Hilton, "Sketch of Gus Ingwersen," ca. May 17, 1970, Tannenbaum Collection, Box 2, FF 31.

8. Dr. Roland Brett to District Judge Robert T. Kingsley, report, Mar. 9, 1970, Tannenbaum Collection, Box 1, FF 16, 13.

9. Tannenbaum to Hilton, "Sketch of Gus Ingwersen."
10. Tannenbaum to Hilton, "Sketch of Gus Ingwersen."
11. Leighton Whitaker, psychological report, Mar. 18, 1970, Tannenbaum Collection, Box 1, FF 16.
12. Dr. Roland Brett to District Judge Robert T. Kingsley, report, Mar. 9, 1970, Tannenbaum Collection, Box 1, FF 16, 18.
13. Brett to Kingsley, report, 18.
14. Brett to Kingsley, report, 2.
15. Brett to Kingsley, report, 8.
16. Brett to Kingsley, report, 19.
17. "Forgery Suspect Arrested," *Denver Post,* Mar. 13, 1970.
18. Galya Tannenbaum, sketch, Tannenbaum Collection, May 22, 1970, Box 1, FF 16.
19. Jo Ann Norton, interview by author, Sept. 30, 2013.
20. Gayle and Jo Ann Norton, deposition, Tannenbaum Collection, Feb. 15, 1974, Box 4, FF 57, 23.
21. G. and J. A. Norton, deposition, Feb. 15, 1974, 24.
22. G. and J. A. Norton, deposition, Feb. 15, 1974, 16–17.
23. Galya Tannenbaum to Mr. and Mrs. Norton, letter 1, n.d., written on Boulder County Jail stationary, courtesy Becky Perkins.
24. Galya Tannenbaum to Gayle Norton, letter 2, n.d., courtesy Becky Perkins.
25. Tannenbaum to Nortons, letter 1, n.d.
26. Tannenbaum to G. Norton, letter 2, n.d.
27. Trial transcript, *State of Colorado v Galya Tannenbaum,* Criminal Action 4971, Colorado State Archives, 186.
28. Trial transcript, 190.
29. Galya Tannenbaum to Gayle Norton, Apr. 14, 1970, courtesy Becky Perkins.

17. THE TRIAL

1. Trial transcript, *State of Colorado v Galya Tannenbaum,* Criminal Action 4971, July 8–10 and July 15, 1970, Colorado State Archives, 257.
2. "Forgotten Envelope Sheds Light on Riha," *Denver Post,* Jan. 15, 1978.
3. John M. Macdonald, *The Murderer and His Victim* (Springfield, IL: Charles C. Thomas, 1961), 193.
4. Trial transcript, 35.
5. Trial transcript, 24.
6. Trial transcript, 35.
7. Trial transcript, 30.
8. Trial transcript, 99.
9. Trial transcript, 142.
10. Trial transcript, 103.
11. Trial transcript, 21.
12. Trial transcript, 12.
13. Trial transcript, 29.
14. Trial transcript, 36–37.
15. Trial transcript, 16.
16. Trial transcript, 29.
17. Trial transcript, 11.

18. Trial transcript, 39.
19. Trial transcript, 43.
20. Trial transcript, 46–47.
21. Trial transcript, 51.
22. Macdonald, *The Murderer and His Victim*, 203.
23. Macdonald, *The Murderer and His Victim*, 204.
24. Macdonald, *The Murderer and His Victim*, 204–5.
25. Trial transcript, 52–53.
26. Trial transcript, 57.
27. The hospitalizations are as follows:
   • Dec. 16, 1948: Gloria McPherson, age twenty, was admitted to the Bolling
     Air Force Base hospital after being unable to move her left arm or leg for
     two weeks. Her facial muscles twitched and she talked rapidly, exhibiting the
     "flight of ideas" that was consistent with a diagnosis of manic depression.
   • Mar. 22, 1952: Gloria McPherson, age twenty-two, was admitted to St. Louis
     University Hospital. She was pregnant at the time, but denied her condition,
     weeping during interviews and asking for advice on how to get her boy-
     friend to marry her and provide a home for her little girl. She also said she
     could hear people talking, but couldn't understand what they were saying.
   • Mar. 12, 1954: Gloria McPherson, age thirty-three, a Baptist, arrived in a
     coma at St. Louis County Hospital after trying to kill herself by ingesting
     bichloride of mercury, chloral hydrate, and Nembutals. When she came out
     of the coma, she said she was an air force captain and seven years earlier
     had had a malignant tumor on her pancreas removed. Hospital staffers diag-
     nosed her with inadequate personality and sociopathic personality.
   • June 2, 1955: Gloria McPherson, age thirty-four, was admitted to St. Louis's
     Jewish Hospital in a coma after ingesting a large quantity of barbiturates
     and morphine. She said she had lung cancer and was dying. The coma was
     so deep that a spinal tap was performed to make sure she wasn't suffering
     from brain hemorrhage.
   • June 5, 1955: Gloria Ann McPherson, age twenty-five, was admitted to
     Barnes Hospital in St. Louis after ingesting twenty Nembutals and leaving
     behind her last will and testament.
   • Sept. 12, 1963: Gloria Ann Zakharovna, age forty-three, admitted to the Uni-
     versity of Illinois Research and Educational Hospital, telling doctors that her
     lesbian roommate was trying to poison her because Galya had rebuffed her
     sexual advances. When Galya's mother arrived on the ward, Galya admitted
     she had falsified some of her background to "make herself appear interesting."
   • Oct. 2, 1965: Galya Tannenbaum, age forty-five, was admitted to Michael
     Reese Hospital. She was five months pregnant and told the medical staff she
     had been incarcerated in a German concentration camp during World War II
     and that a monkey fetus had been implanted in her.
28. Trial transcript, 96.
29. Trial transcript, 112.
30. Trial transcript, 149.
31. Trial transcript, 159.
32. Trial transcript, 154.
33. Trial transcript, 174.

34. Trial transcript, 179.
35. Trial transcript, 182.
36. Trial transcript, 185–86.
37. Trial transcript, 193.
38. Trial transcript, 201.
39. Trial transcript, 205.
40. Trial transcript, 204–5.
41. Trial transcript, 210.
42. Zdenek Cerveny, interview by author, Oct. 9, 2014.
43. Trial transcript, 209.
44. Trial transcript, 218.
45. Trial transcript, 221–22.
46. Trial transcript, 222.
47. Trial transcript, 225.
48. Trial transcript, 239.
49. Trial transcript, 243.
50. Trial transcript, 249.
51. Trial transcript, 242.
52. Trial transcript, 253.
53. Trial transcript, 256–57.
54. Trial transcript, 259.
55. Trial transcript, 286–87.
56. Trial transcript, 287.
57. Trial transcript, 293.
58. Trial transcript, 296.
59. Carol Word, interview by author, Nov. 11, 2013.
60. Trial transcript, 302.
61. Trial transcript, 323–24.
62. Trial transcript, 347–48.
63. Trial transcript, 354.
64. Trial transcript, 354–55.

18. THE SMELL OF ALMONDS

1. Hospital description taken from Nell Mitchell, *The 13th Street Review, A Pictorial History of the Colorado State Hospital* (Pueblo, CO: My Friend, the Printer Inc., 2009), 47.
2. Charles Meredith, deposition, Feb. 1, 1973, Tannenbaum Collection, Box 3, FF 50.
3. Dr. David Olenik, deposition, Nov. 28, 1973, Tannenbaum Collection, Box 3, FF 54, 65.
4. Fred Gillies, notes, n.d., Gillies Collection.
5. Galya Tannenbaum to Dr. Hilton, July 30, 1970, Tannenbaum Collection, Box 1, FF 16.
6. Olenik, deposition, Nov. 28, 1973, 57.
7. Olenik, deposition, Nov. 28, 1973, 68.
8. Olenik, deposition, Nov. 28, 1973, 56.
9. Colorado Bureau of Investigation, report, Apr. 8, 1971, 15; hereafter known as "CBI report."

10. Olenik, deposition, Nov. 28, 1973, 69.
11. Olenik, deposition, Nov. 28, 1973, 63.
12. CBI report, 34.
13. Olenik, deposition, Nov. 28, 1973, 66.
14. Transcript, Special Review Committee, Sept. 21, 1970, exhibit to Karl Waggener's Oct. 30, 1971, deposition, Tannenbaum Collection. Box 4, FF 55.
15. Transcript, Special Review Committee, Sept. 21, 1970.
16. CBI report, 16–18, 32–34.
17. CBI report, 34.
18. Fred Gillies, "T's Feelings and Attitudes," n.d., Gillies Collection.
19. Kathryn Huskins, deposition, Dec. 30, 1973, Tannenbaum Collection, Box 3, FF 53, 22.
20. Henry Madrid, deposition, Feb. 1, 1973, Tannenbaum Collection, Box 3, FF 49, 14.
21. Madrid, deposition, Feb. 1, 1973, 16.
22. Madrid, deposition, Feb. 1, 1973, 27.
23. Madrid, deposition, Feb. 1, 1973, 22.
24. Madrid, deposition, Feb. 1, 1973, 24.
25. Madrid, deposition, Feb. 1, 1973, 26.
26. Madrid, deposition, Feb. 1, 1973, 27.
27. Madrid, deposition, Feb. 1, 1973, 46.
28. Madrid, deposition, Feb. 1, 1973, 46.
29. Madrid, deposition, Feb. 1, 1973, 48.
30. Madrid, deposition, Feb. 1, 1973, 48.
31. Madrid, deposition, Feb. 1, 1973, 48–49.
32. Madrid, deposition, Feb. 1, 1973, 48.
33. Galya Tannenbaum, jail sketch, n.d., Tannenbaum Collection, Box 1, FF 16.
34. CBI report, 29.
35. CBI report, 29.
36. "Galya Ordered Held in Arapahoe Jail," *Rocky Mountain News,* Dec. 10, 1970.
37. CBI report, 28.
38. "Witness Testifies Galya Claimed Stove Invention," *Rocky Mountain News,* Dec. 18, 1970.
39. "Curator Heard in Galya Case," *Denver Post,* Dec. 12, 1970.
40. Dr. Ian McNickle to Haydee Kort, report, Dec. 23, 1970, Tannenbaum Collection, Box 3, FF 53.
41. Madrid, deposition, Feb. 1, 1973, 34.
42. Madrid, deposition, Feb. 1, 1973, 40.
43. Olenik, deposition, Nov. 28, 1973, 34.
44. Galya Tannenbaum to Margie, Mar. 4, 1971, courtesy Becky Perkins.
45. Galya Tannenbaum to John Kokish, Mar. 4, 1971, BPD files.
46. Madrid, deposition, Feb. 1, 1973, 16.
47. Madrid, deposition, Feb. 1, 1973, 20.
48. CBI report, 26.
49. Galya Tannenbaum, suicide note, Mar. 6, 1971, Tannenbaum Collection, Box 1, FF 16.
50. Fred Gillies, "Treatment for T," n.d., Gillies Collection.
51. CBI report, 40.
52. CBI report, 4.
53. CBI report, 7.

54. CBI report, 10.
55. CBI report, 10.
56. CBI report, 32.
57. CBI report, 41.
58. Olenik, deposition, Nov. 28, 1973, 48.
59. Madrid, deposition, Feb. 1, 1973, 59.
60. Olenik, deposition, Nov. 28, 1973, 50.
61. Olenik, deposition, Nov. 28, 1973, 51.
62. Olenik, deposition, Nov. 28, 1973, 70–71.
63. Olenik, deposition, Nov. 28, 1973, 69.

19. TORPEDOES AND SUBMARINES

1. William C. Sullivan and Bill Brown, *The Bureau: My Thirty Years in Hoover's FBI* (New York: W. W. Norton & Company, 1970), 107.
2. Mark Felt and John O'Connor, *A G-Man's Life* (New York: Public Affairs, 2006), 115.
3. Sullivan and Brown, *The Bureau*, 204.
4. Sullivan and Brown, *The Bureau*, 266.
5. W. Mark Felt to John Edgar Hoover, Apr. 30, 1971, https://archive.org/details/MarkFelt/1124498-000%20---%2067E-HQ-276576%20---%20Section%205%20%28880209%29/page/n239/mode/2up?q=portrait.
6. Felt and O'Connor, *A G-Man's Life*, 118.
7. Sullivan and Brown, *The Bureau*, 243.
8. Sullivan and Brown, *The Bureau*, 223.
9. W. M. Felt to Director, Oct. 6, 1971, https://archive.org/details/WilliamC.Sullivan/Sullivan%2C%20William%20C.%20-8/page/n29/mode/2up?q=purloined.
10. O. T. Jacobson to Mr. Walters, May 12, 1973, "Sensitive Coverage Placed at Request of the White House," May 12, 1973, https://archive.org/details/WilliamC.Sullivan/Sullivan%2C%20William%20C.%20-8/page/n199/mode/2up?q=Mardian.
11. Sullivan and Brown, *The Bureau*, 276–77.
12. J. Edgar Hoover to Mr. Tolson et al., Oct. 1, 1971, https://archive.org/details/WilliamC.Sullivan/Sullivan%2C%20William%20C.%20-8/page/n1/mode/2up?q=insolence.
13. Mr. Felt to Mr. Tolson, Oct. 5, 1971, https://archive.org/details/WilliamC.Sullivan/Sullivan%2C%20William%20C.%20-8/page/n25/mode/2up.
14. Felt and O'Connor, *A G-Man's Life*, 120.
15. Sullivan and Brown, *The Bureau*, 248.
16. William M. Kunstler to Griffin B. Bell, Apr. 21, 1978, https://archive.org/details/WilliamC.Sullivan/Sullivan%2C%20William%20C.%20-9/page/n277/mode/2up?q=Griffin.

20. THE FINK

1. David Robarge, "The James Angleton Phenomenon," *Studies in Intelligence* 53, no. 4, 2010, https://www.cia.gov/library/center-for-the-study-of-intelligence/csi-publications/csi-studies/studies/vol53no4/pdf/U-%20Robarge-Passages-17Nov09.pdf.

2. US Senate, Senate Historical Office, "Senate Select Committee to Study Governmental Operations with Respect to Intelligence Activities," synopsis, https://www.senate.gov/about/powers-procedures/investigations/church-committee.htm.
3. "Huge C.I.A. Operation Reported in U. S. against Antiwar Forces, Other Dissidents in Nixon Years," *New York Times,* Dec. 22, 1974.
4. "Huge C.I.A. Operation Reported in U. S. Against Antiwar Forces, Other Dissidents in Nixon Years."
5. US Senate, Senate Historical Office, synopsis of Church Committee.
6. Mary Ferrell Foundation, "Post-Watergate Intelligence Investigations," https://www.maryferrell.org/pages/Main_Page.html. The Mary Ferrell Foundation (maryferrell.org), contains an extraordinary amount of information about the JFK assassination, the MLK assassination, the RFK assassination, the assassination of Malcolm X, the Watergate burglary, and other issues.
7. "Howard Baker: The Real Story of His Famous Watergate Question," *Christian Science Monitor,* June 26, 2014, https://www.csmonitor.com/USA/Politics/Decoder/2014/0626/Howard-Baker-the-real-story-of-his-famous-Watergate-question.
8. Katherine Seekatz to author, Feb. 21, 2014.
9. Gary Hart to Fred Gillies, Mar. 6, 1975, Gillies Collection.
10. Below are some questions Fred Gillies prepared for submission to the CIA. Nearly identical questions were also posed to the FBI, INS, and military intelligence:
    - Does the CIA have any information that Riha is in Czechoslovakia, the Soviet Union, or any other country?
    - Does the CIA have evidence or belief that Riha is dead? What is the evidence for this belief? How did he die?
    - Was Thomas Riha known to the agency? If so, when was he first known to the agency and why?
    - Was Riha employed by the CIA? In what capacity? When?
    - Did Riha report contacts with a "Mr. Chrpa" in Prague, Czechoslovakia, in 1958 and a later contact that same year with "Chrpa" in Moscow? Did Riha inform the CIA that Chrpa tried to recruit him as a Red-bloc intelligence agent?
    - Was Riha an agent for the Soviet Union?
    - Was Riha a double agent?
    - What does the CIA know about the Treasure Tours International Travel Agency in Montreal, Canada? Is this travel agency a "front" for CIA agents traveling abroad?
    - Was Mrs. Gloria Tannenbaum ever employed by the CIA? If so, in what capacity?
    - Was Mrs. Tannenbaum sent by the CIA from Chicago to Boulder, Colorado, in 1968 to check on Riha or on Boulder attorney Dennis Blewitt?
    - Were CIA agents trailing Riha in early 1969?
    - What knowledge does the CIA have about Mrs. Gloria (Galya) Tannenbaum's reported suicide by swallowing cyanide at the Colorado State Hospital in March 1971? Is the CIA acquainted with one of the hospital's technicians, Henry Madrid, and for what reason?
11. Robert Byrnes to Donald Fanger, Nov. 5, 1973, Gillies Collection.
12. Donald Fanger to Robert Byrnes, Dec. 10, 1973, Gillies Collection.
13. Fanger to Byrnes, Dec. 10, 1973.

14. Fanger to Byrnes, Dec. 10, 1973.
15. "Report Calls Riha Intelligence Agent," *Denver Post,* July 26, 1976.
16. US Senate, 94th Congress, 1st Session, Select Committee to Study Governmental Operations with Respect to Intelligence Activities, vol. 2, Huston Plan, Sept. 23, 24, and 25, 1975, 83–84, courtesy Mary Ferrell Foundation.
17. US Senate, Select Committee to Study Governmental Operations, 127–28.
18. "Statement of Gary Hart," Staff of the Senate Select Committee on Intelligence Activities, "The Riha Inquiry," Feb. 1976, Gillies Collection.
19. Zdenek Cerveny, interview by author, Oct. 9, 2014.
20. Robert F. Byrnes to Martin D. Buckley, June 18, 1976, in *Zdenek Cerveny v Central Intelligence Agency,* US District Court for the District of Colorado, CV No. 76 M 690.
21. Byrnes to Buckley, June 18, 1976.
22. Stansfield Turner, affidavit, in *Cerveny v Central Intelligence Agency,* Oct. 8, 1977.
23. Zdenek Cerveny, affidavit, in *Cerveny v Central Intelligence Agency,* [date illegible], 9.
24. "U. S. Judge Declines to Review CIA's Records on Riha," *Rocky Mountain News,* Jan. 25, 1978.
25. Attachment in letter to Martin Buckley from US Army Intelligence and Security Command, Sept. 29, 1977, in *Cerveny v Central Intelligence Agency.*
26. Attachment in letter to Buckley from US Army Intelligence and Security Command, Sept. 29, 1977.
27. Philip Lozinski, invoice, Dec. 15,1969, BPD files.
28. Attachment in letter to Buckley from US Army Intelligence and Security Command, Sept. 29, 1977.
29. Attachment in letter to Buckley from US Army Intelligence and Security Command, Sept. 29, 1977.
30. Lawrence B. Havelock, death certificate, July 3, 1973, Gillies Collection.

21. MISSPELLINGS AND MURDER

1. Galya Tannenbaum to Margie, Mar. 4, 1971, courtesy Becky Perkins.
2. Ursula M. Wilder, "The Psychology of Espionage," *Studies in Intelligence* 61, no. 2 (2017): 21, https://www.cia.gov/library/center-for-the-study-of-intelligence/csi-publications/csi-studies/studies/vol-61-no-2/pdfs/psychology-of-espionage.pdf.
3. Paul Babiak et al., "Psychopathy: An Important Forensic Concept for the 21st Century," *FBI Law Enforcement Bulletin,* July 1, 2012, 2, https://leb.fbi.gov/articles/featured-articles/psychopathy-an-important-forensic-concept-for-the-21st-century.
4. Fydor Dostoyevsky, *Crime and Punishment,* originally published in the series, *The Russian Messenger* (Moscow: N.p., 1866).
5. "Galya's Attorney Asks for Mistrial," *Rocky Mountain News,* Dec. 15, 1970.
6. Denver police notes, Sept. 24, 1969, DPD records.
7. John M. Macdonald, *The Murderer and His Victim,* (Springfield, IL: Charles C. Thomas, 1961), 204.
8. Macdonald, *The Murderer and His Victim,* 122.
9. Zdenek Cerveny, interview by author, Nov. 1, 2016.
10. Zdenek Cerveny, interview by author, Oct. 9, 2014.

11. Galya Tannenbaum to Denver Art Museum, Mar. 1, 1969, Gillies Collection.
12. Robert Stroessner, interview by Fred Gillies, Dec. 23, 1969, Gillies Collection.
13. The words "concidered" and "concideration" show up in a Jan. 2, 1969, letter written by Galya; "concideration" in a Jan. 8, 1969, letter; "concidering" in a Jan. 10, 1969, letter, and "concideration" in a Jan. 29, 1969, letter. "Concider" shows up in the Mar. 8 and Mar. 9, 1969, letters purportedly written by Hana. All letters found in BPD files. The word "extremely" shows up in letters written by Galya on Jan. 8, 1969, Jan. 27, 1969, Jan. 31, 1969, and Feb. 4, 1969. All letters found in BPD files.
14. These words show up in letters that Galya wrote to relatives and others between 1968 and 1970. All letters found in BPD files.
15. Thomas Riha to First National Bank, Apr. 28, 1969, BPD files.
16. All the letters allegedly from Thomas Riha that were forged by Galya can be found in the BPD files.
17. Ben Garcia to Willard H. Spier, Jan. 27, 1970, BPD files.
18. Galya endorsed and cashed checks for $2,685 and $202 from Thomas Riha's bank account; received $1,200 from the sale of the Pietà to the Denver Art Museum; charged $1,213.08 on Riha's credit card; received $1,392.25 from Wheeler Realty for the sale of Riha's house, received $2,100 in royalties from his books, and $1,200 from the sale of his car. BPD files.
19. Gustav Ingwersen, will, June 5, 1969, DPD records; emphasis added.
20. Det. C. B. McCormick Jr. to Sgt. M. J. Mullins, Feb. 1, 1971, DPD records.
21. Barbara Egbert to Whom It May Concern, n.d., DPD records; emphasis added.
22. Police notes, Oct. 2, 1969, DPD records.
23. Charles McCormick, interview by author, Sept. 14, 2020.
24. McCormick Jr. to Mullins, Feb. 1, 1971.
25. R. B. Smith, Oct. 14, 1969, BPD files; also police notes, Jan. 29, 1970, BPD files, and Lee Hedenburg, police statement, Oct. 2, 1969, DPD records.
26. Katherine Ramsland, book review, *Psychology Today,* July 17, 2016, https://www.psychologytoday.com/us/blog/shadow-boxing/201607/staging-murder.
27. McCormick interview, Sept. 14, 2020.
28. McCormick Jr. to Mullins, Feb. 1, 1971.

22. THE INFORMANT AND THE "USEFUL IDIOT"

1. FBI report, June 23, 1954, FBI-FOIA response to author.
2. W. M. Felt to Mr. Tolson, "Inspection—Domestic Intelligence Division," May 26, 1969, https://archive.org/details/WilliamC.Sullivan/Sullivan%2C%20William%20C.%20-10/page/n19/mode/2up.
3. Mary Alice Hilton, "Cyberculture: The Age of Abundance and Leisure," *Michigan Quarterly Review* 30, no. 4 (Oct. 25, 1964): 217–29, https://quod.lib.umich.edu/m/mqrarchive/act2080.0003.004/00000018.
4. SAC, New York, to Director, FBI, June 3, 1965, FBI-FOIA response to author.
5. Dennis Blewitt, interviewed by author, Sept. 3, 2013.
6. Hana Riha, interview by author, Aug. 29, 2020.
7. H. Riha interview, Aug. 29, 2020.
8. H. Riha interview, Aug. 29, 2020.

9. H. Riha interview, Aug. 29, 2020.
10. H. Riha interview, Aug. 29, 2020.
11. "Galya Called 'Very Bright,'" *Denver Post,* Dec. 15, 1970,
12. H. Riha interview, Aug. 29, 2020.
13. After interviewing Hana, I recontacted Robert Schwind and asked him if he truly thought Riha was indeed the oversexed GI he remembered. He responded, "I can only speak about his behavior as *he* related it to us. You see, I never followed him around on his expeditions into town. I remember what he would tell us. I found it extremely lewd. That was Tom. He was smart, very, very smart. Erudite. He was sort of like an early version of Donald Trump." Robert Schwind, interview by author, Oct. 14, 2016.
14. James Gleason, "LGBT History: The Lavender Scare," National LGBT Chamber of Commerce, Oct. 3, 2017, https://www.nglcc.org/blog/lgbt-history-lavender-scare.
15. Staff of the Senate Select Committee on Intelligence Activities, "The Riha Inquiry," Feb. 1976, Gillies Collection.
16. SAC Boston to Director, FBI, May 25, 1960, FBI-FOIA response to author.
17. Francis Randall, interview by author, Mar. 6, 2020.
18. Randall interview, Mar. 6, 2020.
19. T. S. Kozanecki to Embassy of the Soviet Union, Mar. 10, 1971, BPD files.
20. Zdenek Cerveny, interview by author, May 24, 2016.

EPILOGUE

1. Fred Gillies, notes, interview with Howard A. Dougherty, Oct. 8, 1975, Gillies Collection.
2. R. R. Ruzicka and Robert Diezi to District Attorney Stanley Johnson, Feb. 25, 1970, BPD files.
3. Ted Curran, interview by author, Sept. 17, 2013.
4. Fred Gillies, interview with Libor Brom, n.d., Gillies Collection.
5. J. Edgar Hoover to Scott Werner, Feb. 13, 1970, FBI-FOIA response to author.

INDEX

Chicago Council of American-Soviet Friendship, 220

Chicago Star, 55

Choquette, Sonia, 104

Chrpa, Karel, 45, 48

Church, Frank, 155, 205

Church Committee, 21, 119–20, 152, 154, 205–9, 224, 228; James Jesus Angleton testimony, 204–5

CIA, 42–43, 51, 55, 79, 80, 110, 118, 133, 151, 205–6, 224, 226, 229; counterintelligence division, 89, 204–5; Denver office, 82, 84, 141; Domestic Contact Office, 84; files on Thomas Riha, 86–87; HTLINGUAL (mail-opening program), 16, 47, 210, 221; Mexico City station, 228; partnership with FBI, 143–46, 151–52, 156, 202, 208; recruiters, 4, 38, 82, 84; surveillance tools, 153, 155, 205; Thomas Riha's disappearance and, 3, 81, 86–89, 121, 125–27, 141–42, 152, 156, 207–11, 223, 227–28; travel agencies and, 224–25; Vietnam War protests, 20

Clarridge, Duane, 38

COINTELPRO, 119, 155, 200, 226

Collector of Customs, 47

Colorado Bureau of Investigation (CBI), 115, 135, 193–95

Colorado Daily, 88

Colorado Psychiatric Hospital, 135, 157–61

Colorado State Hospital, 180–92, 213; Special Review Committee, 184–85; Ward 69, 183–84, 190

Columbia University, 39, 82, 114, 224, 228; Inter-University Committee on Travel Grants, 43–44; Russian Institute, 38

Communist Party USA, 16, 17, 19, 55, 149, 199, 220

Continental Airlines, 86

Cook, Howard, Jr., 40, 125, 223

Cook, Ruth Ann, 50–51, 68, 207, 222–23; death, 126; divorce from Viktor Riha, 37, 223; marriage to Howard Cook Jr., 40, 223; move to United States, 37; in Prague, 31–32, 35–37; on Thomas Riha's disappearance, 79, 125–26

Cook County House of Corrections, 54

Coors, Adolf, III, 85, 86

Coors, Joseph, 63

Coors brewery, 85

Corbett, Joseph, 85–86

Cornell University, 82

Coroner's Office, 97–98

Crime and Punishment (Dostoyevsky), 213–14

Crippen, Dale, 97, 99

Croiset, Gerard, 130–31

Crown, Henry, 168

Curran, Ted, 39, 228

cyanide, 110, 113, 115, 139, 158, 214, 217, 222, 227; potassium, 98, 108, 130–31, 174, 193–94; sodium, 107–8, 133, 174, 193–94; symptoms of poisoning, 98–99, 193–94

Czech Embassy, 61

Czech Housing Bureau for Foreigners, 43

Czechoslovakia: Communist control of, 43–45, 61, 66–67; Nazi occupation of, 33–36, 62; Prague Spring, 66; Soviet Union invasion of, 67; Wenceslas Square, 33, 67

Czechoslovakia College, 37

Daily Californian, 40

Daniels, Robert, Jr., 203

Darvon, 108

Dean, John, 154

Defense Department, 38

Defense Intelligence Agency, 20, 151

DeLoach, Deke, 153

Denisov, Vladimir V., 220

Denver Art Museum, 127, 189, 214

Denver County Jail, 114–15, 163–64, 188

Denver County Sheriff's Department, 189

Denver Crime Lab, 97

Denver District Court, 137

Denver General Hospital, 98

Denver Lunacy Commission, 175

Denver Medical Examiner, 98

Denver Mint, 94

Denver Police Department, 99, 112, 114, 125, 133, 214, 217; Intelligence Bureau, 124–25

Denver Post, 59, 66, 92, 115, 122–23, 125, 135, 146, 157, 205–6

Diem, Ngo Dinh, 86, 211

Diezi, Robert, 129–30, 133–34

Dill, Arthur "Art," 133–34, 166

Dillinger, John, 18

Dodgin, Claude D. *See* Doreal, Maurice

Doreal, Maurice, 104–5, 110

Dorsey, Douglas J., 8–10, 15

Dostoyevsky, Fydor, 213–14

Dougherty, Howard, 226

Douglas County Sheriff's Department, 131